# Family Tourism

FSC
www.fsc.org

MIX
Paper from
responsible sources
FSC® C014540

## ASPECTS OF TOURISM

*Series Editors:* Chris Cooper, *Oxford Brookes University, UK*; C. Michael Hall, *University of Canterbury, New Zealand*; and Dallen J. Timothy, *Arizona State University, USA*

**Aspects of Tourism** is an innovative, multifaceted series, which comprises authoritative reference handbooks on global tourism regions, research volumes, texts and monographs. It is designed to provide readers with the latest thinking on tourism worldwide and push back the frontiers of tourism knowledge. The volumes are authoritative, readable and user-friendly, providing accessible sources for further research. Books in the series are commissioned to probe the relationship between tourism and cognate subject areas such as strategy, development, retailing, sport and environmental studies.

Full details of all the books in this series and of all our other publications can be found on http://www.channelviewpublications.com, or by writing to Channel View Publications, St Nicholas House, 31–34 High Street, Bristol BS1 2AW, UK.

# Family Tourism

## Multidisciplinary Perspectives

Edited by

**Heike Schänzel, Ian Yeoman and Elisa Backer**

**CHANNEL VIEW PUBLICATIONS**
Bristol • Buffalo • Toronto

Library of Congress Cataloging in Publication Data
A catalog record for this book is available from the Library of Congress.
Family Tourism: Multidisciplinary Perspectives/Edited by Heike Schänzel, Ian Yeoman
and Elisa Backer.
Aspects of Tourism: 56
Includes bibliographical references and index.
1. Tourism. 2. Families--Travel. 3. Family recreation. I. Schänzel, Heike. II. Yeoman, Ian.
III. Backer, Elisa.
G155.A1F255 2012
338.4'791–dc23 2012009346

British Library Cataloguing in Publication Data
A catalogue entry for this book is available from the British Library.

ISBN-13: 978-1-84541-327-9 (hbk)
ISBN-13: 978-1-84541-326-2 (pbk)

**Channel View Publications**
UK: St Nicholas House, 31–34 High Street, Bristol BS1 2AW, UK.
USA: UTP, 2250 Military Road, Tonawanda, NY 14150, USA.
Canada: UTP, 5201 Dufferin Street, North York, Ontario M3H 5T8, Canada.

The policy of Multilingual Matters/Channel View Publications is to use papers that
are natural, renewable and recyclable products, made from wood grown in sustainable
forests. In the manufacturing process of our books, and to further support our policy,
preference is given to printers that have FSC and PEFC Chain of Custody certification.
The FSC and/or PEFC logos will appear on those books where full certification has been
granted to the printer concerned.

Typeset in Schneidler and Officina Sans by R. J. Footring Ltd, Derby.
Printed and bound in Great Britain by Short Run Press Ltd.

# Contents

**Part 2: The Experiences of Family Tourism**

# Figures

# Tables

# Contributors

## Editors

**Elisa Backer**

Elisa is a senior lecturer in tourism at the Business School, University of Ballarat, Australia; she previously lectured at Southern Cross University. Before working in academia, Elisa acquired industry experience through working in management positions at three destination marketing organisations. Elisa has also worked as a tourism and marketing consultant, and has managed the marketing for a large shopping centre complex. Elisa has a particular interest in destination marketing, technology applications in education, and the field of visiting friends and relatives (VFR), in which she is now considered a world expert. She has presented both domestically and internationally at conferences, and has published in leading international journals.

**Heike Schänzel**

Heike is a lecturer in tourism studies at AUT University in Auckland. She previously worked at Victoria University of Wellington as a teaching and research fellow in tourism management. Her doctoral thesis examined family holiday experiences for the whole family group from a New Zealand perspective, and won her a Dean's Award in 2010 from Victoria University. Heike has a particular interest in family tourism and children in tourism, tourist behaviour, and innovative research methodologies and the development of critical theory in tourism and hospitality. She has published several papers in refereed academic journals on family holidays, methodologies and fathers in tourism and is now considered an expert in the field of family tourism.

**Ian Yeoman**

Ian is possibly the world's only professional crystal-ball gazer or futurologist specialising in travel and tourism. Ian learned his trade as the scenario planner for Visit Scotland, where he established the process of futures thinking within the organisation using a variety of techniques, including economic modelling, trends analysis and scenario construction. In July 2008, Ian was appointed Associate Professor of Tourism Management at Victoria University of Wellington, New Zealand. Ian has published extensively within the field of tourism futures, with articles in leading academic journals such as *Tourism Management*, *Journal of Travel Research* and *Journal of Vacation Marketing*, on a variety of topics from climate change to the future of energy and consumer trends, all within the context of travel and tourism. He is a popular speaker at conferences and was described by the UK *Sunday Times* as the country's leading contemporary futurologist. Ian is the holder of a number of honorary positions, including Visiting Professor at the European Tourism Futures Institute at Stenden University of Applied Sciences, the Netherlands, and Visiting Research Fellow at Sheffield Hallam University, England. Ian has undertaken consultancy projects for the United Nations World Tourism Organization and is sought by many organisations for advice about the future. Ian is presently undertaking research for the New Zealand Ministry of Tourism, examining the future of tourism in New Zealand in 2050 (see http://www.tourism2050.com). His most recent book, *2050 – Tomorrow's Tourism* (Channel View Publications, 2012), examines tourism through the lens of science fiction in order to present a new radical picture. Other books include *Tomorrow's Tourists: Scenarios and Trends* (Elsevier, 2008), *Tourism and Demography* (Goodfellows, 2010) and *Revenue Management* (Palgrave, 2010).

## Contributors

### Melanie Howard
Melanie was a co-founder in 1996 and is now chair of the Future Foundation, an international trends and insight consultancy that helps clients to identify and capitalise on emerging market opportunities and to reduce risk. Passionate about the value of futures thinking to organisations of all sizes and sectors, Melanie speaks frequently, writes often and grabs any chance to communicate how and why understanding consumer trends can really make a difference to effectiveness and creativity. As well as acting as chief networker, proselytiser and chair for the Future Foundation, she is also a Visiting Business Fellow at Innovation RCA at the Royal College of Art, a visiting professor at Henley Business School, where she is running master classes in Futures Thinking, an advisor to social business 'beehive' clearlyso.com and a trustee of the Institute of Direct and Digital Marketing and the Women's Sport and Fitness Foundation.

### Howard Hughes
Howard was Professor of Tourism Management at Manchester Metropolitan University until retirement in 2010. He is the author of three books, including, most recently, *Pink Tourism: Holidays of Gay Men and Lesbians* (CABI, 2006).

He has published numerous papers in refereed academic journals on the relationship between the arts and tourism and on holidays of gay men and lesbians. His research in this latter field has investigated holidays and gay identity, gay tourism and spatial transformation, holiday destination choice by gay men, marketing of gay-friendly destinations, holidays of older gay men and residents' attitudes towards gay tourists. Other research interests have included cultural tourism, especially in Central and Eastern Europe, entertainment in British seaside resorts and holidays of the Irish Diaspora.

**Damian Lord**
Damian joined the Future Foundation in August 2007, after working in media research for the market research company SPA Future Thinking. He is currently the Foundation's Intelligence Manager, working across both UK and global nVision services, maintaining and refreshing all nVision content. Additionally, he regularly writes nVision sector reports across the Foundation's services, as well as bespoke client reports on a variety of themes. Alongside this main role, he is also the manager and director for a number of key accounts across sectors, such as advertising, media and tourism, while further managing the Future Foundation's expert insight community, nVoys. Damian possesses an MA in sociology from the University of Manchester and has a particular professional interest in the lives of children and young consumers, travel and tourism, global luxury markets and media consumption habits.

**Una McMahon-Beattie**
Una is Head of the Department of Hospitality and Tourism Management at the University of Ulster. She has a PhD from the University of Gloucestershire (UK) in the area of relationship marketing, pricing and consumer trust in tourism. She also has an interest in tourism futures. She has published widely in these areas, with articles in leading academic journals such as the *Journal of Travel Research, Journal of Vacation Marketing, Journal of Strategic Marketing* and *Tourism Management*. Una is the author or editor of a number of books, including *Festival and Events Management: An International Arts and Culture Perspective* (Elsevier, 2004) and *Revenue Management: A Practical Pricing Perspective* (Palgrave Macmillan, 2001).

**Lynn Minnaert**
Lynn is a lecturer in tourism and events at the University of Surrey. She has published extensively on the topic of social tourism, and has conducted research projects in the UK and Belgium with social tourism users and organisations. She is one of the editors of *Social Tourism in Europe: Theory and Practice* (Channel View Publications, 2011), the first book about social tourism in English to compare theoretical perspectives and practical implementations of social tourism across Europe. Her work also focuses on the

social sustainability of tourism and events. She has conducted research in practices for the Olympic Games and business events.

## Luke Parker-Hodds
Luke is a third-year placement student at the Future Foundation in London. He is studying economics and international development at Bath University, and has five 'A's at A-level, in economics, geography, financial studies, maths and further maths. The blend of economics and geography provides a background and interest in how tourism affects trade, aid and population movement. Outside work Luke plays football, rugby and cricket, and is a keen traveller, with a trip to Bangladesh in spring 2012.

## Carol Southall
Carol is a lecturer in tourism and event management at Staffordshire University. With over 20 years of experience in the tourism industry, in contract and operations management, and 16 years of experience in teaching in further and higher education, much of which was gained alongside industry experience, Carol continues to apply the practical elements of her operational role in an academic context. Research interests include the relationship between cultural awareness and perceptions of service quality in tourism, as well as lesbian, gay, bisexual or transgender (LGBT) tourism and family tourism. She is a member of the ERRIN (European Regions Research and Innovation Network) Tourism Working Group in Brussels. Alongside teaching and research, Carol continues to work as a tour manager and driver (she hold a licence for passenger-carrying vehicles), escorting tours to diverse destinations in the UK and Europe.

## Sally Webster
Sally is an author, academic and marketing communications professional with more than 20 years' experience in marketing communications in government, politics, education, tourism and the arts. She is currently a lecturer in marketing communications at Victoria University, Melbourne, Australia, and is completing her PhD in communication, which investigates the use of travel novels as a new destination marketing tool to creatively market a city (the city of Barcelona) while also supporting cultural education. Her academic research focuses on creative tourism marketing, tourism writing, place branding and identity, cultural education, and the influence of young people as the current and future tourists. Sally is a social commentator for Australian and international media. She regularly speaks at conferences on her areas of research and advertising/marketing communications, and in 2011 was invited to present at TEDx Canberra on her PhD research.

# Foreword

Given that the family is the most universal, enduring and adaptable social institution through which the vast majority of the world's (now) 7 billion inhabitants will derive their principal source of identification, support and meaning in life, it seems astonishing that the subject of this book hasn't been tackled in such depth before. After all, tourism is now the world's largest industry. By implication, at the very least, these two significant spheres of influence on the lives of so many must have considerable degrees of overlap and a huge amount to illuminate within each other. The need to develop new tools and concepts in order to research and understand this relationship is pressing and the light the book shines on the subject should be of enormous benefit to the academic, government and commercial audiences that it addresses.

Findings from the consumer research business of which I am chair, the Future Foundation, confirm time and time again that the family – despite the long-term trend to greater individualism and self-expression – remains at the emotional heart of every society. The profound effects of liberalism, demographic shifts and the growing economic engagement of women have changed a significant proportion of families to more fluid, flexible and cross-generational groupings – often characterised by sociologists as a network, or even a personal community. That might be going a bit far for some, but it is certainly the case that active engagement with other family members remains a key component of day-to-day relationship building and emotional satisfaction – with new technologies playing a growing part in facilitating the arrangement of such activities. For many, the word family is becoming as much of a *verb* as a noun – defined by what members do with each other as much as formal blood ties and co-residence.

Nowadays it seems indisputable that travel and tourism are one of the most significant means by which the modern family in all its myriad forms invests time and energy in forging strong connections and generating invaluable social and cultural capital by which it can flourish and generate additional meaning and well-being for its members. The emotional and cultural ties that endure across continents and across decades in our increasingly multicultural and mobile world are profound and determine extensive travel investments that criss-cross the globe. The demands of work and the pressures of time that shape the daily patterns of life for so many families ensure that the few short weeks in which they can enjoy each other's company unconfined by such stresses become the highlight of the year and an important contributor to each family's narrative and sense of specialness.

Looking ahead, the extent to which the unfolding story of tourism in the 21st century will continue to be driven by the needs and development of the family cannot be underestimated. The family will continue to adapt to the circumstances and social norms that surround it. Ageing and longevity will drive more cross-generational family groups to travel together. Divorce and reconstitution will result in less predictable mixes of step-parents and step-siblings needing to be accommodated in new ways in holiday destinations. The experiences generated through travel and tourism will continue to be used to reinforce and build the emotionally meaningful ties at the core of family life, both nuclear and extended. I am sure this book will provide fascinating insights and powerful tools that will help reach to the heart of analysing and understanding this important subject and its implications in an ever-more global economy.

Professor Melanie Howard
*Chair, Future Foundation*

# 1 Introduction: Families in Tourism Research

## Why Study Families in Tourism?

Families with dependent children account for just under half of the population and comprise 29% of all households in the UK (Beioley, 2004), which is comparable to other Western countries. In New Zealand, about 26% of the population are under 18 years old and most children are nurtured within the context of the family (Statistics New Zealand, 2006). Families with dependent children (who encompass adolescents as well as babies) thus represent a significant proportion of the population and an important current and future market for the tourism industry. For example, families generate about one in four of all holiday trips made in the UK (Mintel, 2004) and account for 30% of leisure travellers in the USA (Travelhorizons, 2009). Consequently, it is not surprising that the family holiday market has been identified as constituting a major portion of leisure travel around the world (Shaw *et al.*, 2008). Peter Yesawich predicted that family travel (defined as that undertaken by adults, including grandparents, with children) will continue to grow at a faster rate than all other forms of leisure travel, partly because it represents a way to reunite the family and for family members to spend time with each other, away from the demands of work (Yesawich, 2007). Families seem to put a high priority on taking holidays. For many families in the UK an annual holiday is now seen as essential rather than a luxury (Beioley, 2004). The importance placed on the family market within the tourism industry is, however, not reflected in tourism research.

The American humourist Nathaniel Benchley (2001) stated that 'there are two classes of travel – first class, and with children', referring to the burdens associated with travelling with children. While research that addresses travel has focused on the 'first class' holiday, very little is known about holidays with children, which are deemed to be a more 'mundane' and trivial type of tourism (Bærenholdt *et al.*, 2004). In tourism research, the family holiday has been awarded far less attention than it deserves for its overall market share and size. One area of family tourism in which the invisibility of the family is especially disconcerting is coastal mass tourism (Obrador, 2012); the invisibility results partly from the general vilification of mass tourism. Another area where family tourism has been ignored is domestic tourism, despite the predominance of families with children travelling within their own countries. In New Zealand, for example, domestic tourism has generally been the neglected cousin of international tourism (Pearce, 2001) because of the emphasis placed on export earnings. Both of these shortcomings can be linked back to the perception of ordinariness and the taken-for-granted nature of family travel. It is the purpose of this multidisciplinary book to expand in a comprehensive manner our understanding of families who travel with children. It results from the collaboration of international tourism experts and is the first book to disseminate original thinking and research on family tourism from a variety of disciplinary backgrounds. The chapters in Part 1 of the book provide some context by looking at the social, demographic and historical trends affecting families and their holiday behaviour before Parts 2 and 3 respectively provide a comprehensive reflection on family holiday experiences now and into the future, from a range of perspectives. A more holistic, multidisciplinary, global and future-orientated approach is taken here to understand family tourism by acknowledging its underlying social dynamics, fluidity and multidimensionality. What emerges is that family tourism is far more complex and noteworthy than has been appreciated.

## Definition of Families and Family Holidays

This is a pertinent time for a comprehensive consideration of families in tourism. The concept of the 'family' is itself in question. There is recognition of the plurality of family forms, to the effect that many would refer to *families* rather than to 'the family', in that different family members are likely to perceive the composition of their families in different ways (Dumon, 1997; Shaw, 1997). Nevertheless, despite the diversity of family forms, a common denominator is that 'they all serve as *person-supporting networks*' (Dumon, 1997: 181, original emphasis). Defining 'family' is not only a complex undertaking for researchers but also a problem that confronts society with new challenges. The concept of relationships and interaction between family members is essential to any notion of family and underlies most literature on family leisure and family tourism. Researching the family holiday must be considered within the context of changing family structures and values, and wider societal trends. In the UK, a family holiday is most commonly defined in the literature and policy as a recreational break of four or more nights away from home (Hazel, 2005). A more widely accepted definition of family holidays is that it involves leisure travel away from home for more than one day undertaken by a family group, itself defined as at least one child and one adult (Schänzel et al., 2005). The adult here can be a parent, legal guardian or caregiver (although in the present work the term 'parent' will be used throughout, for the sake of simplicity). These definitions are fairly narrow, in that they are based merely on length of stay and minimum size of the travelling group, and do not take into account the different experiences of children and parents.

Holidays are commonly defined around push motivations that are orientated either towards escape (Iso-Ahola, 1982) or towards a break from routine (Crompton, 1979) but this does not necessarily apply to family holidays. According to Shaw et al. (2008) parents with children differ from other tourists in their strong focus on social values, such as family togetherness, creating family memories and generativity. This indicates a purposive element to family holidaying that involves connections with, rather than escape from, social relations (Larsen et al., 2007). While parents seek togetherness on holiday they may also desire personal space, which can be a source of conflict and requires compromise. Gram (2005) identified an inherent dilemma in family holidays: because parents seek relaxation and children seek activities, the ideal of togetherness is hard to achieve. Gram's study, however, was largely based on the parental perspective rather than being informed by the individual members of the family. According to Schänzel (2008), who included the voices of all family members, family holidays are primarily about doing activities that are different to normal routines and that involve spending time together 'with' the family (including extended family) rather than being an escape or break 'from' home routines. They serve a purpose of (re)connecting people, through tourism, and can be seen as a social practice that involves networking, family capital formation and social obligations. Because Schänzel included the voices of children it became evident that fun was an important factor, as evidenced by the comments of an eight-year-old boy: 'It is not a holiday if it is not fun. If it is fun then it is a holiday' (Schänzel, 2008). As a result, the following definition of 'family holidays', based on the experiences of all family members, was adopted for this book:

> A purposive time spent together as a family group (which may include extended family) doing activities different from normal routines that are fun but that may involve compromise and conflict at times.

## The Under-representation of Families in Tourism Research

Despite the economic significance of family tourism for the tourism industry, holidays with children have largely been marginalised in academic research (Schänzel et al., 2005). Most tourism research focuses on the individual and emphasises detachment, and so has effectively de-socialised tourist subjects, rendering such approaches unsuitable for research into families (Obrador, 2012). Research has also not kept pace with the change in family forms and structures. This has led to limited, fragmented and individualised research on family holiday experiences. Most family tourism research is market and consumer driven and focused on the themes of decision processes and roles (Lehto *et al.*, 2009), and even here relatively few studies have included children (Blichfeldt *et al.*, 2011; Nickerson & Jurowski, 2001). Some research has been carried out at family-centred tourist attractions (Hallman *et al.*, 2007; Johns & Gyimothy, 2003) and there are historical accounts of family holidaying (Inglis, 2000; Rugh, 2008). A historical development of family tourism in the UK is given in Chapter 4. Specialised studies on the benefits of social tourism coming out of Europe (Hughes, 1991; McCabe *et al.*, 2011; Minnaert *et al.*, 2009) are increasingly identifying the link between tourism for disadvantaged families and increases in family social capital, as discussed in Chapter 7. Families also form an important part of travel for visiting friends and relatives (VFR), which is perpetually underestimated in tourism research (Backer, 2012) and is discussed in Chapter 6.

Also evident is a lack of research into the broader experiential dimensions of family holidays that takes into account the perspectives of all family members and the increasing diversity of family groups. There have been studies of family holiday experiences that are mainly informed by feminist perspectives and thus focused on mothers' family holiday experiences (Deem, 1996; Small, 2005). There is little published on the holiday experience of fathers, apart from their joint parenting voice (Schänzel & Smith, 2011) and, again, few studies have investigated the family holiday experiences of children (Carr, 2006, 2011; Cullingford, 1995; Hilbrecht *et al.*, 2008; Small, 2008). This is in contrast to a research tradition that is inclusive of children and fathers in related social sciences such as family studies and leisure studies (Daly, 1996b; Jeanes, 2010; Kay, 2009). This means that little is known about children as family tourists and how they can be better attended to. Children are the consumers of tomorrow and their influence on travel decisions and tourism experiences should not be underestimated. This is discussed with regard to marketing to young tourists in Chapter 10. Relatively little attention has been paid to the meaning of family holiday experiences to parents (Blichfeldt, 2006; Shaw *et al.*, 2008). The dearth of research on the family group (Gram, 2005) and on family group dynamics on holiday (Schänzel, 2010) has resulted in a poor understanding of how group dynamics can inflame or heighten the individual holiday experience (Pritchard & Havitz, 2006). This is despite the fact that potentially different generational and gender needs and desires can lead to social tensions and conflicts on holiday, as discussed in more detail in Chapter 5.

As mentioned above, holidays with children are different from other holidays and can involve family group conflicts (Gram, 2005; Schänzel,

2010) and added stresses that require careful family organisation. There is scant literature on the work involved in and the difficulties with facilitating positive family experiences (Shaw, 2008). Even less is known about the stress factors in family holidays, despite the significant influence these can have on overall satisfaction with the holiday experience, as discussed in Chapter 8. Instead, the notion of families spending happy times together on holiday is a persistent marketing image that has long been part of the 'mythology of tourism' (Seaton & Tagg, 1995). The image of the happy family on holiday is also largely based on white, middle-class and nuclear families, and does not reflect the growing diversity of family forms. According to Carr (2011), it can be construed that the non-nuclear family is an unhappy family who cannot be together because it does not fit within conceptualisations of the tourism experience as a time of family togetherness. Yet this is clearly erroneous, as demonstrated by the discussion in Chapter 9 of the significant potential of tourism to strengthen and consolidate sexual identities and family relationships for gay and lesbian families. The increasing proportion of people who exist outside the traditional family life cycle in tourism (Bojanic, 1992; Lawson, 1991), such as families with different sexual orientations, is discussed in Chapter 11. It debates whether a model of set stages that people are expected to go through during their life needs updating to reflect societal changes.

Apart from the under-representation of families in tourism research there is also a disconnection between tourism studies and other social sciences concerned with families. This is despite the significant influence that society and dominant ideologies of parenting and childhood can exert on family holiday experiences. Much can be gained from the literature in sociology, family studies and leisure studies (Daly, 2004; Handel et al., 2007; Shaw, 2010) for the deeper understanding of trends and behaviours shaping family tourism experiences, as discussed in Chapter 2. The idealisation of family time in Western societies (Daly, 1996a) and changing gender roles (Harrington, 2006; Shaw, 2008) can then be traced from the home and leisure realms to the holiday realm. While tourism has some unique qualities that may not be found in everyday leisure activities or in the home, such as the 'notion of departure' from what is routine (Urry, 1990), this neglects the concept that family tourists' behaviour is influenced by a combination of socio-cultural and personal values that are present in both the home and holiday environment (Carr, 2002). In fact, family holidays are also about the supporting experiences and interactions that are intrinsic to everyday life (McCabe, 2002). The implication here is that changes in domestic family life and family leisure also affect family behaviours on holiday, and this needs wider recognition in tourism research. The prominence of families with children in tourism contrasts with the neglect within academic research of the relations between tourism and domesticity, sociality, broader experiential dimensions, diversity and ideologies.

It would be a huge undertaking to try to fill the apparent gaps in our knowledge on family tourism. This book, though, is a first coming together of different perspectives and disciplines to provide better understandings of what holidays for families entail. It provides a broad ideological context, societal trends and historical background as well as discussions and empirical findings on a variety of topics concerning family tourism behaviours; the future implications are also considered. In this way, experts in the incongruent field of family tourism are brought together for the first time to disseminate to a wider audience their knowledge of aspects such as: social and demographic trends; historical developments; fathers, children and family groups; gay and lesbian families; VFR travel; social tourism; stress on holiday; consumer kids; and the life cycle models. Much of this breaks new ground and addresses some of the gaps in the research literature highlighted above. It also emphasises that more research is needed to keep pace with the increasingly changing and diversifying tourism market that is made up of families in all their shapes and forms. The concluding chapter suggests research topics in order to capture the fluid and dynamic nature of modern families. Families make up a substantial and robust market segment for the tourism industry, generating about 30% of tourism receipts (Mintel, 2004) and warrant much more attention in research than they are currently awarded. What is needed is a better conceptualisation of the family in tourism that takes account of its unique social qualities, multiple dimensions and idiosyncrasies.

## Conceptualisation of Families in Tourism

The fragmented and limited research on family tourism might explain why there is no conceptual framework for it in the literature. Instead, most studies that deal with tourism experiences discuss representations of the self (tourist) and the other (host), usually in an international (exotic) holiday environment (e.g. Wearing & Wearing, 2006), or external factors such as the weather (e.g. Pritchard & Havitz, 2006). Yet the host–guest structure that is applied to international tourism is not well suited to family group travel because it neglects issues of group dynamics and sociality with 'significant others' (i.e. within the family group) (Larsen et al., 2007), and simply grafting theories about individual tourist behaviour onto group contexts may not work (Yarnal & Kerstetter, 2005). This has led to a de-socialisation of tourism subjects, which makes such research approaches unsuitable for families (Obrador, 2012). One way to 'de-exoticise' and 're-socialise' tourism theory is by placing family and friendship relations at the centre of tourism research through the social turn (Larsen, 2008). What is needed, then, is a familial perspective (Smith & Hughes, 1999) which puts the social into travel and is inclusive of the views of all family members.

Accordingly, a conceptual framework is developed here that centres on the holiday experiences of all family members. It moves from an individual perspective (one dimensional) and a dyadic or gendered perspective (two dimensional) to a more inclusive triangular family group perspective (three dimensions of mothers, fathers and children) with its implicit gender, generation and group dynamic perspectives (see Figure 1.1). This means that the generational perspective (parents–children) must be considered alongside a gender perspective (mother–father, daughter–son) and that individual family members must be understood as part of a group dynamic. Further explanation of the three-dimensional conceptualisation of families in tourism is in order.

The tourist experience is currently depicted as an obscure and diverse phenomenon which is essentially constituted by the individual consumer (Uriely, 2005). In fact, much of the initial research on tourism was concerned with the individual tourist and the part that holidays play in establishing self-identity (Wearing & Wearing, 2001). The figure of the primarily male tourist is presented as a disembodied and asocial subject who has no family, no private life, no social obligations, no children, not even any friends (Obrador, 2012). This has led to a mainly one-dimensional understanding of tourism experiences, unsuitable for family groups. Gender considerations have appeared in the tourism literature since the 1990s (Kinnaird & Hall, 1994; Swain, 1995), and a growing body of research on the female travel experience now attests to the unique needs, motivations and constraints that women face (Harris & Wilson, 2007). However, the objects of gender research to date have almost exclusively been women (rather than women *and men*) (Pritchard *et al.*, 2007). There is recognition that an intersection between gender and other social roles is needed, or true gender scholarship (Stewart & McDermott, 2004). For example, a gendered approach to the study of parents (fathers as well as mothers) in family tourism is much neglected (Schänzel & Smith, 2011) and is absent in the study of children (boys and girls). And even a two-dimensional gendered approach is itself unsuited to the study of group dynamics and generational perspectives in family tourism. Turley (2001) and Carr (2006) recognised that a more comprehensive approach to tourism research is needed for family groups, an approach that triangulates the views of children and adults, but neither offered a conceptualisation of such an approach. In effect, there is little research on how social interaction and travel party composition intersect with the holiday experience (Yarnal & Kerstetter, 2005). There are few generational comparisons in family tourism research (Carr, 2006, 2011) but what is needed is a three-dimensional conceptualisation of family tourism experiences that is inclusive of gender, generation and group dynamic perspectives (Schänzel, 2010) (see Figure 1.1).

The strength of this conceptualisation is that extended families (for example ones that include grandparents) could be accommodated through

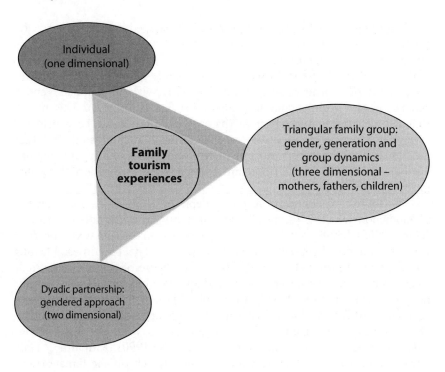

**Figure 1.1** Conceptual triangular framework of the three dimensions of family tourism experiences

a multigenerational approach, although the focus here is on nuclear families. Single parents and gay/lesbian families would require a more complex framework that could go beyond triangulation. Richardson and St Pierre (2005) suggested the crystal as a central image for such a conceptualisation because it offers a large variety of shapes and many angles of approach. Crystals can grow and change just like modern family forms. The important recognition here is that family groups entail social realities that cannot be captured by conventional one-dimensional or two-dimensional perspectives and theorisations in tourism. Instead a three-dimensional or familial perspective is needed that allows for group dynamics and generational considerations alongside potential gendered approaches. While this conceptualisation has been applied in only some of the present chapters, it highlights the need for a reappraisal of families in tourism research that is inclusive of the sociality and multidimensionality of family groups.

# Intentions and Structure of the Book

We as the editors are excited to introduce this rich and much needed compilation of chapters on family tourism. The varied subject matter, disciplinary approaches, theoretical positioning and methodologies signal the salience and importance of families within tourism. The chapters address some of the shortcomings in tourism research and provide better linkage to other social sciences, notably family studies and leisure studies. The following 11 chapters bring together a variety of perspectives on families within tourism and illustrate the many approaches that can be taken. Much of the material is based on empirical research but there are also reviews where primary research is still lacking. Many of the findings are reported here for the first time, illustrating the infancy of academic family tourism research, one consequence of which is the notable absence here of considerations of single parents, families from ethnic minorities and other non-Western families. Despite repeated attempts to commission a chapter on Asian families on holiday, no author could be found. Although the Asian family market is predicted to grow and take on more importance (United Nations World Tourism Organization, 2006) this is not yet captured in academic tourism research, and hence its absence in this volume.

It is the expectation of the editors and contributors that this book will stir interest and create further debate about families in tourism. The intention here is to build a solid base from which future research on families can emerge and grow in a more systematic fashion. What are still needed are more fundamental discussions about the place of families in tourism research; such research should not only be on a scale that reflects the economic relevance of family tourism but more importantly acknowledges its unique social realities and value to society. Any research into families also provides a social lens on contemporary life (Lashley *et al.*, 2007), as most of us are connected to families (past and present) in some way.

*Family Tourism: Multidisciplinary Perspectives* begins with three chapters outlining the ideological influences, social trends and historical developments that impact on families and their holiday behaviour. Together they provide a broad sociological context for the discussions and empirical findings in the remaining chapters. Families on holiday cannot be seen in isolation from their domestic behaviours, as becomes apparent in Chapter 2. There have been profound changes in ideologies and parental roles in Western society and these are traced through the family studies and leisure studies literature to see how they might influence our understanding of family time in tourism. Chapter 3 continues to add to our understanding of demographic and social change, by disseminating some current trend data. Rather than providing theoretical underpinnings, as in Chapter 2, this chapter illustrates the effect of demographic influences and broader structural changes on family tourism. Chapter 4 provides a historical background to the current family tourism market and discusses social and economic influences affecting its future.

The next five chapters discuss the tourism experiences of families from different disciplinary perspectives and methodological approaches. Chapter 5 begins by introducing a novel whole-family methodology, which includes the hitherto silenced voices of fathers, children and the whole family group within our understanding on family holiday experiences. It provides a more inclusive familial perspective that highlights the specific roles of the father, the social needs of the children and family group dynamics. Chapter 6 shows the importance that VFR travel has for family tourism, by highlighting the robustness of this market. Specific marketing strategies are suggested to tap into this growing market. The increasingly debated value of social tourism is raised in Chapter 7, which emphasises that holidays for disadvantaged families can have significant benefits for their members. The stress of the family holiday is discussed in Chapter 8, another based on empirical research. Families have unique requirements that require better attendance from accommodation providers if the desired stress relief of a holiday is to be achieved. Chapter 9 provides an overview of the potential for gay and lesbian family tourism and draws attention to some of the challenges in overcoming fears and stereotyping.

The last three chapters deal with the future of family tourism in different ways. Chapter 10 discusses the importance of marketing to young tourists and stresses that more engaging strategies are needed to appeal to this next generation of consumers. The future of the family life cycle is empirically debated in Chapter 11, which argues that traditional models are outmoded and do not reflect societal changes. Chapter 12, by way of conclusion, identifies the contribution of each chapter to the theory and practice of family tourism through a cognitive mapping approach. An aggregated map of the chapter themes presents both the present state of family tourism and directions for the future, and suggestions for further research are made.

## Conclusion

This book brings together current research topics from leading experts in the wide-ranging field of family tourism and thereby adds to an under-developed knowledge base. *Family Tourism: Multidisciplinary Perspectives* underlines the infancy of academic family tourism research that belies its market importance and advises readers of the implications and theoretical debates about the place of families within tourism. This is an edited collection, and so the chapters are independent and can be read in any order, but we do recommend that readers begin at the beginning to get a sense of the wider context affecting family tourism. We appreciate that this book is not complete but is rather a first international engagement with families in tourism that highlights the richness of the field, along with the need for further research to address its shortcomings. The contribution this book makes to the tourism literature, then, is threefold:

- It is the first 'encyclopaedia' of family tourism – a compendium that summarises contemporary information relating to the study of families in tourism now and in the future.
- It provides an academic foundation for the field of families in tourism by way of a conceptual framework, definition, theorisation, contextualisation and social lens.
- It presents a comprehensive, multidisciplinary, global and future-orientated approach to understanding families on holiday that acknowledges their sociality, domesticity, fluidity, multidimensionality and ideology.

What emerges is that family holidays are far from being mundane and trivial but are much more complex and intriguing than previously acknowledged in research debates. We hope that you will enjoy reading the various chapters in this book as a demonstration of the application of the study of families to tourism.

*Heike Schänzel*
*Ian Yeoman*
*Elisa Backer*
The Editors

# References

Backer, E. (2012) VFR travel: it is underestimated. *Tourism Management*, 33(1), 74–79.

Bærenholdt, J.O., Haldrup, M., Larsen, J. and Urry, J. (2004) *Performing Tourist Places*. Aldershot: Ashgate.

Beioley, S. (2004) Meet the family – family holidays in the UK. *Tourism Insights*, January. Retrieved 19 September 2011 from http://www.insights.org.uk/articleitem.aspx?title=Meet+the+Family+-+Family+Holidays+in+the+UK.

Benchley, N. (2001) *The Benchley Roundup: A Selection by Nathaniel Benchley of His Favorites*. Chicago, IL: University of Chicago Press.

Blichfeldt, B.S. (2006) *A Nice Vacation* (IME Report 8/06). Esbjerg: University of Southern Denmark. Retrieved 19 September 2011 from http://static.sdu.dk/mediafiles//Files/Om_SDU/Institutter/Miljo/ime/rep/blichfeldt8.pdf.

Blichfeldt, B.S., Pedersen, B.M.I., Johansen, A. and Hansen, L. (2011) Tweens on holidays. In-situ decision-making from children's perspective. *Scandinavian Journal of Hospitality and Tourism*, 11(2), 135–149.

Bojanic, D.C. (1992) A look at a modernized family life cycle and overseas travel. *Journal of Travel and Tourism Marketing*, 1(1), 61–79.

Carr, N. (2002) The tourism–leisure behavioural continuum. *Annals of Tourism Research*, 29(4), 972–986.

Carr, N. (2006) A comparison of adolescents' and parents' holiday motivations and desires. *Tourism and Hospitality Research*, 6(2), 129–142.

Carr, N. (2011) *Children's and Families' Holiday Experiences*. London: Routledge.

Crompton, J.L. (1979) Motivations for pleasure vacation. *Annals of Tourism Research*, 6(4), 408–424.

Cullingford, C. (1995) Children's attitudes to holidays overseas. *Tourism Management*, 16(2), 121–127.

Daly, K. (1996a) *Families and Time: Keeping Pace in a Hurried Culture*. Thousand Oaks, CA: Sage.

Daly, K. (1996b) Spending time with the kids: meanings of family time for fathers. *Family Relations*, 45(4), 466–476.

Daly, K. (2004) *The Changing Culture of Parenting*. Ottawa: Vanier Institute of the Family.

Deem, R. (1996) Women, the city and holidays. *Leisure Studies*, 15(2), 105–119.

Dumon, W. (1997) The situation of families in Western Europe: a sociological perspective. In S. Dreman (ed.), *The Family on the Threshold of the 21st Century* (pp. 181–200). Hillsdale, NJ: Lawrence Erlbaum Associates.

Gram, M. (2005) Family holidays. A qualitative analysis of family holiday experiences. *Scandinavian Journal of Hospitality and Tourism*, 5(1), 2–22.

Hallman, B.C., Mary, S. and Benbow, P. (2007) Family leisure, family photography and zoos: exploring the emotional geographies of families. *Social and Cultural Geography*, 8(6), 871–888.

Handel, G., Cahill, S.E. and Elkin, F. (2007) *Children and Society: The Sociology of Children and Childhood Socialization*. Los Angeles, CA: Roxbury.

Harrington, M. (2006) Sport and leisure as contexts for fathering in Australian families. *Leisure Studies*, 25(2), 165–183.

Harris, C. and Wilson, E. (2007) Travelling beyond the boundaries of constraint: women, travel and empowerment. In A. Pritchard, N. Morgan, I. Ateljevic and C. Harris (eds), *Tourism and Gender: Embodiment, Sensuality and Experience* (pp. 235–250). Wallingford: CABI.

Hazel, N. (2005) Holidays for children and families in need: an exploration of the research and policy context for social tourism in the UK. *Children and Society*, 19(3), 225–236.

Hilbrecht, M., Shaw, S.M., Delamere, F.M. and Havitz, M.E. (2008) Experiences, perspectives, and meanings of family vacations for children. *Leisure/Loisir*, 32(2), 541–571.

Hughes, H.L. (1991) Holidays and the economically disadvantaged. *Tourism Management*, 12(3), 193–196.

Inglis, F. (2000) *The Delicious History of the Holiday*. London: Routledge.

Iso-Ahola, S.E. (1982) Toward a social psychological theory of tourism motivation: a rejoinder. *Annals of Tourism Research*, 9(2), 256–262.

Jeanes, R. (2010) Seen but not heard? Examining children's voices in leisure and family research. *Leisure/Loisir*, 34(3), 243–259.

Johns, N. and Gyimothy, S. (2003) Postmodern family tourism at Legoland. *Scandinavian Journal of Hospitality and Tourism*, 3(1), 3–23.

Kay, T. (ed.) (2009) *Fathering Through Sport and Leisure*. London: Routledge.

Kinnaird, V. and Hall, D. (eds) (1994) *Tourism: A Gendered Analysis*. Chichester: John Wiley.

Larsen, J. (2008) De-exoticizing tourist travel: everyday life and sociality on the move. *Leisure Studies*, 27(1), 21–34.

Larsen, J., Urry, J. and Axhausen, K.W. (2007) Networks and tourism: mobile social life. *Annals of Tourism Research*, 34(1), 244–262.

Lashley, C., Lynch, P. and Morrison, A. (eds) (2007) *Hospitality: A Social Lens*. Oxford: Elsevier.

Lawson, R. (1991) Patterns of tourist expenditure and types of vacation across the family life cycle. *Journal of Travel Research*, 29(4), 12–18.

Lehto, X.Y., Choi, S., Lin, Y.-C. and MacDermid, S.M. (2009) Vacation and family functioning. *Annals of Tourism Research*, 36(3), 459–479.

McCabe, S. (2002) The tourist experience and everyday life. In G.M.S. Dann (ed.), *The Tourist as a Metaphor of the Social World* (pp. 61–75). Wallingford: CABI.

McCabe, S., Minnaert, L. and Diekman, A. (eds) (2011) *Social Tourism in Europe*. Bristol: Channel View Publications.

Minnaert, L., Maitland, R. and Miller, G. (2009) Tourism and social policy: the value of social tourism. *Annals of Tourism Research*, 36(2), 316–334.

Mintel (2004) *Family Holidays, Leisure Intelligence, June*. London: Mintel International Group.

Nickerson, N.P. and Jurowski, C. (2001) The influence of children on vacation travel patterns. *Journal of Vacation Marketing*, 7(1), 19–30.

Obrador, P. (2012) The place of the family in tourism research: domesticity and thick sociality by the pool. *Annals of Tourism Research*, 39(1), 401–420.

Pearce, D. (2001) Tourism. *Asia Pacific Viewpoint*, 42(1), 75.

Pritchard, A., Morgan, N., Ateljevic, I. and Harris, C. (2007) Editor's introduction: tourism, gender, embodiment and experience. In A. Pritchard, N. Morgan, I. Ateljevic and C. Harris (eds), *Tourism and Gender: Embodiment, Sensuality and Experience* (pp. 1–12). Wallingford: CABI.

Pritchard, M.P. and Havitz, M.E. (2006) Ratios of tourist experience: it was the best of times, it was the worst of times. *Tourism Analysis*, 10(3), 291–297.

Richardson, L. and St Pierre, E.A. (2005) Writing a method of inquiry. In N.K. Denzin and Y.S. Lincoln (eds), *The SAGE Handbook of Qualitative Research* (pp. 959–978). Thousand Oaks, CA: Sage.

Rugh, S. (2008) *Are We There Yet? The Golden Age of American Family Vacations*. Lawrence, KA: University Press of Kansas.

Schänzel, H.A. (2008) The New Zealand family on holiday: values, realities and fun. In J. Fountain and K. Moore (eds), *Proceedings to the New Zealand Tourism and Hospitality Research Conference*. Canterbury, New Zealand: Lincoln University.

Schänzel, H.A. (2010) Whole-family research: towards a methodology in tourism for encompassing generation, gender, and group dynamic perspectives. *Tourism Analysis*, 15(5), 555–569.

Schänzel, H.A. and Smith, K.A. (2011) The absence of fatherhood: achieving true gender scholarship in family tourism research. *Annals of Leisure Research*, 14(2–3), 129–140.

Schänzel, H.A., Smith, K.A. and Weaver, A. (2005) Family holidays: a research review and application to New Zealand. *Annals of Leisure Research*, 8(2–3), 105–123.

Seaton, A.V. and Tagg, S. (1995) The family vacation in Europe: paedonomic aspects of choices and satisfactions. *Journal of Travel and Tourism Marketing*, 4(1), 1–21.

Shaw, S.M. (1997) Controversies and contradictions in family leisure: an analysis of conflicting paradigms. *Journal of Leisure Research*, 29(1), 98–112.

Shaw, S.M. (2008) Family leisure and changing ideologies of parenthood. *Sociology Compass*, 2(2), 688–703.

Shaw, S.M. (2010) Diversity and ideology: changes in Canadian family life and implications for leisure. *World Leisure Journal*, 52(1), 4–13.

Shaw, S.M., Havitz, M.E. and Delemere, F.M. (2008) I decided to invest in my kids' memories: family vacations, memories, and the social construction of the family. *Tourism Culture and Communication*, 8(1), 13–26.

Small, J. (2005) Women's holidays: disruption of the motherhood myth. *Tourism Review International*, 9(2), 139–154.

Small, J. (2008) The absence of childhood in tourism studies. *Annals of Tourism Research*, 35(3), 772–789.

Smith, V. and Hughes, H. (1999) Disadvantaged families and the meaning of the holiday. *International Journal of Tourism Research*, 1(2), 123–133.

Statistics New Zealand (2006) New Zealand census of population and dwellings, individual form. Retrieved 2 September 2006 from http://www.stats.govt.nz.

Stewart, A.J. and McDermott, C. (2004) Gender in psychology. *Annual Review of Psychology*, 55, 519–544.

Swain, M.B. (1995) Gender in tourism. *Annals of Tourism Research*, 22(2), 247–266.

Travelhorizons (2009) Leisure travel profiles July. Retrieved 19 September 2011 from http://www.ustravel.org/research/domestic-research/travelhorizons.

Turley, S.K. (2001) Children and the demand for recreational experiences: the case of zoos. *Leisure Studies*, 20(1), 1–18.

United Nations World Tourism Organization (2006) *Mega-Trends of Tourism in Asia-Pacific*. Retrieved 19 September 2011 from http://www.tourism.wu-wien.ac.at/summit/material/megatrend_in_asia-pacific.pdf.

Uriely, N. (2005) The tourist experience: conceptual developments. *Annals of Tourism Research*, 32(1), 199–216.

Urry, J. (1990) *The Tourist Gaze: Leisure and Tourism in Contemporary Societies*. London: Sage.

Wearing, S. and Wearing, B. (2001) Conceptualising the selves of tourism. *Leisure Studies*, 20(2), 143–159.

Wearing, S. and Wearing, M. (2006) 'Rereading the subjugating tourist' in neoliberalism: postcolonial otherness and the tourist experience. *Tourism Analysis*, 11(2), 145–162.

Yarnal, C. and Kerstetter, D. (2005) Casting off: an exploration of cruise ship space, group tour behavior, and social interaction. *Journal of Travel Research*, 43(4), 368–379.

Yesawich, P. (2007) *Ten Travel Trends to Watch in 2007*. Retrieved 17 November 2011 from http://www.hospitalitynet.org/news/4029930.html.

# Part 1
# The Context of Family Tourism

# 2 Society and Ideology: Changes in Family Time Perceptions with Implications for Tourism

Heike Schänzel

## Introduction

Increasing importance is placed by society on families spending time together at home, during leisure time and on holiday. Several online and printed magazines are available in Europe, North America and Australasia dedicated to 'family times' (e.g. http://www.familytimes.biz and http://www.familytimesinc.com) and newspaper articles urge parents 'to turn off phones, computers to spend more time with children' (Doherty, 2011). The idealisation of family time in Western societies has led to growing societal pressure on parents through the media and peers to ensure 'good' parenting (Daly, 1996a). This comes despite the common misconceptions that parents are too busy to spend enough time with their children and that families have less time to relax, play, communicate and sit down for meals together (Mintel, 2009). In fact, most studies of family time use suggest that parents are now more involved in their children's leisure life than were previous generations (e.g. Bianchi *et al.*, 2006; Gauthier *et al.*, 2004). Instead, a dominant ideology of parenting has emerged with higher valuation of family time, which has led to a new orthodoxy about leisure (Shaw, 2010) and tourism. Within this context, family holidays are perceived as opportunities for bonding to ensure the happiness and togetherness of the family, away from the distractions of everyday life (Carr, 2011). Obrador (2012) found that family package holidays are saturated with ideas of intimacy, love and togetherness. This chapter examines the changing perceptions of time and roles within the family by reviewing the academic literature on family and leisure studies. It presents a theoretical discourse and sociological context for the changes that influence family tourism and provides understandings for trends and findings explored in other chapters of this book. It highlights a generational and ideological disjuncture in understandings of family time as affected by individual realities and discusses the relationship between and implications of societal trends in family life, family leisure and family tourism.

# The Changing Nature of Family Time in Western Society

Family time is now a central part of the Western discourse when referring to the day-to-day experiences of families. In response to the fast pace of technology and the dramatic increase of women in the paid labour force, family time has been idealised as the private still point in an otherwise frenzied pattern (Daly, 1996a). One of the repercussions of this is the emergence of a discourse in the popular and academic press that emphasises a 'growing *time famine* in families' (Daly, 2004: 9, original emphasis). In spite of this perception that parents are spending less time with their children, national time studies indicate that parents are actually spending more time with their children (e.g. Gauthier *et al.*, 2004; Sandberg & Hofferth, 2001; Zuzanek, 2001). In fact, parents report spending more time with their children today than in the 1960s, particularly fathers (Sayer *et al.*, 2004). One explanation is that the time that families spend together has become more goal oriented, structured and saturated with activity (Daly, 2004), and there is increased emphasis on the 'consumption' of experiences and the phenomenon of 'time deepening' (doing more things, more quickly) (Robinson & Godbey, 1997). Paradoxically, it is the very abundance of family time that is contributing to the sense that there is not enough time for family. The proliferation of family 'occasions' and the high standard expected of them have added to the effort and sense of busyness that characterises family life today (Gillis, 2001). It is important here to discuss how contemporary families perceive their time together and the cultural changes accompanying this. The time families live *by*, as captured by quantitative studies, might not be the same as the quality of time they live *with*, which is grounded in experience.

The ideals of quality family time and child-centredness are important guiding principles for modern Western families. Although family time is subject to serious competition from changing work and societal structures, ideas on family time seem resistant to change (Mestdag & Vandeweyer, 2005). There is discordance between the traditional ideal of family togetherness and the reality of everyday experiences. Parents today may feel increased cultural pressure to provide large amounts of time to children in order to be considered 'good parents' (Sayer *et al.*, 2004; Snyder, 2007). According to Giddens (1984) time has both lived, inter-subjective aspects and a structured, normative dimension. With regard to family life, it is the normative dimension that directs families to act in certain ways (Daly, 2001). Everyone has two different families that live in a state of tension, 'one that they live *with*, and another that they live *by*' (Gillis, 1996: xv). The strong cultural standards that families 'live by' play an important role not only in preserving continuity with traditional values but also in leading to dissatisfaction with family time, which is usually expressed as guilt (Daly, 2001). Instead of changing ideals about family time and being more realistic about it, the achievement of family time is seen as a personal trouble that requires a private solution rather than as a systemic or public dilemma applying to all families (Daly, 2002). Today's families live by what they call 'quality time', which is different to the time they actually share together, in routines and rituals.

Within the home the routines of meals are still the most important activity done as a family (Mestdag & Vandeweyer, 2005). Increasing literature on shared meals is spurred by its perceived reduced frequency; this literature documents positive impacts, such as enhancement of the socioemotional and cognitive development of children (Davidson & Gauthier, 2010). This idealisation of the family meal receives increasing media exposure (Gibbs, 2006).

In contrast, there are also a range of rituals in contemporary family life, including everything from special family meals to family holidays, which are not like other times but rather a time out of time, a social and cultural construction (Gillis, 2001). These ritualised times are different, in that they require anticipation and preparation, are the subject of extensive remembering, and provide a sense of identity (Fiese et al., 2002). Rituals such as family holidays stand out as more symbolic, steeped in memories and spanning across generations compared with everyday routines. However, the scientific study of routines and rituals remains relatively immature (Fiese et al., 2002) and tends to reproduce privatised notions of family life (DeVault, 2000). In fact, while family holidays are mentioned in the family literature (e.g. Gillis, 2000; Snyder, 2007), little is known about the symbolic and enduring meanings of family time on holiday. Discussions of family time also do not typically include any negative aspects (Daly, 2001) or capture the increasing diversity among families in terms of cultural background and family composition.

## Gender and Generational Perspectives on Family Time

Families cannot be considered as separate from society and can be understood only in relation to the broader social context. The meaning of family time can differ by gender and generation because of the relative weight that mothers, fathers and children place on their family identities. The term *gender* has been adopted by feminist scholars as acknowledging the influence of social structures on family roles. In general, there are quantitative gender differences, in that mothers overall spend more time with their children than fathers, regardless of their work status (Sayer et al., 2004). There are also qualitative gender differences, in that a substantial amount of the time mothers spend with their children involves childcare and maintenance, whereas fathers spend more time with their children playing (Craig, 2006; Roxburgh, 2006). This leads to gendered and generational differences in the way family time is defined within contemporary Western society.

According to McMahon (1995), contemporary *motherhood* is contested terrain. It is often defined as a state of being, but women usually describe their mothering as activity-based rather than identity-based (Maher, 2005). Douglas and Michaels' (2004) analysis of the context for mothering outlines unattainable ideals for 'moms' that promulgate standards of perfection beyond their reach. Maume (2006) suggests that these cultural messages have intensified with time in the popular literature, and women are now deemed responsible for all aspects of preparing their children for adulthood. This prevailing ideology of *intensive mothering* declares that mothering is wholly child-centred, emotionally involving and time-consuming (Arendell, 2000). While mothers continue to exert more control over the organisation of time in families, thus taking on a more traditional role, time negotiations have become a more complex and demanding activity (Daly, 2002), such as the struggle to meet the schedule demands of their children (Hochschild & Machung, 1989). Also, mothers preserve time for interacting with their children by accepting greater task density, in other words, working harder than fathers (Craig, 2006). As a result, mothers want slower, high-quality time with their children (Roxburgh, 2006). Cowdery and Knudson-Martin (2005) suggest that many couples hold contradictory ideologies related to parenting. These couples want fathers to be involved but the ideology of mothering as a gendered talent perpetuates separate spheres of parenting and gender inequality. The meaning of family time for mothers is thus linked to the ideology of motherhood, which is intricately related to how fatherhood is constructed.

The family literature on *fatherhood* has mushroomed since the 1990s (Marsiglio *et al.*, 2000). Most has been grounded in feminist concerns regarding the division of labour, gender, power and fairness. Studies have, in the main, been quantitative in nature (e.g. Blair & Johnson, 1992; Craig, 2006) and there has been less focus on the qualitative dimensions of father-hood, such as the important social role of fathers in teasing, talking to and teaching children (Lareau, 2000). Scholars have realised that fathering must be understood in its own context and not simply as an adjunct to maternal caring (Brotherson *et al.*, 2005), yet research is still dominated by the challenges faced by working mothers (Daly & Palkovitz, 2004). Social expectations of the father's role have changed considerably, from the father being mainly an economic provider to now being the 'new father' who is expected to provide as much care to children as the mother (Yeung *et al.*, 2001). This led to a disjunction between the ideals and the realities of being a provider and an engaged father, and a discrepancy between fathers' desire to spend more time with their children and work constraints (Daly, 1996b; McDonald & Almeida, 2004), which might explain why fathers are more likely than mothers to feel time deficits with their children (Milkie *et al.*, 2004). This all points to conflicts experienced by fathers as they seek to navigate their work and family lives while embracing greater responsibilities at home.

Fathers, in general, are spending significantly more time in childcare activities today than in the past (Sayer *et al.*, 2004). Yet, they are relatively rarely alone with their children and instead join their wives as helpers in the task (Craig, 2006), which has potential effects on father–child relations. Dollahite *et al.* (1997) developed the concept of *generative fathering* to describe fathering that responds readily and consistently to a child's developmental needs over time. Fathers primarily connect with their children through shared leisure activities (Brotherson *et al.*, 2005), which makes them more satisfied with their lives (Eggebeen & Knoester, 2001). Spending time with the kids is also a notion that is deeply embedded in the social discourse about being a good father (Daly, 1996b) rather than being inherited from their own fathers. The ideology of fatherhood has an effect not only on the meaning of family time for fathers and their desire for more time with their children but also on their identity formation (Allen & Daly, 2005) and is embedded in their parenthood role.

It has to be remembered in any discussion of gender that a review of the literature concluded that men and women are far more alike than they are different (Kimmel, 2004). Hence *parenthood* is all about collaboration and sharing of similar goals in rearing children. Current cultural ideals of parent-hood are shaped by both inherited gender traditions and the desire for new and more balanced practices which convey a sense of what parents should do (Daly, 2004). For example, parents in the USA engage in 'concerted culti-vation' by actively fostering children's talents and skills through organised activities at the expense of the parents' leisure preferences (Lareau, 2003), which points to behavioural shifts that privilege time with children over other activities (Bianchi *et al.*, 2006). This is coupled with people having smaller families, in which it is possible for each child to be in a sense 'more precious' (Sayer *et al.*, 2004), resulting in shifting power relationships between parents and children, especially parents' increasing psychological investment in their children (Mintz, 2004). The age of the youngest child is another factor that shapes parental feelings about time with children. Parents of young children tend to spend more focused time with them and feel more time strain than do those with older children (Milkie *et al.*, 2004). It can be with a tone of self-sacrifice that parents emphasise the greater importance of family time for their children (Daly, 2001). The culture of parenting is one that not only requires adaptability to societal change but also involves fundamental change in the generational relationship, affecting the meaning of family time for children.

The conception of *childhood* in today's society is built around the emotionally priceless child (Zelizer, 1985). Many years of study have shown that parents are the key in predicting child developmental outcomes, but parents are also influenced by their children and the child has a key influence in family dynamics (Crouter & Booth, 2003). The parent–child relationship, then, becomes an interactive process, one of mutual influence (Handel *et al.*,

2007) which involves a concept of contestation and negotiation (Thorpe & Daly, 1999). However, there is little research that compares parents' and children's perspectives on family time (Carr, 2011; Daly, 2001). Two studies found that children like family time to be less rushed (Galinsky, 1999) and that it is not the quantity of time but *how* parents spend it with their children that is important to them (Christensen, 2002). Also, children are happier with the amount of family time they have than are their parents (Christensen, 2002; Galinsky, 1999; Kränzl-Nagl & Beham, 2007), highlighting a potential generational disjuncture in understandings of family time. This indicates that the importance of family togetherness as espoused by adult society may not hold the same significance for children (Carr, 2011). In fact, Christensen (2002: 85) reports that the call for parents to spend more 'quality time' with their children is problematic if this 'denies children their need to be both with and without their families'. All this underlines the gendered and generational differences in the social meaning of family time, in that mothers seek higher-quality family time and fathers seek quantitatively more family time, while children want unstressed time together.

## The Idealisation of Family Leisure in Western Society

Leisure researchers have devoted considerable attention to family leisure. Most of this work is driven by the popular sentiment that 'a family that plays together stays together', based on the recognition that leisure experiences provide the context in which most family members establish, maintain and develop relationships with each other (Siegenthaler & O'Dell, 2000). The positive contributions of family leisure to family cohesion, family interaction and overall satisfaction with family life dominate the literature (Orthner & Mancini, 1990). Zabriskie and McCormick (2003) found that having both 'core' (i.e. everyday, home-based) and 'balance' (i.e. less common, away from home) family leisure activities was associated with higher levels of family functioning. Family leisure is also advanced as a key context in which most children develop lifelong skills and values (Mannell & Kleiber, 1997; Shaw & Dawson, 2001). Family leisure has been reported to have benefits by researchers operating from a social psychological paradigm, but this work did not consider gender inequality (Shaw, 1997), societal influences, children's perspectives or conflict.

There is a realisation among researchers that 'family leisure' has an underlying ideological notion that reflects a hegemonic and romanticised version of family life that reifies family leisure; this notion permeates not only leisure studies but also the popular media (Harrington, 2001; Hilbrecht *et al.*, 2008). This idealisation of family leisure can have negative consequences for parents through increased feelings of guilt and stress, especially among mothers, when the ideal of family togetherness is difficult for them to achieve (Shaw, 2001). Increasing research evidence emphasises that family leisure activities may not always be a positive experience for all family members (Larson *et al.*, 1997; Shaw & Dawson, 2001); a common example is conflict over watching television (Harrington, 2001). Harrington's (2001) study highlights how parents feel pressured to put their children always first, at the expense of their own leisure. Acknowledgement of both the benefits and the difficulties of family leisure can lead to a more realistic view of this valued aspect of family life (Shaw & Dawson, 2003/2004). This also includes recognising the implications that new ideologies of parenthood and parental responsibilities have for family leisure and the disjuncture with children's perceptions.

From the parents' perspective, family leisure in fact involves work as well as fun, and has been characterised as 'purposive leisure' (Shaw & Dawson, 2001), where the focus is on planning and facilitating leisure for the purpose of health, developmental and educational benefits for the children and the family as a unit. This idea of an instrumental or goal-directed orientation for family leisure activities can be linked to changed parental ideologies but has received little attention in the literature (Shaw, 2010). Another increasing trend has been towards organised activities for children – notably sports activities – which are perceived by parents as safe and 'good', at the expense of free play; this trend has been lamented by child development experts (Guldberg, 2009). Parents, and particularly fathers, are often involved in the organisation, management and coaching of children's sports as avenues to strengthen and enhance their relationship with their children (Coakley, 2006; Harrington, 2006; Kay, 2009). The facilitation of children's participation in organised leisure activities clearly ties to new ideas of parenting and the fulfilment of parental responsibilities (Trussell, 2009) along with changing gender roles.

Understanding fatherhood is a relatively new pursuit for family leisure scholarship (Kay, 2009; Such, 2006). Leisure-based activities seem to be more prominent in fathering than they are in mothering (Kay, 2006). For example, in Australia sport is perceived as a major site at which 'fathering' can occur and at which fathers can show an emotional connection to their children (Harrington, 2006). Recent publications on fatherhood in leisure (Kay, 2006, 2009) show that mothers perceive family leisure as more work-like or 'being there' for the children. In contrast, fathers describe leisure to mean 'being with' their children, resulting in a kind of 'leisure-based' parenting (Such, 2006), including the opportunity for non-resident fathers 'to parent' (Jenkins & Lyons, 2006). There is also a sense of fostering the next generation through children's leisure activities which is central to the generative notion of fathering (Harrington, 2006). Despite this, the evidence to date shows that mothers continue to facilitate most leisure experiences for their families, which adds to their overwhelming workloads (Shaw, 2010).

Fathers still see the traditional provider role as the defining function of fathering, which can be contextualised by an 'ethic of work' with an emotional dimension (Kay, 2006), while also feeling under increasing pressure to fulfil modern expectations of their role (Lewis, 2000). This disjunction between ideals and realities is not unique to fathers and also applies to working mothers. Strong ideological notions of how parents ought to behave underpin much family leisure. There are cultural standards of putting children first whereby the character and achievements of children are linked to the moral worth of parents (Coakley, 2006). Fathers are expected to be more intimate and have greater involvement with their children (Kay, 2003), while social pressures of being a 'good mother' and an 'ethic of care' prevail for women (Miller & Brown, 2005). This leads to feelings of guilt for taking time out for their own leisure (Harrington, 2001), although more mothers today believe that they have a right to time and space for themselves (Spowart et al., 2008). Family leisure is seen as an obligatory aspect of parental responsibility (Shaw, 2010), yet the achievement of family leisure, just as with family time, is perceived as a personal problem rather than a societal dilemma. Those ideologies are further highlighted when the children's perspective is taken into account.

The limited research on family leisure that has included children's perspectives highlights some generational differences in experience and even conflicts (Jeanes, 2010). Zabriskie and McCormick (2003) found that parents were more satisfied when providing 'purposive leisure' that was new and challenging, while children and particularly adolescents were more likely to value ordinary leisure activities, such as watching television together. Especially as children move through adolescence, the amount of leisure time spent with the family decreases, along with parental influence (Siegenthaler & O'Dell, 2000). Instead, young adolescents gain more pleasurable leisure experiences outside the family context (Larson et al., 1997), which is connected to the fun factor with friends (Francis & Kentel, 2008). Adolescents in particular may not enjoy family leisure as much as younger children because it does not provide excitement or an opportunity to fulfil their age-related needs (Larson et al., 1997). Family holidays can be perceived as an extension to family leisure but few tourism studies have included children. Carr (2011) states that the ideal image of the 'happy family' on holiday, which is viewed by society as a product of family togetherness, is unrealistic to live up to because of the differences between parents' and children's holiday desires and needs. The holiday experience may actually increase the potential for conflict as family members are in closer contact for longer periods than in the home environment and without any outside distractions. A Canadian study found that parents viewed some types of family leisure as 'purposive' while children rarely noticed this and instead viewed the purpose of holidays as having fun (Hilbrecht et al., 2008). For parents, family leisure on holiday is then more influenced by society and current ideologies of what constitutes 'good' parenting, whereas for children the focus is more immediate and also mediated by needs for sociality with peers.

# Conclusion

The change in societal perceptions of family time has implications for family holidays in that they are perceived by parents as opportunities for 'quality family time' or 'purposive leisure time' away from everyday distractions, and they form part of the image of the 'happy family'. In fact, holidays are often the only time the whole family spends together for an extended period and seemingly offer a balance to family life at home. The instrumental or purposive aspect of holidays and the emphasis put on family togetherness and harmony disguise individual needs for personal leisure and free or own time. There is a disjuncture between societal ideologies and individual realities and also between children's and parents' understandings of what constitute quality family time. In fact, holidays can give rise to intra-family conflicts, in that parents seek relaxation and children seek activities, which makes the ideal of togetherness hard to achieve (Gram, 2005). Stresses can also be added when family needs are not met by tourism operators, as discussed in Chapter 9. While the notion of spending 'quality time' together is dictated by adult society and endorsed as the Holy Grail for family leisure and holiday providers (Mintel, 2009), other aspects of time and the desires of all family members need to be included. This calls for a methodology inclusive of children's voices and the whole family group, as illustrated in Chapter 5. A move away from overly idealistic notions of family holidays is required, towards more realistic understandings that are accepting of individual needs for own time, free play and social time with peers. The idealisation of family time is also conceptualised around the white Anglo-Saxon nuclear family, which needs extension to other family forms. Thus, a more complete and privatised understanding is required of the different roles and desires on holiday, from a diversity of family forms. The inclusion of individual realities and lived experiences would provide a more sustainable representation of family holidays (or indeed any family situation). This chapter, then, provides a theoretical and sociological context for the ideological changes that influence family tourism and offers deeper insights into the trends and findings explored in other chapters of this book.

# References

Allen, S.M. and Daly, K. (2005) Fathers and the navigation of family space and time. In W. Marsiglio, K. Roy and G.L. Fox (eds), *Situated Fathering: A Focus on Physical and Social Spaces* (pp. 49–70). Oxford: Rowman and Littlefield.

Arendell, T. (2000) Conceiving and investigating motherhood: the decade's scholarship. *Journal of Marriage and Family*, 62(4), 1192–1207.

Bianchi, S.M., Robinson, J.P. and Milkie, M.A. (2006) *Changing Rhythms of American Family Life*. New York: Russell Sage Foundation.

Blair, S.L. and Johnson, M.P. (1992) Wives' perceptions of the fairness of the division of household labor: the intersection of housework and ideology. *Journal of Marriage and the Family*, 54(3), 570–581.

Brotherson, S.E., Dollahite, D.C. and Hawkins, A.J. (2005) Generative fathering and the dynamics of connection between fathers and their children. *Fathering*, 3(1), 1–28.

Carr, N. (2011) *Children's and Families' Holiday Experiences*. London: Routledge.

Christensen, P.H. (2002) Why more 'quality time' is not on the top of children's lists: the 'qualities of time' for children. *Children and Society*, 16(2), 77–88.

Coakley, J. (2006) The good father: parental expectations and youth sports. *Leisure Studies*, 25(2), 153–163.

Cowdery, R.S. and Knudson-Martin, C. (2005) The construction of motherhood: tasks, relational connection, and gender equality. *Family Relations*, 54(3), 335–345.

Craig, L. (2006) Does father care mean father share? A comparison of how mothers and fathers in intact families spend time with children. *Gender and Society*, 20(2), 259–281.

Crouter, A.C. and Booth, A. (eds) (2003) *Children's Influence on Family Dynamics: The Neglected Side of Family Relationships*. Mahwah, NJ: Lawrence Erlbaum Associates.

Daly, K. (1996a) *Families and Time: Keeping Pace in a Hurried Culture*. Thousand Oaks, CA: Sage.

Daly, K. (1996b) Spending time with the kids: meanings of family time for fathers. *Family Relations*, 45(4), 466–476.

Daly, K. (2001) Deconstructing family time: from ideology to lived experience. *Journal of Marriage and Family*, 63(2), 283–294.

Daly, K. (2002) Time, gender, and the negotiation of family schedules. *Symbolic Interaction*, 25(3), 323–342.

Daly, K. (2004) *The Changing Culture of Parenting*. Ottawa: Vanier Institute of the Family.

Daly, K. and Palkovitz, R. (2004) Guest editorial: reworking work and family issues for fathers. *Fathering*, 2(3), 211–213.

Davidson, R. and Gauthier, A.H. (2010) A cross-national multi-level study of family meals. *International Journal of Comparative Sociology*, 51(5), 349–365.

DeVault, M.L. (2000) Producing family time: practices of leisure activity beyond the home. *Qualitative Sociology*, 23(4), 485–503.

Doherty, E. (2011) Parents urged to turn off phones, computers to spend more time with children. *Courier-Mail* (Brisbane), 10 May.

Dollahite, D.C., Hawkins, A.J. and Brotherson, S.E. (1997) Fatherwork: a conceptual ethic of fathering as generative work. In A.J. Hawkins and D.C. Dollahite (eds), *Generative Fathering: Beyond Deficit Perspectives* (pp. 17–35). Thousand Oaks, CA: Sage.

Douglas, S.J. and Michaels, M.W. (2004) *The Mommy Myth: The Idealization of Motherhood and How It Has Undermined Women*. New York: Free Press.

Eggebeen, D.J. and Knoester, C. (2001) Does fatherhood matter for men? *Journal of Marriage and Family*, 63(2), 381–393.

Fiese, B.H., Tomcho, T.J., Douglas, M., Josephs, K., Poltrock, S. and Baker, T. (2002) A review of 50 years of research on naturally occurring family routines and rituals: Cause for celebration? *Journal of Family Psychology*, 16(4), 381–390.

Francis, N. and Kentel, J.A. (2008) The fun factor: adolescents' self-regulated leisure activity and the implications for practitioners and researchers. *Leisure/Loisir*, 32(1), 65–90.

Galinsky, E. (1999) *Ask the Children*. New York: Harper Collins.

Gauthier, A.H., Smeeding, T.M. and Furstenberg, F.F. (2004) Are parents investing less time in children? Trends in selected industrialized countries. *Population and Development Review*, 30(4), 647–672.

Gibbs, N. (2006) The magic of the family meal. *Time Magazine*, 167, 50 (12 June).

Giddens, A. (1984) *The Constitution of Society: Outline of the Theory of Structuration*. Berkeley, CA: University of California Press.

Gillis, J.R. (1996) *A World of Their Own Making: Myth, Ritual and the Quest for Family Values*. New York: Basic Books.

Gillis, J.R. (2000) *Our Virtual Families: Toward a Cultural Understanding of Modern Family Life*. Atlanta, GA: Emory Center for Myth and Ritual in American Life.

Gillis, J.R. (2001) Never enough time: some paradoxes of modern family time(s). In K.J. Daly (ed.), *Minding the Time in Family Experience: Emerging Perspectives and Issues* (pp. 19–36). New York: JAI Press.

Gram, M. (2005) Family holidays. A qualitative analysis of family holiday experiences. *Scandinavian Journal of Hospitality and Tourism*, 5(1), 2–22.

Guldberg, H. (2009) *Reclaiming Childhood: Freedom and Play in an Age of Fear*. Abingdon: Routledge.

Handel, G., Cahill, S.E. and Elkin, F. (2007) *Children and Society: The Sociology of Children and Childhood Socialization*. Los Angeles, CA: Roxbury.

Harrington, M. (2001) Gendered time: leisure in family life. In K.J. Daly (ed.), *Minding the Time in Family Experience: Emerging Perspectives and Issues* (vol. 3, pp. 343–382). Oxford: Elsevier Science.

Harrington, M. (2006) Sport and leisure as contexts for fathering in Australian families. *Leisure Studies*, 25(2), 165–183.

Hilbrecht, M., Shaw, S.M., Delamere, F.M. and Havitz, M.E. (2008) Experiences, perspectives, and meanings of family vacations for children. *Leisure/Loisir*, 32(2), 541–571.

Hochschild, A.R. and Machung, A. (1989) *The Second Shift: Working Parents and the Revolution at Home*. New York: Viking.

Jeanes, R. (2010) Seen but not heard? Examining children's voices in leisure and family research. *Leisure/Loisir*, 34(3), 243–259.

Jenkins, J. and Lyons, K. (2006) Nonresident fathers' leisure with their children. *Leisure Studies*, 25(2), 219–232.

Kay, T. (2003) Leisure, gender and self in the analysis of family. *World Leisure*, 45(4), 4–14.

Kay, T. (2006) Where's dad? Fatherhood in leisure studies. *Leisure Studies*, 25(2), 133–152.

Kay, T. (ed.) (2009) *Fathering Through Sport and Leisure*. London: Routledge.

Kimmel, M. (2004) *The Gendered Society* (2nd edition). New York: Oxford University Press.

Kränzl-Nagl, R. and Beham, M. (2007) *Time Poverty or Time Welfare in Austrian Families? Impact of Family Factors on Children's School Achievements*. Policy brief. Vienna: European Centre for Social Welfare Policy and Research.

Lareau, A. (2000) My wife can tell me who I know: methodological and conceptual problems in studying fathers. *Qualitative Sociology*, 23(4), 407–433.

Lareau, A. (2003) *Unequal Childhoods: Class, Race, and Family Life*. Berkeley, CA: University of California Press.

Larson, R.W., Gillman, S.A. and Richards, M.H. (1997) Divergent experiences of family leisure: fathers, mothers, and young adolescents. *Journal of Leisure Research*, 29(1), 78–97.

Lewis, C. (2000) *A Man's Place in the Home: Fathers and Families in the UK*. York: Joseph Rowntree Foundation.

Maher, J. (2005) A mother by trade: Australian women reflecting mothering as activity, not identity. *Australian Feminist Studies*, 20(46), 17–29.

Mannell, R.C. and Kleiber, D.A. (1997) *A Social Psychology of Leisure*. State College, PA: Venture.

Marsiglio, W., Amato, P., Day, R.D. and Lamb, M.E. (2000) Scholarship on fatherhood in the 1990s and beyond. *Journal of Marriage and the Family*, 62(4), 1173–1191.

Maume, D.J. (2006) Gender differences in taking vacation time. *Work and Occupations*, 33(2), 161–190.

McDonald, D.A. and Almeida, D.M. (2004) The interweave of fathers' daily work experiences and fathering behaviors. *Fathering*, 2(3), 235–251.

McMahon, M. (1995) *Engendering Motherhood: Identity and Self-transformation in Women's Lives*. New York: Guilford Press.

Mestdag, I. and Vandeweyer, J. (2005) Where has family time gone? In search of joint family activities and the role of the family meal in 1966 and 1999. *Journal of Family History*, 30(3), 304–323.

Milkie, M.A., Mattingly, M.J., Nomaguchi, K.M., Bianchi, S.M. and Robinson, J.P. (2004) The time squeeze: parental statuses and feelings about time with children. *Journal of Marriage and Family*, 66(3), 739–761.

Miller, Y. and Brown, W. (2005) Determinants of active leisure for women with young children – an 'ethic of care' prevails. *Leisure Sciences*, 27(5), 405–420.

Mintel (2009) *Family Leisure, Leisure Intelligence, December*. London: Mintel International Group.

Mintz, S. (2004) *Huck's Raft: A History of American Childhood*. Cambridge, MA: Harvard University Press.

Obrador, P. (2012) The place of the family in tourism research: domesticity and thick sociality by the pool. *Annals of Tourism Research*, 39(1), 401–420.

Orthner, D.K. and Mancini, J.A. (1990) Leisure impacts on family interaction and cohesion. *Journal of Leisure Research*, 22(2), 125–137.

Robinson, J.R. and Godbey, G. (1997) *Time for Life: The Surprising Ways Americans Use Their Time*. University Park, PA: Pennsylvania State University Press.

Roxburgh, S. (2006) 'I wish we had more time to spend together…': the distribution and predictors of perceived family time pressures among married men and women in the paid labor force. *Journal of Family Issues*, 27(4), 529–553.

Sandberg, J.F. and Hofferth, S.L. (2001) Changes in children's time with parents: United States, 1981–1997. *Demography*, 38(3), 423–436.

Sayer, L.C., Bianchi, S.M. and Robinson, J.P. (2004) Are parents investing less in children? Trends in mothers' and fathers' time with children. *American Journal of Sociology*, 110(1), 1–43.

Shaw, S.M. (1997) Controversies and contradictions in family leisure: an analysis of conflicting paradigms. *Journal of Leisure Research*, 29(1), 98–112.

Shaw, S.M. (2001) The family leisure dilemma: insights from research with Canadian families. *World Leisure*, 43(4), 53–62.

Shaw, S.M. (2010) Diversity and ideology: changes in Canadian family life and implications for leisure. *World Leisure Journal*, 52(1), 4–13.

Shaw, S.M. and Dawson, D. (2001) Purposive leisure: examining parental discourses on family activities. *Leisure Sciences*, 23(4), 217–231.

Shaw, S.M. and Dawson, D. (2003/2004) Contradictory aspects of family leisure: idealization versus experience. *Leisure/Loisir*, 28(3/4), 179–201.

Siegenthaler, K.L. and O'Dell, I. (2000) Leisure attitude, leisure satisfaction, and perceived freedom in leisure within family dyads. *Leisure Sciences*, 22(4), 281–296.

Snyder, K.A. (2007) A vocabulary of motives: understanding how parents define quality time. *Journal of Marriage and Family*, 69(2), 320–340.

Spowart, L., Hughson, J. and Shaw, S. (2008) Snowboarding mums carve out fresh tracks: resisting traditional motherhood discourse? *Annals of Leisure Research*, 11(1/2), 187–204.

Such, E. (2006) Leisure and fatherhood in dual-earner families. *Leisure Studies*, 25(2), 185–199.

Thorpe, K. and Daly, K. (1999) Children, parents, and time: the dialectics of control. In C.L. Shehan (ed.), *Contemporary Perspectives on Family Research* (vol. 1, pp. 199–223). Stamford, CT: JAI Press.

Trussell, D.E. (2009) *Organized Youth Sport, Parenthood Ideologies and Gender Relations: Parents' and Children's Experiences and the Construction of 'Team Family'*. Unpublished doctoral dissertation, University of Waterloo, Waterloo, Ontario.

Yeung, W.J., John, F.S., Pamela, E.D.-K. and Sandra, L.H. (2001) Children's time with fathers in intact families. *Journal of Marriage and Family*, 63(1), 136–154.

Zabriskie, R.B. and McCormick, B.P. (2003) Parent and child perspectives of family leisure involvement and satisfaction with family life. *Journal of Leisure Research*, 35(2), 163–189.

Zelizer, V. (1985) *Pricing the Priceless Child: The Changing Social Value of Children*. New York: Basic Books.

Zuzanek, J. (2001) Parenting time: enough or too little? *Isuma – Canadian Journal of Policy Research*, 2(2), 125–133.

# 3 Demography and Societal Change

Ian Yeoman, Una McMahon-Beattie,
Damian Lord and Luke Parker-Hodds

## Introduction

Children and families form the closest and most important emotional bond in humans. The relationship is what drives humanity and society, and as such the family is the centre of human activity (Yeoman, 2008). As a consequence, family tourism is one of the most important sectors in the tourism industry and constitutes 25% of all trips by domestic tourism in the UK (VisitBritain, 2011). There are many futurists and commentators (Yeoman, 2012) arguing that in an uncertain world the only thing that is certain in life is birth and death. In between those certainties, social structures with families are changing. The OECD (2008) identifies higher rates of female participation in the labour market, higher divorce rates, more single parents, rising and longer enrolment in education, growing numbers of elderly, higher numbers of foreign-born population and ethnic diversity as demographic trends that will change structures in society.

The purpose of this chapter is to identify the core demographic changes that are occurring in society and identify the implications for tourism, as summed up in the concluding Figure 3.9. Why? Families are all about demography, therefore understanding the future of families and the direction of these trends is extremely important for the family tourism market. The chapter observes those changes that are occurring in the UK, as those changes are representative of similar patterns occurring in the advanced economies of the OECD. The data for this chapter were provided by the Future Foundation, a London-based consumer think-tank, whose six-times-a-year survey of 11,000 UK households enables organisations to identify changes in society from longitudinal data, thus identifying and forecasting social and consumer trends that are relevant across Western societies.

# Changes That Will Shape the Future of the Family

Changes in social structures tend to be slow-moving. Many of these gradual changes that have been taking place in those countries comprising the membership of the Organisation for Economic Co-operation and Development (OECD) are likely to continue and in some cases intensify their impact on the traditional family (OECD, 2008). These include increasing longevity leading to stronger multigenerational ties; trends to smaller families leading to stronger social networks outside the immediate family; and increasing blurring between various forms of partnerships. From another perspective, family relations may in the future be reconfigured on new, more sustainable foundations. Society may increasingly see networks of loosely connected family members from different marriages, partnerships and generations emerging, who devise fresh approaches to cohesion and solidarity. Growing, better-integrated ethnic communities may help to instil more positive family values (old and new) into mainstream society. This section identifies the key trends that are shaping families in the UK before the following section assesses what it all means for the tourism businesses.

## The decline of the nuclear family

The most noticeable and well established trend in British family life has been the decline of the nuclear family and the rise of the household comprising a single person under pensionable age. It is predicted that in the 60 years from 1961 to 2021 (Figure 3.1), households consisting of a couple with children will have declined from about half of all households to around a fifth. During the same time period, single-person households will have increased from less than 5% to nearly a 20%. However, other types of household, such as couples without children, lone parents and single persons over pensionable age, are forecast to remain relatively steady. Hence, it is clear that the decreasing number of nuclear families is due not to a decline in partnerships but to people remaining childless for various reasons. For a growing segment of society, having children is increasingly thought of as a lifestyle choice; as a result of our 'have it all' society, a growing proportion of women who aspire to have children are postponing childbirth until later or indefinitely (Future Foundation, 2006). Additionally, financial pressures may have deterred some couples from having children. What is certain is that the nuclear family is certainly in decline as a result of shifting priorities, at least within among those in early adult life. Basically, in the future the number of households will grow but there will be fewer households with children.

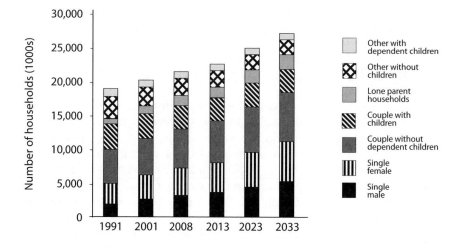

**Figure 3.1** Household composition, 1991–2033: Numbers of households in England by household type (projections are 2010 forecasts based on 2008 data). *Source*: Future Foundation

## Falling marriage rates and increasing divorce rates

As outlined in Figure 3.2, the number of marriages taking place has fallen to a new low in recent years. At the same time, divorce rates have remained relatively stable, which means that the proportion of marriages ending in divorce has been steadily growing. It seems clear that the growing divorce rate has brought a kind of instability to the family concept.

However, what is often overlooked is the detailed analysis (Figure 3.2), which shows the family is being reconstituted, even in light of divorce statistics, as a great proportion of divorcees remarry and cohabit. Indeed, higher proportions of divorced people cohabit than any other marital group. Hence, while families are separating through divorce, people are forming new families, while often still being networked to their old ones through the children. Social, as opposed to biological, parenting is an increasing phenomenon in family life. More and more men and women are raising children who are not biologically their own. For example, research by the Future Foundation (2006) found that 17% of men born in 1970 are stepfathers, nearly double the proportion among men born just 12 years earlier. Since the majority of children remain with their biological mother after divorce, most stepfamilies will have a stepfather rather than a stepmother. Most non-resident fathers have regular contact with their children, with nearly a half seeing them every week and a further fifth at least once a month. In

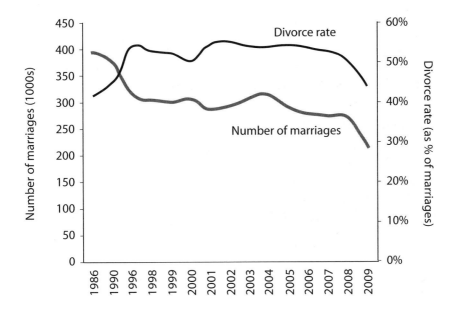

**Figure 3.2** Number of marriages and divorce rate, 1986–2009 (2009 figures are based on that year's first three quarters only). *Source*: Future Foundation

the UK, only 3% of non-resident fathers never see their children, although a further 18% have effectively no contact, since they meet their children less than once a year.

## An ageing society

Life expectancy in the UK in 2011 stood at 78.4 years for men and 82.6 years for women. This was a 10-year increase for both men and women since 1950 (Yeoman, 2012). Society is rapidly ageing; by 2023, the over-75s will constitute over a tenth of the population (Office of National Statistics, 2010b). This has several major implications for the family. Firstly, the family will become increasingly multigenerational as grandparents survive into an older age. This greatly contrasts with the beginning of the century, when the average woman would have died not long after her last child reached 15. Secondly, longevity has the potential to create a false sense of security in relation to postponing childbirth; while women in their thirties are far from being considered 'middle aged', those approaching their thirties may not realise that their fertility will be rapidly dissipating within the next few years. Finally, with people having children later in life as well as living longer, the 'family life-stage' is no longer the period in our lives which dominates as it had in the past. In fact, in terms of time, the predominant stage in a person's life is now after the children have left home.

## Emotional attachments

According to research by the Future Foundation (2006), half the UK population claims that they get all or most of their satisfaction from family life, while another 41% state that they experience equal satisfaction from family life and from other activities. Indeed, only a minority do not cite the family as a prime source of happiness. Family life seems to make us more satisfied as consumers become older, suggesting that children may be the main source of happiness or that they create new bonds and closeness within the family.

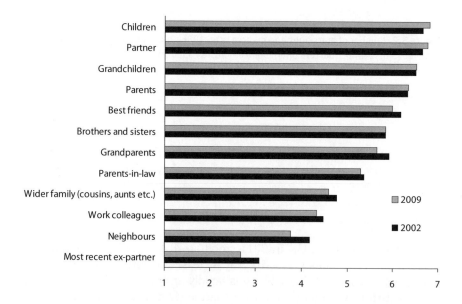

**Figure 3.3** Closeness of emotional attachments: Mean scores given to emotional attachment to selected types of people, 2002 and 2009. A sample of 1200 adults, all with a relation in question, responded to the following item: 'We usually have close emotional ties to some people, and more distant ties, or none at all, to others. From this list of types of people, can you tell me how close you feel your emotional attachment is to them? Please use a scale of 1 to 7, where 1 is no particular emotional attachment at all, and 7 is a very close emotional attachment.' *Source*: Future Foundation

Figure 3.3 reveals that respondents considered children, partner, parents, grandchildren and best friends as being extremely close to them (with an attributed score of attachment being higher than six out of seven). Best friends rated at almost the same level of closeness to respondents as parents and they were considered closer than siblings. As such, it appears that friends are expected to play an even greater role in people's emotional lives. There is no demise of the family as far as emotional attachments are concerned. As the nuclear family morphs, networks of emotional closeness are reconstituted. For example, a husband may become an ex-partner and become less close to his ex-wife; nonetheless, his children will still remain close to him.

## The effect of migration

As a consequence of globalisation, there is no corner of the world that remains untouched by migration. As European Union citizens, people in the UK can take advantage of free movement and are resettling, often in the preferred destinations of Spain and France. Indeed, the landscape of the UK is changing as inbound migration has made London, for example, a melting pot of international inhabitants from a multitude of countries, from anywhere from Poland to Somalia. Simply put, people no longer live next door to many of their family members. Diasporas of this kind will, of course, affect everyday family life (Future Foundation, 2006).

## The democratic family

The family is not only changing in structure but also in the attitudes which govern relationships within it. As shown in Figure 3.4, family members were revealed in the research by the Future Foundation (2006) as becoming more open with each other than ever before. Parents are increasingly including children in any major decision-making and are giving children more autonomy in their personal consumption. Additionally, traditional domestic roles, such as women being the primary carer for children, are starting to become slightly less rigid. This is what is known as the democratic family. As a result of this democratisation, children's quarrels with parents are becoming more infrequent. At present, one-third of 11–16-year-olds quarrel with their mothers once a week and one-fifth quarrel with their fathers. As a consequence, children are becoming more involved in the decisions about holiday destination and activities.

## The family network

The family plays a central role in daily life. As Castells (2009) suggests, 'it is the psychological lynchpin of people's lives'. While the modern family is as strong as its predecessors, it is being reconstituted from a family unit to

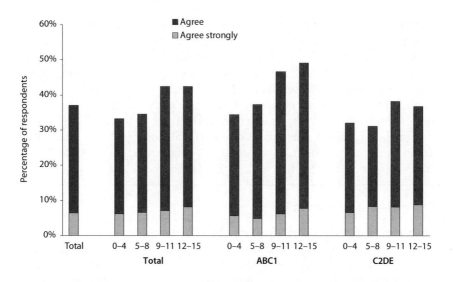

**Figure 3.4** The democratic family: The percentage of respondents who agree or agree strongly with the statement 'In my family, children have a say in important family spending decisions', by age of child and by age of child within social grade. (Data from 5000 respondents to an online survey, 2010.) *Source*: The Future Foundation

a family network. There are numerous reasons why the authors consider this to be so. Firstly, a network transcends time and space. Today's family is likely to experience some level of dispersion as migration becomes more common. A family unit, on the other hand, is more linked to actual location. Secondly, as families become smaller and move around more, new networks of reciprocal support are built. These networks may include anyone from close friends to distant relatives. Children are increasingly being brought up by non-biological parents. Thus, love and trust are decreasingly being defined by blood and so the notion of family is becoming more fluid and flexible. While at present in the majority of traditional two-parent families the man is still the primary breadwinner and the woman is the primary carer for children, it is now socially accepted to not adhere to this formulation. With women strengthening their position in the workplace, women may be the breadwinners in many families and husbands may opt to be a stay-at-home dad. The change to a network is then not a dramatic change in behaviour but a shift in cultural paradigm, where the emphasis within each family is on flexibility and multiple roles.

## The connected family

As each generation of parents becomes increasingly techno-literate, technology plays an important role in the family network. For example, Skype (http://www.skype.com) is making speaking to family on the other side of the world easy and free, and Facebook (http://www.facebook.com) is allowing family members to see what each other is doing, and the Story Before Bed website (http://www.astorybeforebed.com) provides a platform for families to read interactive stories online using different social media platforms. The internet and other technology platforms have become facilitators of communication in which distance is no longer a barrier (Yeoman, 2008).

## The vertical family

Longevity and smaller core families have led to the family becoming more vertical rather than statically horizontal in form. Grandparents as they live longer are enjoying more time with their grandchildren. Consider the following: in 1960, the life expectancy of a woman was 73 and the mean age for giving birth was 27. Presently, life expectancy for a woman in the UK is 82.6 (Office for National Statistics, 2010b). Thus, although the age for giving birth is increasingly in the thirties, present-day grandparents

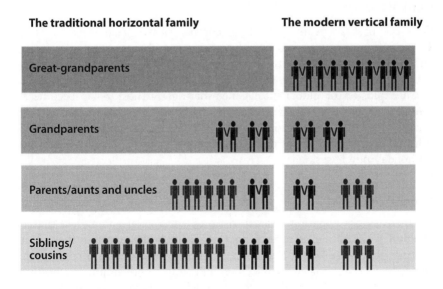

**Figure 3.5**  The vertical family. *Source*: Briggs (2001)

can expect to enjoy several more years with their grandchildren than those of the 1960s. The verticalisation of the family is apparent through more grandparents becoming involved in caring for their grandchildren. Where siblings within a larger family would have previously been responsible for baby-sitting duties, grandparents in the vertical family are now taking their place. As Young (cited in Briggs, 2001) pointed out, these inter-generational relationships play a central role in the family network, as a prominent part of this process of verticalisation (see Figure 3.5). Indeed, as people live to a greater age and childcare becomes more expensive, some parents are relying on grandparents to play an active role in their grandchildren's lives.

## Ethnic minorities

The nuclear family is not the force it was within the majority of the population. However, within certain segments of the population, such as certain Asian communities, the nuclear family still exists. Within Indian, Pakistani and Bangladeshi groups, the traditional nuclear family still comprises over half of all households. In contrast, people of Black ethnic origin are the least likely to live within a nuclear family. Additionally, all ethnic minorities are far more likely to have a much smaller proportion of people of pensionable age. Ethnic minority groups are also more likely than the majority White ethnic group to see their non-immediate family such as their grandparents, aunts and uncles on a regular basis (Future Foundation, 2006).

## Word of mouth

Over the past 25 years, distrust of companies has been steadily rising. At the moment, over a quarter of consumers feel that companies in the UK (Figure 3.6) are unfair to consumers and nearly half agree that multinational companies cannot be trusted. Concurrently, the internet has led to an explosion of global intelligence-sharing. Authority has become so fragmented that the real challenge is choosing the best sources rather than finding the bare information (Future Foundation, 2006; Yeoman, 2008). Within this context, the family has become a growing source of influence for holiday purchases.

## Anxious parents

An increasingly apparent characteristic of the modern family is that of parental responsibilities stretching further into the lives of their 21st-century offspring. The 2010s decade is likely to see a continuation of the trend, given the rising costs associated with higher education and housing and a less than stellar employment market for new entrants. As calling on parental assistance – emotionally and financially – becomes a necessity for

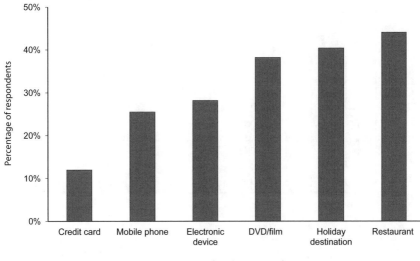

**Figure 3.6** Family as a source of influence, by market. The proportion of a sample of 1,200 adults (UK, 2006) who were influenced by their family when choosing a product or service in each market (proportion of 'family' responses to the question 'When you last did each of the following things, which of the following sources, if any, was influential in choosing it? So, the last time you...?'). *Source*: Future Foundation

many, numerous opportunities present themselves to the savvy brands of the day. According to the UK's Office for National Statistics (2010b), 29% of men and 18% of women aged 20–34 live with their parents (including one-quarter of 25–29-year-old men), up from 27% and 15% respectively in 2001. This is a trend with international parallels; 'boomerang kids', for example, is a term used to describe the increasing numbers of young adults returning to the family home in the USA. In Japan, the prominent stay-at-home demographic is affectionately referred to as 'parasite singles' (Nishi & Kan, 2006). In Australia, too, one in four people aged 20–34 now live with their parents, up from one in five during the mid-1980s (Weston *et al.*, 2001). The phenomenon known as 'helicopter parenting' (Yeoman, 2008) has become well and truly entrenched in the US cultural lexicon. Appearing first in the 1990s, the term is used to describe how some parents 'hover' above the lives of their children, ready to swoop at a moment's notice either to intervene in their child's interest or to contribute to key life decisions traditionally taken independently by the young adult.

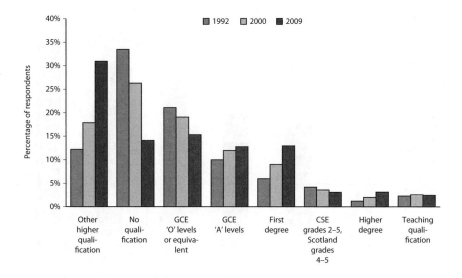

**Figure 3.7** Educational attainment, 1992–2009. Proportion of a sample of 7179 British adults endorsing selected educational qualifications in response to the question 'Which of these is your highest qualification?' *Source*: Future Foundation

Figure 3.7 indicates significant increases in those completing further and higher education. In 2009, 2.9 million school-leavers in England and Wales went on to higher education, compared with 0.7 million in 1970. Attainment in higher education is a key attribute of the modern family, resulting in discerning consumers and the choices they make regarding cultural experiences. As a consequence of higher participation rates in all levels of education, structures in society are changing, especially as women participate at a higher rate than men in higher education. As a consequence, certain professions are becoming dominated by women. Penn (2008) terms this 'wordy women'. For example, in the Church of England, more women than men have been ordained as clergy since 2006. In that year, Church statistics showed that 244 of the 478 clergy ordained were women and the other 234 were men (Yeoman, 2008).

## An affluent society and family spending

In the UK, household disposable income grew threefold in real terms between the early 1950s and 2008, an annual growth rate of 2.5% per annum (Yeoman, 2008), with tourism being a beneficiary of this growth as families

**Table 3.1** Expenditure of households by gross income group, 2009

| Commodity or service | One-adult household with one child | Two-adult households with two children | *HRP aged 65–74 | *HRP aged under 30 |
|---|---|---|---|---|
| Food and non-alcoholic drinks | £36.70 | £76.50 | £50.10 | £58.70 |
| Clothing and footwear | £15.40 | £32.70 | £72.60 | £28.00 |
| Transport | £29.10 | £76.70 | £43.20 | £72.70 |
| Recreation and culture | £32.50 | £98.10 | £55.70 | £68.90 |
| Restaurants and hotels | £19.60 | £54.50 | £25.90 | £49.70 |

* HRP – Household Reference Person (the person within the household who is chosen to characterise the household's social position)

*Source*: Office for National Statistics (2010a)

with increased disposable income spent more on culture, experiences and out-of-home expenditure during that period.

Table 3.1 shows the average weekly household expenditure across all UK households in 2009 on five key commodities and services. The inclusion of the five commodities and services listed is designed to show a comparison between expenditure on what may be classified as essential items, namely food and clothing, and those services which may be classed as non-essential or luxury items. It is recognised, however, that a significant component of transport expenditure is likely to be on accessing the workplace. Although expenditure differed across income groups, in some cases quite significantly, as is evident from a more detailed statistical comparison, what is clear is that many households, regardless of their make-up (for example one or more children or different ages of household reference person), allocated a significant proportion of their weekly expenditure to tourism and leisure products and services. In most cases, more money was allocated to the pursuit of recreational and cultural activities than to the basic essentials of food, clothing and footwear.

## Obesity

In 1980 only 6% of men and 8% of women were obese, whereas in 2007 nearly 25% of the UK population was obese, including over 10% of children aged 2–10. In 2007, the government-commissioned Foresight (2007) report predicted that if no action was taken, 60% of men, 50% of women and 25% of children would be obese by 2050. As a consequence, obesity is an important trend in a health conscious world. Being healthy is a preoccupation for most consumers. Since the mid-1980s, UK consumers' desire to stay fit and well has increased significantly (jumping from 20% to 75%) with consumption of health foods doubling (Yeoman, 2008). However, consumers' desire for well-being coexists with a thirst for indulgence. Consumers take steps to become healthier but are unwilling to sacrifice many aspects of a modern lifestyle which bring pleasure.

## Age compression

Eager to grow up, today's tweens (8–12-year-olds), like youngsters before them, are zealously trying to emulate the consumer habits of those older than them. Businesses have been quick to recognise that the growing distinction between children's ages is pronounced enough to warrant products and services specifically focused on those tweens who are aspiring to become more like teenagers and adults (Yeoman, 2010), as illustrated in Figure 3.8. Children have always had specific consumer needs. The difference today compared with earlier is perhaps that more and more products are targeting these tween needs from an earlier age. Whether society thinks this a blameworthy development (laid at the door of the media and marketing communities) or whether children are just evolving faster than before, something of a shrinking of childhood seems to have taken place. This phenomenon is often referred to as 'age compression' or 'children growing older younger'. As illustrated in Figure 3.8, the blurring of the boundaries between childhood and full-blown adolescence is happening at an earlier age than just a generation or two ago. In the 1960s, childhood was a distinct stage and it had been only roughly a decade since the world had discovered or invented the 'teenager'. Today, children seem to adopt the habits and attitudes of what has so far been considered the teen domain at an earlier age than previously – hence the emergence of the 'tween' (preadolescence, that is, the stage between middle childhood and adolescence in human development, in the range of 9–12 years old). There can be no doubt that the concepts of both 'childhood' and 'youth' are being redefined and that, as consumers, today's kids are very different.

Today, increasingly sophisticated merchandise is being pitched at much younger children, with far more advertising. A whole new consumer industry has developed trying to lure tweens with toys that are edgy or sophisticated

Age                                                                          Age

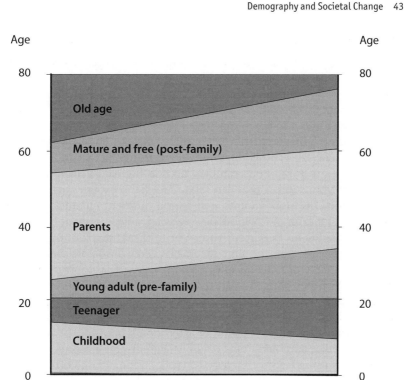

**Figure 3.8** Age compression: changing age range characterising each of six life-stages. *Source*: Future Foundation

enough for their taste. Producers of make-up, clothes, toiletries, electronics, food and drink, music and games treat children as a current 'market'. At the retail level, such outlets as video arcades, shopping centres, restaurants and cinemas also recognise that tweens are an important segment, with money to spend.

## So, What Does All This Mean For Tourism Businesses?

The previous section discussed the core trends that are shaping families and society from a demographic perspective. The next section addresses the more practical implications for businesses that these demographic and societal changes bring to family tourism.

## Democracy and anxious parents

Children are part of the decision-making process regarding where to go and what to do on holiday. As such, tourism businesses need to develop innovative and effective communication methods that engage all family members from the start of the family holiday planning process. This means designing websites and brochures for all the family rather than just the key decision-makers. Business will increasingly wish to engage with children, although there are ethical dilemmas concerning marketing to children. Anxious parents mean that families need a higher level of reassurance, particularly from sources that can relate first-hand experiences before they make the final decision. Parents will search different channels for recommendations, for example from http://www.tripadvisor.com or from friends. As the internet is an important source of information, tour operators and travel agents need to host online forums (where consumers exchange ideas and have a source of truthful information) and virtual tours of properties. All of this provides parents with reassurance in making a decision. These anxious parents have a tendency to over-schedule every aspect of their children's lives. For a growing number of middle-class children especially, their free time is a constant round of afternoon school clubs, music lessons and organised leisure activities. Anxious parents may monitor children's whereabouts using GPS technology to track children: Lok8u (http://www. lok8u.com) is one such company that offers GPS wristwatches to keep tags on children. Therefore, tourism businesses may want to consider how innovations such as these can add value to their service offering.

From a destination branding perspective, it is important for organisations to meet the needs of anxious parents through quality assurance. VisitScotland's Children's Welcome Scheme is a voluntary scheme that signals to families that children are welcome here and the establishment has a minimum number of facilities and procedures geared towards families. The scheme covers self-catering establishments, serviced apartments, restaurants, holiday parks, caravan parks and visitor attractions.

As every trend has a counter-trend, the desire from parents for children to be carefree, just play and not be overprotected is the basis of the website http://freerangekids.wordpress.com. Here, children are encouraged to be children and companies are creating opportunities for children to roam free and discover their creative potential. This is why camping and caravanning have remained popular among families (Mintel, 2009; Yeoman, 2008). Camp sites are safe places, offer flexibility and affordability with recognisable parameters, minimum interference and control; children are allowed to explore their environment. In addition, the UK scouting movement saw consecutive years of growth over the period 2006–2010, with membership growing to 499,323, the largest growth spurt since 1972 (Scouts, 2011), a recognition of a back-to-basics culture as a trend which is the opposite of Louv's (2010) argument that children are losing a connection with playing outdoors.

## Price

As families are more price sensitive today (Yeoman, 2012) and will keenly understand differences in service offers, suppliers must be able to segment tourists by value and life cycle in order to build a relationship and encourage repeat purchase at different life-stages. Suppliers should consider loyalty schemes or cash-back offers for those regular and repeat purchase tourists. For example, having found that more and more customers were wishing to holiday with both children and grandparents together, Eurocamp, a holiday accommodation company, decided to waive the adult fee for grandparents who share the same accommodation as the rest of their family. Where consumers want difference and activity, the trend towards healthy activity is important and providers should focus on the values, safety and benefits of doing such activity. According to research by VisitEngland (2011), as the global financial crisis deepened, pessimism about the economy grew, and therefore the trend towards the 'staycation' picked up pace, with two in 10 consumers taking a short break in England in 2010 rather than going abroad. In particular, 18–34-year-olds were more likely to staycation.

## Family bond

Research by Mintel (2009) suggests that the family leisure time is shrinking. Families have less time to relax and play together; therefore time together becomes the new luxury (Yeoman, 2008) and tourism is the facilitator of quality time. As a consequence, family tourism has an opportunity to be the social glue that increases the opportunity for family interaction. Independent domestic holidaymakers simply want to relax and unwind and hand over childcare to someone else. Parents who go on package family breaks are the most likely to spend time with their children (Mintel, 2009). The same can be said for family consumers who go on short breaks, although they are slightly more inclined to choose to relinquish childcare to someone else, who is likely to be a trusted friend or relative. Therefore, tourist businesses can no longer differentiate themselves based on price alone and need to formulate distinctive approaches to target different family holidaymaker types. Facilities alone are insufficient to attract all segments of the family market. Clear and different messages for each target group are essential. For instance, companies targeting independent family holidaymakers should emphasise the opportunities for parents to relax and unwind without the children.

## Ageing population

As society ages, the elderly population has an important caregiving role in looking after children. Closer bonding between young and old (as illustrated by the Disney-Pixar film *Up* – http://adisney.go.com/disney videos/animatedfilms/up) is an important social phenomenon, along with the growing opportunities for grandparents and grandchildren to holiday together (called 'grandtravelling'). As families are more mobile and grandparents live more active and independent lives than any previous generation and as grandparents and grandchildren often live too far apart to see each other regularly, so grandparents are always looking for ways to draw their families together and strengthen the relationship with their grandchildren. Characteristics of the elderly population include lots of free time, willingness to travel and a desire to spend time with their family, especially grandchildren. The baby boomer generation, in particular, is better off than any other generation has been and, consequently, its members are spending more money on grandchildren. Hence, the grandtraveller is born, especially during school holidays, when parents may have to work.

The concept of grandtravel was first put into practice by Helena Koenig, who set up the tour operator Grandtravel in 1989 in Maryland (Yeoman, 2008). Grandtravel runs escorted tours and has received over 15,000 enquiries without any advertising. The Walt Disney Corporation was another pioneer of the idea of grandparents travelling with their grandchildren. In 1998, Disney recognised opportunities to attract grandparents and grandchildren to Disney theme parks for holidays and the company offered special packages and travel arrangements specifically for this market. Grandtravelling is popular because it offers something for everyone involved, even the parents, who are not travelling. Grandparents are able to spend quality time with their grandchildren without interference from the parents. The parents are able to relax, knowing their children are away with someone they trust.

## Family models

The family structure is changing from a horizontal to a vertical model (see Figure 3.5), therefore tourism suppliers need to provide for a diversity of facilities and/or offer a high degree of flexibility such as 'family tickets' that extend beyond the norm of two adults and two children. In order to further create value, providers should facilitate the process of bonding by bringing parents and children closer together to share experiences, whether that is music or hobbies. Indeed, as the 'experience economy' grows, family cultural visits are on the rise (Mintel, 2009); in particular, we are noticing an increase in parents and children attending pop concerts together as different generations become more likely to share similar values and tastes (for example, the Glastonbury festival is increasingly popular with families). According to Mintel (2009) the 'family life-stage' penetration of concerts and festivals increased from 25% to 48% in the decade up to 2009. This trend of vertical families doing things together has seen attractions such as Alton Towers (http://www.altontowers.co.uk) and Warwick Castle (http://www.warwick-castle.com) promote themselves as 'true family resorts', with attractions from '3 to 83'. The latter offers an edutainment-based approach to history (where education and entertainment come together), with interactive experiences such as jousting tournaments and falconry alongside guided tours of the castle, and the former appeals to parents as well as children with a broad mix of rides. Attending live sports events as a family remains a favourite activity of dads, along with trips to the zoo.

The family tourism market also faces the challenge of responding to demographic trends, including the rise of single-parent families, which has created more female-led and part-time working family structures. There has being an increase in suppliers who provide specialist websites, holidays and facilities, such as http://www.familienhotel-laurentius.com, where children are given the opportunity to quickly find friends to play with while parents have time for some relaxation.

A more educated society means greater awareness of what is happening in society and a desire for edutainment, hence the importance of culture, museums and theatres in the future. Indeed, since 2000 there has been a steady increase in theatre and art attendance, along with an increase in family life-stage reading. Films and books such as *Harry Potter* have rekindled children's interest in reading (Mintel, 2009). Tourism businesses need constantly to innovate as leisure-savvy families are saying 'seen it, done it'; for example, Thorpe Park (http://www.thorpepark.com) is constantly introducing new rides. The 'seen it, done it' families are driven by a need to find value for money against a trend of seeking novelty and the desire for new experiences (Yeoman, 2008).

## Concluding Remarks

Changing family structures and relationships are affected by population patterns, with implications for family tourism, as shown in Figure 3.9. It is recognised that:

- As longevity continues to rise, adults are marrying and having children at later ages. The average age of a mother at childbirth will reach 30.7 years by 2025; meanwhile, the mean age at first marriage stood at 32.2 years for men and 30.05 for women in 2009 (Office for National Statistics, 2010b).
- Grandparents are playing an ever more active role in family lives but are increasingly techno-savvy and dismissive of age stereotypes. Research by the Future Foundation (2011) suggested that nearly a third of those aged over 65 will be social networkers by 20151 and around a quarter will be mobile internet users.
- The ethnic market is growing in size and will comprise over 7 million people by 2020, with these households typically being comparatively young, large and urban (Office for National Statistics, 2010b).
- Nearly 80% of people now agree that children are financially dependent on their parents for longer than in previous generations. Furthermore, as

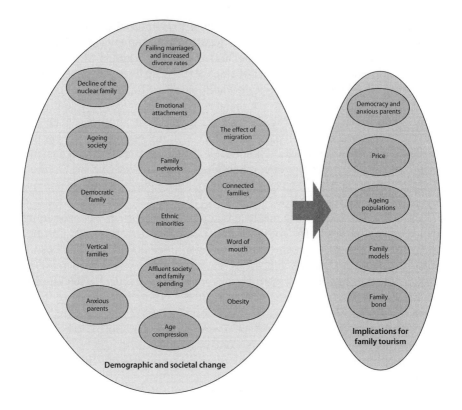

**Figure 3.9** Core demographic and societal changes shaping the future of family tourism

the age at which adults buy their first property rises, so greater numbers of children are living in their parents' homes into adulthood (Future Foundation, 2011).

- In an ever more urban society, enthusiasm for nature and the countryside is pronounced; over 80% of parents agree that children should know as much as possible about nature (Future Foundation, 2011).

Many commentators have stated that the family is in destructive decline, yet there is very little evidence to support such a proposition (Future Foundation, 2011). What is changing is the structure of families as a result of demographic changes. As a consequence, families are becoming more democratic, hence destination choice and holiday activities are discussed more among all family members. Fewer children in society mean they become more important and the focus of attention across the generations. Grandparents live longer and are seen as caregivers and are part of a new market called grandtravellers. What this chapter has highlighted are the demographic changes that are occurring and the practical implications they can have for tourism business, thus providing insight and direction.

## References

Briggs, A. (2001) *Michael Young: Social Entrepreneur*. Basingstoke: Palgrave Macmillan.

Castells, M. (2009) *The Power of Identity: The Information Age – Economy, Society, and Culture*. New York: Wiley-Blackwell.

Foresight (2007) *Tackling Obesities: Future Choices*. London: Department for Business, Innovation and Skills. Retrieved 26 June 2011 from http://www.bis.gov.uk/foresight/our-work/projects/published-projects/tackling-obesities/reports-and-publications.

Future Foundation (2006) *Networked Family*. nVision Trend Report. London: Future Foundation.

Future Foundation (2011) *Multigenerational Family*. Retrieved 14 June 2012 from http://www.futurefoundation.net.

Louv, R. (2010) *Last Child in the Woods: Saving Our Children from Nature-Deficit Disorder*. New York: Atlantic Books.

Mintel (2009) *Reports Family Leisure – UK*. London: Mintel International Group. Retrieved 22 June 2011 from http://academic.mintel.com/sinatra/oxygen_academic/my_reports/display.

Nishi, F. and Kan, M. (2006) Current situation of parasite singles in Japan. Retrieved 27 May 2011 from http://www.metlink.org.nz/timetables/train/HVL.

OECD (2008) *The Future of the Family to 2030*. Retrieved 28 June from http://www.oecd.org/dataoecd/11/34/42551944.pdf.

Office for National Statistics (2010a) *Family Spending*. Newport: Office of National Statistics. Retrieved 27 June 2011 from http://www.statistics.gov.uk/downloads/theme_social/familyspending2010.pdf.

Office for National Statistics (2010b) *National Population Projections, 2010 based projections*. Retrieved 28 November 2011 from http://www.ons.gov.uk/ons/rel/npp/national-population-projections/2010-based-projections/index.html.

Penn, M. (2008) *Microtrends: Surprising Tales of the Way We Live Today*. New York: Penguin.

Scouts (2011) Scouting sees biggest membership surge in 40 years. Retrieved 2 August 2011 from http://www.scouts.org.uk/news/288/scouting-sees-biggest-membership-surge-in-40-years.

Southall, C. (2010) Family tourism. Retrieved 22 June 2011 from http://www.insights.org.uk/articleitem.aspx?title=Family+Tourism

VisitBritain (2011) Inbound visitor statistics. Retrieved 10 July 2011 from http://www.visitbritain.org/insightsandstatistics/inboundvisitorstatistics/index.aspx.

VisitEngland (2011) *The Staycation: 2011 and Beyond?* Retrieved on 28 July from http://www.visitengland.org/Images/Staycation%202011%20March%202011%20Debrief_for%20internet_tcm30-26164.pdf.

Weston, R., Lixia, Q. and Soriano, G. (2001) The changing shape of Australia's population. Retrieved 23 November 2011 from http://www.aifs.gov.au/institute/pubs/briefing10.pdf.

Yeoman, I. (2008) *Tomorrow's Tourist: Scenarios and Trends*. Oxford: Elsevier.

Yeoman, I. (2010) Consumer kids and tourism. Retrieved 29 May 2011 from http://www.tomorrowstourist.com/kids.php.

Yeoman, I. (2012) *2050: Tomorrow's Tourism*. Bristol: Channel View Publications.

# 4 UK Family Tourism: Past, Present and Future Challenges

Carol Southall

## Introduction

Increasingly the diversity of the family tourism market appears to be the subject of limited and somewhat narrow considerations by tourism organisations. The growing importance of this market should not be underestimated and, despite the prevailing economic climate, tourism organisations that recognise and accommodate the changing 'make-up' of families are more likely to attract significant economic returns. The result of quality time spent together on holiday is likely to be improved family relationships and, for some, increased engagement with learning. The purpose of this chapter is to encourage recognition not only of family diversity in a tourism context, but also the social and economic benefits of accommodating the needs of diverse families.

The family is 'the fundamental social unit of group formation in society ... [and therefore] the influence of the family on tourism demand is extremely important' (Cooper *et al.*, 2008: 50). Research indicates that, even in difficult economic circumstances, many families are unwilling to forgo their family holiday. This chapter clearly defines the family market segment in all its complexity before focusing on the historical development of the family holiday in the UK, considering the early days of the 1930s holiday camps pioneered by Butlin and Pontin through to the overseas package holidays facilitated by developments in transportation. The impact of the changing make-up of families on the family tourism product is considered, alongside the factors influencing family participation in tourism.

There are numerous challenges facing both the generic family tourism market and organisations catering for this segment, not least rising socio-economic inequalities, the proliferation of 'alternative' families, a rise in the proportion of ABC1 families (composed of skilled workers and professionals, likely therefore to have higher disposable incomes), an ageing population, 'pester power', exponential growth in the use of social media and a corresponding rise in the availability of electronic entertainment as a prerequisite for travel. What is clear is that tourism organisations will need to develop multigenerational products and services to accommodate the needs of the family market.

It is argued that recognition of the specific needs of this market proves, for many tourism organisations, to be the differentiator between long-term success and failure, and that the search for *quality* time together is the key to understanding this highly price- and quality-sensitive market. The notion of quality versus quantity of time is explored below from a family perspective. Supported by current statistics related to family tourism expenditure and participation in the UK, the chapter also considers current trends in the UK family tourism market, including the notion of the 'staycation' and the trend towards camping and 'glamping'. Additionally, legislative issues such as those involved in taking family holidays in the school's academic year are explored. The idea of children within today's families being the customers of tomorrow is one which is briefly explored in a concluding section. The notion that their consumption, experiences and level of enjoyment will shape the way they structure their own family holidays in future is an important consideration in any discussion of family tourism.

## Definition of the family in this context

The introductory chapter established some clarity in the definition of family in this context, where families are defined as social groups including at least two family members. The Office for National Statistics (ONS) defines families 'by marriage, civil partnership or cohabitation or, where there are children in the household, child/parent relationships' (ONS, 2011: 3). The family unit is generally considered to consist of one or more parents together with one or more children. The extended family is likely to consist of grandparents, aunts, uncles and other family members. Family tourism therefore involves the family unit and their participation in diverse forms of tourism activity.

# Historical Development of Family Tourism in the UK

> Holidays are dreamed of as restoring the abandon and bliss of childhood. They will repair the ravages of old time. Once away from work-discipline where time is spent and time is money, away also from the industrial city, its dirt and noise and fearful, nameless crowds of people, we shall restore time's losses, rediscover the magnificent freedoms of both famili-arity and strangeness, natural beauty and civic ritual. (Inglis, 2000: 4)

The family holiday was firmly embedded in working-class culture as far back as the late 1800s. According to Walton (2000: 15), 'working class demand first became an important influence on resorts close to industrial population centres in the late-nineteenth century (although "excursionists" and "cheap trippers" made their presence felt on summer weekends as soon as the railways arrived around mid-century)'.

However, for the middle and upper classes, the family holiday dates back further. As Inglis (2000: 6) states, 'it was the idle rich who took all the vacations during the eighteenth century, and what they did and had became obvious models for those who aspired to that condition of life to copy'. Historically, before the 16th century, people travelled for religious festivals, trade and even war but it was only really people travelling for the purpose of pilgrimage who could be described as travelling for reasons other than work. While some provision was made for these people, in the form of basic inn accommodation, there was little in the way of comfort and pilgrimages were not a family pursuit.

In the 17th century it was unquestionably the Grand Tour of Europe which became the forerunner of tourism as we know it today. The tour involved the sons of rich families travelling in Europe, with the aim of broadening their minds before the commencement of their career in UK government. The Grand Tour became a well trodden route around the cities and cultural sites of mainland Europe and included Paris, Florence and Rome on its itinerary. Still, this form of tourism was hardly a family travel experience as, deemed suitable for men only, given the social conformity expected of women of the day, it was designed for a very different market.

It was also in the 17th century that medical circles in the UK proposed the benefits of bathing in mineral water for its healing properties. Although the Romans had recognised the health-giving properties of mineral water centuries previously, and travelled to spas and seaside resorts for health reasons, centuries of European upheaval were to pass before spa bathing became a fashionable activity (Inglis, 2000). The proliferation of spa resorts across the UK and Europe and the subsequent growth in popularity of sea bathing for health benefits quickly boosted the fortunes of UK towns and cities such as Bath, Brighton and Scarborough, as well as numerous European destinations. Spa bathing had been for adults only, but increasingly popular with families by the 18th and 19th centuries were seaside resorts, where a range of facilities and attractions had started to flourish, catering for the needs of an increasingly diverse range of visitors. With developments in transportation in the form of steamships and railways, the popularity of holidays soared. The Bank Holiday Act 1871 turned a number of religious festivals into holidays and by 1936 the Annual Holiday Bill finally gave workers a week's holiday with pay.

Perhaps most influential in his impact on the British family holiday market was the entrepreneur Billy Butlin, who was one of the first to recognise the growing importance of the family holiday. In the mid-1930s Butlin opened his first holiday camp, in Skegness, on the north-east coast of England, to accommodate the growing number of families looking for an escape from daily routine. The holidays, initially advertised in the *Daily Express* newspaper, were priced between 35 shillings (£1.75) and £3 per week. By 1939 (at the start of the Second World War) 11 million people in the UK were able to take holidays with pay, and Butlin had opened another camp, at Clacton in Essex; the two camps combined attracted almost 100,000 visitors (Page, 2009). The type of holidays offered by early entrepreneurs such as Butlin, and later Fred Pontin, enabled families to seek a brief respite from historically dark and depressing times. For the families not previously in a position to afford such luxuries as holidays, the camps offered a welcome break.

As access to land-based transportation increased, so the coast and countryside became more accessible to the masses, thus increasing the types of holiday available to families. With the advent of affordable commercial aviation came greater opportunities for family holidays outside the UK. Vladimir Raitz organised the first package tour by air to Corsica in 1949 and key developments in air transportation quickly followed with the entry into commercial service of the Boeing 707 in the late 1950s and Boeings 727 and 747 in the 1960s. Capable of seating almost 500 passengers, the Boeing 747, or jumbo jet, has since been instrumental in transporting millions of people worldwide. In 2009, of the 58.6 million visits abroad by UK residents, 46.7 million were made by air (ONS, 2010c).

The package holiday market grew considerably in the 1970s, with Spain quickly becoming the preferred destination for UK travellers, thanks to cheap transportation and a proliferation of affordable accommodation complexes and support services to cater for inbound tourism. Indeed, Spain remains the most popular destination for UK tourists (ONS, 2010c), with 11.6 million visits by UK travellers in 2009.

According to Association of British Travel Agents (ABTA), those people most likely to have young families (i.e. those aged 35–44) are the age group most likely to take a UK domestic holiday (ABTA, 2011). In the current economic climate and with rising costs of foreign exchange within the eurozone in particular, the 'staycation' phenomenon appears to have become more firmly embedded in UK travel culture. The number of visits abroad in 2009 was the lowest since 2001 (ONS, 2010c) and '2009 was an exceptional year for domestic tourism' (VisitEngland, 2010: 1). According to VisitEngland (2010), the volume of domestic overnight trips in the UK, however, declined across all categories, such as visiting friends and relatives (VFR), business and leisure. There were also differences across socio-economic grades, 'with the number of trips taken by the more affluent AB demographic group unchanged compared with 2009 levels while trips taken by the least affluent DE social grade were down by 15 per cent' (VisitEngland, 2010: 1). Importantly, 'households with children maintained trip levels, whereas 7 per cent fewer trips were made by households without children'.

The family holiday is changing and extending beyond the traditional one-week or two-week holiday. There is an increasing desire for parents to expose their children to the cultures and lifestyles of the destinations visited. It is argued that travel is one of the best forms of education for children and the family bond may be cemented through experiential travel, expanding the family's perspective on life, lifestyle and other aspects of culture worldwide. Experiential travel refers to the physical, emotional and psychological benefits of taking a holiday. It is important to consider how the family tourism experience contributes to the overall psychological well-being of the tourist and what implications this might have for operators. Research by VisitScotland (2006) indicated that one-third of consumers with an interest in adventure tourism and sports on holidays and short breaks had children under the age of 15, confirming 'the attractiveness of adventure sports for the family audience'.

Families with children are increasingly finding that participation in 'soft' adventure tourism can yield significant benefits in terms of family bonding through the shared experience of exciting activities combined with some mild exercise. The most common motivators for outdoor recreation are fun, relaxation, health and exercise, stress reduction, to experience nature, the thrill of learning and family togetherness. The most common barriers to outdoor recreation are lack of time, interest and money, and lack of instructional programmes in recreational areas (Recreation Roundtable, 1995, cited in Neirotti, 2003: 17). The current trend in the UK towards camping and 'glamping' (a form of luxury camping with facilities under canvas equal to those found in hotel accommodation) indicates recognition of the benefits of outdoor recreation combined with a more cost-effective way for the family to holiday together.

What is clear from an analysis of the historical development of the family holiday market is that while the family holiday is changing and extending beyond the traditional one-week or two-week holiday, its main purpose remains much as it was in the late 18th and throughout the 19th century, with the elements of escapism, fun and entertainment at its core. The opportunity for family togetherness is an important factor in today's family tourism market, with parents seemingly working harder to afford a basic quality of life and at the same time compensating for time lost during the working week.

## Social Tourism

Social tourism enables people living on low incomes to access leisure and holiday activities. The resulting happiness and perceived healthiness, as a benefit accrued from participation in a holiday or leisure activity, contribute to a happier, healthier and more caring society (Hazel, 2005; Hughes, 1991; Minnaert et al., 2009). Travel and the pursuit of leisure activities as a family cements the family bond and may also serve to expand a family's perspective of what is important in life. Additionally, they allow families to be away from the distractions of everyday problems. What is clear is that the family holiday, despite its perceived benefits, is often the first thing to be sacrificed in poverty (Hazel, 2005; Hughes, 1991), a fact supported by the research cited above carried out by VisitEngland (2010: 1), where 'trips taken by the least affluent DE social grade were down by 15 per cent'. Chapter 8 elaborates on disadvantaged families and the importance of social tourism.

The Family Holiday Association (FHA) is a registered charity that helps approximately 2000 low-income families a year to take a week's holiday. According to the FHA's director, John McDonald, there are at least two and a half million families in the UK who are unable to afford a holiday (*Guardian*, 2011). The FHA stresses that the benefits to families and, indirectly, schools are clear and include children becoming calmer, happier and more engaged with learning (*Guardian*, 2011). In their study of social tourism, Smith and Hughes (1999: 131) explored the significance of the family holiday for those families disadvantaged due to personal economic and social circumstances. They showed, for 'economically and socially disadvantaged families with young children', the importance of relationship enhancement on holiday, where family relationships are improved through participation in leisure-based activities and 'quality' time spent together. Additionally, being removed from daily existence in terms not only of physical location but also of other factors such as financial issues and antisocial behaviour allows the economically and socially disadvantaged a form of escapism not normally encountered in daily routine. Smith and Hughes (1999: 133) concluded that 'any further strategies from the state for widening participation [in tourism], in the current climate, are unlikely and it will fall to the industry itself and voluntary charitable bodies to do this'. Little has changed since this research was presented in 1999. Both Smith and Hughes (1999) and Hazel (2005) discuss the mainstreaming of holiday provision in social care policies in many European countries for economically and socially disadvantaged families as well as concurring that social tourism was not on the UK's political agenda.

It is possible, though, that this is about to change, as, at the time of writing, two investigations into the benefits of social tourism are underway in the UK. The first is an All-Party Parliamentary Group chaired by the MP for Blackpool North and Cleveleys, Paul Maynard, which is focusing on the social and economic benefits of social tourism in the UK. The other investigation, led by Scott McCabe, Nottingham University Business School, also focuses on the physical and economic effects of social tourism. The economic benefits are being considered both from the perspective of the host destinations and in terms of a potential reduction in demand for prescription drugs and support services (*Guardian*, 2011). The study will also explore the possibility of weaving learning opportunities into the 'term time' holiday, to attempt to overcome, at least in part, the engagement and progression problems involved in taking children out of school in term time.

## Impact of the Changing Make-Up of Families on the Family Tourism Product

In many European countries more and more children are living in households with stepfamilies or just one parent. The growth in working mothers has also led to a greater role for family members in informal childcare, grandparents in particular (Grandparents Plus, 2010). Additionally, increased life expectancy and falling fertility rates across Europe mean that there is an ageing population (European Commission, 2010; ONS, 2010a; Royal Geographical Society, 2011) and fewer children per family. Indeed, according to the European Commission (2010) as the baby-boom generation of the late 1940s, 1950s and early 1960s retires, the European Union's active population will start to shrink from 2013/2014 and, with the number of people aged over 60 increasing twice as fast as it did before 2007, there will be additional strains placed on the welfare systems of member states. In the UK there has been an increase of 1.7 million people over the age of 65 in the 25 years between 1984 and 2009 and over the same period there was also a significant reduction in the proportion of the UK population aged under 16. Indeed, it is projected that, by 2034, 23% of the population will be aged 65 or over, compared with 18% aged under 16 (ONS, 2010a). Also of interest is the projected change in the ratio of women to men aged 65 and over, falling from 156 women to 100 men in 1984 to a predicted 118 women to every 100 men by 2034 (ONS, 2010a).

The fall in the dependency ratio (i.e. the number of people of working age supporting each pensioner), from the current 4:1 to a projected 2:1 by 2050, the increasing pressure on health and social services, the current downturn in the global economy, a rise in retirement age and a shortfall in retirement savings are further issues to challenge the tourism industry (Royal Geographical Society, 2011).

The key question is, what do these significant demographic changes mean for the tourism industry and, more specifically, the family tourism market? What is clear is that they will present further challenges and opportunities for the industry in the form of catering for the needs of changing family structures alongside an ageing population. The constraints to the selection of a destination, type of holiday or even a holiday itself centre on personal, family, social and situational influences which include gender, age, stage in the family life cycle or life-stage, social class, income and other work-related issues (Page & Connell, 2009). The family life cycle groups people by age, marital status and whether they have children but does not (necessarily) take account of lesbian, gay, bisexual or transgender (LGBT) families, single-parent families or ethnic considerations (see Chapter 12). The family life cycle model does, however, identify that different life-stages are characterised by different lifestyles in terms of the ways in which people think and pursue activities and interests. These different lifestyles determine travel requirements and may vary at each stage of the life cycle, dependent on commitments (Page & Connell, 2009).

## The Travel Decision-Making Process

What is clear is that 'the presence of children in a household has a significant influence on tourism participation and patterns, and can often create a substantive diversion from the type of pre-family holidays taken by a couple' (Page & Connell, 2009: 89). Furthermore, 'households with children tend to have a more limited choice in terms of travel date and duration, dominated by school holidays'.

The taking of family holidays during school term time is controversial. Family holidays account for a significant number of both authorised and non-authorised absences during the school academic year, with parents attempting to save money by travelling during off-peak periods, when costs are lower. With the travel industry insisting that market forces are to blame for higher prices during school holidays, an increasing number of parents are risking incurring a fine by taking their children out of school to avoid paying premium prices. Having the financial means to take a holiday is a major issue for low-income families in particular. According to Smith and Hughes (1999) for many families it is a choice of a holiday in term time or no holiday at all. With Hazel (2005) describing the benefits of family holidays as including social interaction and strengthening family relationships, it is undoubtedly the case that the controversy surrounding term-time holidays will continue. Certainly the debate between the relationship-strengthening nature of the holiday, or break from routine, and the potential for disruption to a child's learning is ongoing.

The travel/holiday decision-making process is considered to be important for marketers in particular, who could benefit greatly from knowing who makes travel purchase decisions within the family and on what basis those decisions are made. This information is used by tourism marketers to target their material more effectively. It is clear that 'children are an important determining factor of parental holiday satisfaction and can often play a role in the decision-making process, in terms of identifying a holiday desire and negotiating activities' (Page & Connell, 2009: 89). The importance of 'pester power' in the travel decision-making process should not be underestimated (Nickerson & Jurowski, 2001). Indeed, its growing importance is suggested by changes in the birth rate. While UK statistics indicate a declining birth rate over the last 40 years as a whole, there are signs that this is changing.

The last decade has seen a slight rise in birth rates in the UK, to 1.9 children per family. While this is the highest figure since 1973, it is still lower than the 2.93 of 1964 (Royal Geographical Society, 2011).

Nickerson and Jurowski (2001: 19) consider the use of the family holiday as 'a time to reconnect as a family'. With an increase in the proportion of parents who work and, for some, an increase in disposable income, alongside limited time spent with children due to the constraints of working life, participation in family tourism is seen as an opportunity to spend quality time together. Consequently, children may be actively encouraged to participate in the making of purchasing decisions. Research carried out by Eurocamp indicates that even toddlers are instrumental in the holiday decision-making process, with a significant number of parents basing their choice of holiday on the best option for their toddler (Home While Away, 2011). Travelling with young children is considered stressful and it is evident that many operators do not cater well for families with small children (see Chapter 9).

## Family Spending

In order to consider the volume and value of the family tourism market, it is important to consider some statistics related to household composition and family expenditure in the UK. Chapter 3 provides an overview of market structure and size. While the number of households in the UK has increased significantly since 1961, the average household size has decreased, and a smaller proportion of households contain children. Those households that do have children have fewer children than in 1961, concurrent with the lower birth rate evidenced in the UK over the course of the past 50 years (ONS, 2011; Royal Geographical Society, 2011).

## The Role of Grandparents in the Family Structure

In recent years grandparents have started to play a more significant role in family tourism, often accompanying their own offspring and grandchildren on family holidays, as well as taking grandchildren on trips themselves. According to NetMums and Eurocamp there has been a considerable growth in family holidays that have included grandparents in the UK in recent years (Home While Away, 2011). As the role played by grandparents in everyday family life increases, the demand for holidays for the extended family has increased commensurately. The research indicated that 75% of UK families with young children were planning a summer holiday with grandparents in 2011. Just as holidays are seen as a way of reconnecting with family through participation in quality time, so parents see breaks for the extended family as a way of strengthening ties with their own parents, who, research suggests, play an increasingly significant role in everyday life (Home While Away,

2011). Clearly, the tourism industry will need to adapt to such changes and consider how to meet the needs of extended families through the provision of accommodation, activities and deals.

In the period since the Second World War there has been a significant growth in state/governmental family policies, with a clear impact on the structure of family life through benefit payments, social care provision, childbirth, employment legislation and protection, and the implementation and promotion of 'family friendly' policies (Grandparents Plus, 2010). Such policies have, in some respects, changed the nature of families, in the sense that the role of both women and men in the family home, and that of grandparents, has altered. Only in recent years has the essential family role of grandparents been recognised through state policy. For example, from April 2011 UK grandparents who provide childcare for a child under 12 in order that parents can work are able to claim National Insurance credits towards their basic state pension. In Portugal grandparents are entitled to take up to 30 days a year and receive financial support to care for a sick child if the parents have used their parental leave entitlement or have work commitments (Grandparents Plus, 2010).

## Factors Influencing Family Participation in Tourism

A number of factors influence family participation in tourism, not least, at present: the current economic climate; government spending cuts; the recent rise in VAT in the UK to 20%; increases in air passenger duty (APD); developments in technology, in particular the popularity of social media; the growth of the VFR market; and the growth of the 'staycation'. The economic downturn in the UK appears to have promoted a rise in family holidays, with older children electing to travel with their parents rather than alone (Cheapflights, 2009).

According to the ONS (2010b), households with children are more likely to have an internet connection than those without. Social media play a significant role in the tourism industry, in terms of consumer feedback. It is vital for operators to consider how much more involved children are likely to be in the family decision-making process in the future as they communicate increasingly effectively through social media and smartphones. With increasing numbers of people making use of social media to maximise their holiday budget, brand perception is clearly influenced by online information and comments. Smartphone penetration and mobile applications have revolutionised the travel industry in recent months and are likely to continue to do so. According to ABTA (2011: 13) 'social media platforms, such as Facebook, [have] revolutionised global relationships – and reconnected long-lost friends and family, this is set to cement a popular travel trend of visiting friends and relatives abroad in 2011'. The VFR market, although smaller in recent years than previously, has grown faster than both holiday and business travel since 1984, with an average growth of 6% per year (ABTA, 2011; ONS, 2010c).

According to VisitEngland (2011a), 119 million domestic trips were made in the UK in 2010, generating £20.8 billion. Trips, in particular holiday trips, despite being down on 2009, remained above pre-recession levels and it appears that, for now at least, the 'staycation' *is* here to stay. Interestingly, over 70% of trips were for three nights or less, with only around one in 20 being for longer than eight nights, thus indicating that short breaks continue to be popular with UK domestic tourists.

In a 2011 survey on the 'staycation' phenomenon, VisitEngland (2011a) identified two clear types of 'staycation' tourist, the 'switcher' and the 'extra', with 'switchers' taking at least one holiday in England that directly replaced an overseas holiday and 'extras' taking more domestic holidays than they previously had done. The main reason for 'switching' is for financial reasons, although other reasons include the ease of travelling in England and the desire to go somewhere new in the UK and experiencing less hassle than would be expected on an overseas holiday. Interestingly, while an increase in the numbers of people travelling abroad in 2012 was anticipated, this was not felt likely to be at the expense of a holiday in the UK (VisitEngland, 2011b). What is clear is that the 'staycation' continued in 2011, with two in 10 people taking a domestic break in England that would otherwise have been abroad. The report concluded that '18–34 year olds and families in particular are likely to continue taking more holidays in England, in 2012 and beyond' (VisitEngland, 2011b).

## Challenges for the Family Tourism Market

Baby boomers were born between 1945 and 1964, generation X between 1965 and 1980 and generation Y, the dot com generation, were born after 1980 (Cooper *et al.*, 2008). Generations X and Y, according to Cooper *et al.* (2008), 'represent the future of tourism demand for the next 50 years [however] research tends to focus on the current active travel generation – the baby boomers'. What will happen when generation X takes their place, followed by generation Y, is unclear. Similarities and contrasts in the consumer behaviour of baby boomers, generation X and generation Y are summarised in Table 4.1. These technologically oriented generations will challenge the tourism industry. As mentioned above, as the baby-boom generation of the late 1940s, 1950s and early 1960s retires, the European Union's active population will start to shrink from 2013/2014 (European Commission, 2010).

Marconi (2001, cited in Glover, 2010) questioned the benefit of using generations to identify consumption patterns, because it ignores other aspects shaping individuals' behaviour and preferences, such as attitudes, values and beliefs. Nonetheless, while there are clearly a wide variety of

**Table 4.1** Consumer behaviour of baby boomers and generations X and Y

| Baby boomers | Generation X | Generation Y |
|---|---|---|
| Diligent. Prefers stable environment | Independent, self-motivated and self-sufficient | Independent, self-motivated and self-sufficient |
| Search for experiences in a secure environment. Constrained by financial austerity | Search for authentic experiences. Adventurous | Search for authentic experiences. Adventurous |
| Not generally highly technologically savvy | Less technologically savvy than generation Y but demonstrates increasing use of internet for travel research | Highly technologically savvy |
| Enjoys teamwork – possibly supporting the prolific rise in the package holiday of the 1970s and 1980s | Prefers to work as an individual, suggesting that making own travel arrangements is preferable to pre-packaged holiday | 'It is less important to build products *for* them but to build products *with* them' (Cooper *et al.*, 2008: 52). Teamwork and individualism are closely linked |
| Balance work and family | Strong family values and financial conservatism leads them to seek value-for-money travel and family holidays | Ability to be permanently connected to friends and family through social media technology |
| Less geographically aware in terms of destination location, although this is changing as this generation retires and has more time and disposable income for exploration | More geographically aware in terms of destination location | Increasingly geographically aware in terms of destination location |

*Source*: Adapted from Cooper *et al.* (2008); Yu and Miller (2005); Glover and Prideaux (2009)

demand patterns and market segments within each generation, there may be some generation-specific values that are inherent across generations and thus a generational approach is useful in this context.

Supplying the needs of three or more generations can be a considerable challenge for tourism organisations. As each generation grows within a particular social and environmental system their behaviour is shaped by media, culture and world events (Cooper *et al.*, 2008). Modification of tourism products and services will be necessary to avoid the 'product gap' between the pre- and post-war generations (Glover & Prideaux, 2009). Differences in consumption preferences and demand patterns should be considered in today's market. Continuing to focus on the needs of one generation is likely to result in a range of products, attractions and interpretation that will not meet the needs of other generations (Glover & Prideaux, 2009); indeed, Lehto *et al.* (2008: 237–238) argue that 'it would be unwise to assume that people in similar chronological age and life-stages will always have similar travel preferences from generation to generation'.

## Conclusion

With customer service excellence being the differentiator between tourism organisations, catering appropriately for the family market, in all its diversity, is unquestionably one of the keys to long-term business survival. Importantly, value for money rather than lowest price is regarded as an essential element of the holiday experience (ABTA, 2011). Understanding who their customers are and how to engage with them is vital for tourism organisations and the development of multigenerational products and services to accommodate the needs of the family market is imperative. The customer service experience, in all its complexity, will determine consumer perceptions, which will ultimately, through the use of social media, be disseminated globally to interested parties.

As the role of grandparents in the family continues to grow, the tourism industry will need to consider how to adapt to the needs of extended family groups. Traditionally marginalised families such as LGBT, single-parent and ethnic families will also gain increasing recognition as operators seek to cater for a more diverse range of families. Furthermore, holidays of a shorter duration, experiential tourism and all-inclusive holidays are likely to remain popular with the family market due to financial, time and work constraints, as well as increasing recognition, in the case of experiential tourism, of the benefits of outdoor recreation and exposure to other cultures. Children in today's families are the customers of tomorrow and their consumption, experiences and level of enjoyment will shape the way they structure their own family holidays in future. The role of children in the family decision-making process should not be underestimated.

The purpose of this chapter has been to encourage recognition not only of family diversity in a tourism context but also the social and economic benefits of accommodating the needs of diverse families. Recognition and accommodation of the diverse nature of the family tourism market is highly likely to attract significant economic returns for operators, despite the prevailing economic climate. Consideration of the characteristics of generations X and Y presents the tourism industry with a number of challenges which they must face in order to meet the needs of these consumers from the perspective of participation in family tourism. These challenges include the search for authenticity, bridging the gap between the technologically savvy and those who are less so, provision for 'soft' and 'hard' adventure seekers and integration of opportunities for enhancement of family values within value-for-money tourism propositions.

## References

ABTA (2011) *ABTA Travel Trends Report 2011*. London: ABTA.

Cheapflights (2009) Recession prompts surge in 'family holidays'. Retrieved 11 May 2011 from http://news.cheapflights.co.uk/2009/07/recession-prompts-surge-in-family-holidays.

Cooper, C., Fletcher, J., Fyall, A., Gilbert, D. and Wanhill, S. (2008) *Tourism: Principles and Practice* (4th edition). Harlow: Pearson Education.

European Commission (2010) *Europe 2010 – A Strategy for Smart, Sustainable and Inclusive Growth*. Communication from the Commission. Brussels: European Commission.

Glover, P. (2010) Generation Y's future tourism demand: Some opportunities and challenges. In P. Benckendorff, G. Moscardo and D. Pendergast (eds), *Tourism and Generation Y* (pp. 155–163). Wallingford: CABI.

Glover, P. and Prideaux, B. (2009) Implications of population ageing for the development of tourism products and destinations. *Journal of Vacation Marketing*, 15(1), 25–37.

Grandparents Plus (2010) *Grandparenting in Europe Report*. London: King's College.

*Guardian* (2011) Charity holidays widen children's horizons. Retrieved 15 June 2011 from http://www.guardian.co.uk/education/2011/may/03/school-children-charity-holidays.

Hazel, N. (2005) Holidays for children and families in need: An exploration of research and policy context for social tourism in the UK. *Children and Society*, 19(3), 225–236.

Home While Away (2011) Family holidays with grandparents become more popular. Retrieved 25 June 2011 from http://www.homewhileaway.co.uk/family-holidays/2011/04/05/family-holidays-with-grandparents-become-more-popular.

Hughes, H. (1991) Holidays and the economically disadvantaged. *Tourism Management*, 12(3), 193–196.

Inglis, F. (2000) *The Delicious History of the Holiday*. London: Routledge.

Lehto, X.Y., Jang, S., Achana, F.T. and O'Leary, J.T. (2008) Exploring tourism experience sought: a cohort comparison of baby boomers and the silent generation. *Journal of Vacation Marketing*, 14(3), 237–252.

Minnaert, L., Maitland, R. and Miller, G. (2009) Tourism and social policy – the value of social tourism. *Annals of Tourism Research*, 36(2), 316–334.

Neirotti, L.D. (2003) An introduction to sport and adventure tourism. In S. Hudson, (ed.), *Sport and Adventure Tourism* (pp. 1–25). London: Haworth Hospitality Press.

Nickerson, N. and Jurowski, C. (2001) The influence of children on vacation travel patterns. *Journal of Vacation Marketing*, 7(1), 19–30.

ONS (2010a) *Ageing: Fastest Increase in the Oldest Old.* London: ONS.

ONS (2010b) *Family Spending: A Report on the 2009 Living Costs and Food Survey.* London: ONS.

ONS (2010c) *Travel Trends 2009.* London: ONS.

ONS (2011) *Households and families.* London: ONS.

Page, S.J. (2009) *Tourism Management: Managing for Change* (3rd edition). Oxford: Butterworth–Heinemann.

Page, S. and Connell, J. (2009) *Tourism: A Modern Synthesis* (3rd edition). Andover: Cengage Learning EMEA.

Royal Geographical Society (2011) 21st century challenges: Britain's ageing population. Retrieved 24 June 2011 from http://www.21stcenturychallenges.org/focus/britains-greying-population.

Smith, V. and Hughes, H. (1999) Disadvantaged families and the meaning of the holiday. *International Journal of Tourism Research*, 1(2), 123–133.

VisitEngland (2010) UK tourism survey – December 2010 – summary of results. Retrieved 9 September 2011 from http://www.visitengland.org/Images/December%20 2010%20Commentary_tcm30-25399.pdf.

VisitEngland (2011a) *The Staycation: 2011 and Beyond.* London: VisitEngland. Retrieved 10 November 2011 from http://www.visitengland.org/Images/Staycation%202011%20 Autumn%202011_for%20website_tcm30-28685.pdf.

VisitEngland (2011b) *VisitEngland Domestic Overview: UK and England – All Trips.* London: VisitEngland. Retrieved 23 August 2011 from http://www.visitengland.org/Images/ Domestic%20Overview%202010_tcm30-26786.pdf.

VisitScotland (2006) Adventure sports research. Retrieved 23 August 2011 from http:// www.visitscotland.org/pdf/adventure_online_research_2006.pdf.

Walton, J.K. (2000) *The British Seaside: Holidays and Resorts in the Twentieth Century*. Manchester: Manchester University Press.

Yu, H.C. and Miller, P. (2005) Leadership style – the x generation and baby boomers compared in different cultural contexts. *Leadership and Organisation Development Journal*, 26(1), 35–50.

# Part 2

# The Experiences of Family Tourism

# 5 The Inclusion of Fathers, Children and the Whole Family Group in Tourism Research on Families

## Heike Schänzel

## Introduction

This chapter addresses the absence of fatherhood, childhood and collective perspectives in family tourism through the application of the whole-family methodology – a qualitative methodology used in family research that is inclusive of group and individual perspectives of all family members (Schänzel, 2010). Methodological approaches to family tourism research are underdeveloped, which has led to a lack of research into fathers, children and the whole family group. Research on family holiday experiences is largely informed by feminist gender representations, adult perspectives and individualisation, which do not account for the sociality and multivocality present in family groups.

A more holistic and critical approach to tourism research is required, which led to the adoption of whole-family research for this study into domestic summer holiday experiences in New Zealand, based on 10 families (10 fathers, 10 mothers and 20 children). This chapter outlines the methodology of interviewing all family members individually and as a group over three time periods. It goes on to outline the findings on generational differences (children), gender differences (fathers) and group dynamics. The grounded-theory process taken here led to the theoretical modelling of family time (time spent with the family) and own time (time spent away from the family) around these different perspectives. An analytical framework for whole-family experiential dimensions that transcends the complexity and multidimensionality of this study is presented and then illustrated through examples from the findings. The potential is highlighted of including the perspectives of fathers, children and group dynamics within understandings of family holiday experiences and contemporary family life.

## Literature Review

Most tourism research has focused on the individual and emphasises detachment, but thereby has effectively de-socialised tourist subjects, which renders such approaches unsuitable for research on families (Obrador, 2012). This has led to limited and fragmented literature on family holiday experiences. Families travelling with children form the consumer base of most tourism operators and are estimated to generate over a third of receipts within the wider travel industry (Travelhorizons, 2009). Research into family group behaviour, as a collective experience, requires a more inclusive approach, instead of the individual perspectives that have dominated. There have been some studies on the collective perspective of family holiday experiences (Gram, 2005) but most research is either from the individual perspective, usually the mother, or centred on particular attractions (Johns & Gyimothy, 2003; Sterry & Beaumont, 2006). The lack of research into broader understandings of the whole family group raises several unique points in tourism studies: firstly, virtually nothing is known about the father's experience (Schänzel & Smith, 2011); secondly, very little is known about the experiences of children (Small, 2008); and thirdly, very few studies focus on the experiences of different family members together on holiday, or on how group dynamics can inflame or heighten the individual's holiday experience (Pritchard & Havitz, 2006). This calls for a methodology that is inclusive of children, fathers and the whole family group as was applied in the study reported here.

Most family tourism research is market- and consumer-driven and focused on the themes of decision processes and roles (Lehto et al., 2009) and there is a lack of research into broader experiential dimensions. However, the core product of tourism are the experiences gained (Prentice et al., 1998). This is represented by a three-phase realisation of journey experiences (Gyimothy, 1999), albeit with an element of continuation: the anticipation of experiences; the on-holiday experiences; and the recollection of experiences. Relatively little attention has been paid to the meaning of family holiday experiences to parents (see Blichfeldt, 2006; Lehto et al., 2009; Shaw et al., 2008). Even less is known about all the family members' experiences alongside group experiences traced over time, which means that family group dynamic experiences and their temporal dimension are virtually absent in tourism research.

In contrast to fathers, there are studies that are informed by a feminist perspective and are focused on mothers' family holiday experiences (e.g. Anderson, 2001; Davidson, 1996; Deem, 1996; Small, 2005a, 2005b). These studies highlight the never-ending physical and emotional work of motherhood, both at home and when travelling. However, apart from the present investigation (Schänzel & Smith, 2011) no studies have been done on the family holiday experience of fathers (Ryan, 2003). This is surprising given the increasing interest in fathers in the leisure and family literature, as illustrated by recent special publications on fatherhood in leisure (Kay, 2006, 2009) and the establishment of the *Fathering* journal (Fagan, 2003) within family research. Kay (2009) considers fathers and fatherhood as an 'absent presence' in leisure studies but also argues that leisure-based activities (such as sport) are potentially more prominent in fathering than they are in mothering. For example, in Australia, engagement in 'sport is perceived as a major site for fathering to occur' (Thompson, 1999: 53) and for fathers to show emotional connection to their children (Harrington, 2006, 2009). Fathers in the UK described leisure to mean 'being with' their children, resulting in a kind of 'leisure-based' parenting (Such, 2009). Fathers in general use sport and leisure not only to enact their fathering ideology but also increasingly as a strategy to express their masculinities (Kay, 2009).

Few studies have investigated the family holiday experiences of children (e.g. Carr, 2011; Cullingford, 1995; Hilbrecht *et al.*, 2008; Small, 2008). These suggest that, for children, holidays are about physical activity, being involved and having fun rather than relaxing. Differences between children's and parents' holiday needs and desires can lead to intra-family tensions (Carr, 2011). Hilbrecht *et al.* (2008) established that newness within a familiar environment and connections with social relations were important for children on family holidays. This confirmed results reported by Small (2002), who found that for 12-year-old girls sharing holiday experiences with others, such as friends, makes for a good holiday experience.

In the social sciences (more broadly) there has been a methodological shift that has involved repositioning children as the subjects rather than objects of research (Farrell, 2005) and this is reflected in the increasing work on children's experiences (e.g. Freeman & Mathison, 2009; Greene & Hogan, 2005). This is a reminder that tourism research is not only lagging behind other social research but also that children are marginalised in tourism studies and fathers are largely invisible, apart from their joint parenting voice (with no gender consideration), or when they are used as a point of comparison for mothers' perspectives.

To address this, the purpose of this study on family holiday experiences was to understand the perspectives of all family members, including both mothers and fathers, and from their individual and interactive family group perspectives. The study focused on domestic tourism in New Zealand, which accounts for over half of all national tourism earnings; families account for a major part of this market. With the aim of finding out more about family holiday behaviour in New Zealand, a parental survey was distributed through five primary schools in the Wellington region (Schänzel, 2008). The survey also recruited 10 families as research participants in a whole-family study, which is the focus of this chapter.

## Whole-Family Study Methodology and Analysis

The study aimed to understand the individual and collective experiences and meanings of family holidays over time for all family members. Whole-family methodology was adopted from family research (Handel, 1996). This involved a two-stage interview process. To begin with, all family members were interviewed together. The second stage involved each family member being interviewed separately, to capture their collective and individual perspectives. This was repeated three times over one year, once before and twice after their summer holiday, to capture their anticipation as well as short-term and longer-term recollections of their holiday experiences. The inherently private nature of families and their mobility on holiday did not allow for research access during the holiday experience. The application of the whole-family method longitudinally thus gave a temporal, experiential and whole-family understanding of holidays (Schänzel, 2010).

Ten families participated in this element of the study, involving 10 fathers, 10 mothers and 20 children (11 boys and 9 girls, aged 6–16 years). To give a balanced gender perspective on parenthood, only two-parent/guardian families were selected (94% of the 110 initial survey respondents fitted this family form). This allowed for step-parents but in fact no 'blended' families volunteered, meaning the sample was made up of 10 sets of biological parents and their children (between one and three children per family). The participants were all white, Anglo New Zealand, middle class, and residents in the Wellington region, making the families relatively homogeneous and not representative of the diversity of New Zealand families.

The choice of methodology was underpinned by the philosophical perspective of interpretivism, with the goal of understanding the complex world of lived experience from the point of view of those who live it (Denzin & Lincoln, 2000). A symbolic interactionist perspective was adopted for this study, which focuses on the connection between *symbols* (i.e. shared meanings) and *interactions* (i.e. verbal and non-verbal actions and communications); it also formed the basis for a grounded theory methodology (GTM) used for the analysis. This allowed a focus on interpersonal relations within the family group. The interpretive nature of this study not only qualifies as a more critical and reflexive path in tourism research but also invokes new ways of interpreting and expressing the multivocality, textuality and situatedness of its participants (Jamal & Hollinshead, 2001). Case studies of families are mainly based on interviews and a small number of cases (Handel, 1991) and are almost always conducted in the home (LaRossa *et al.*, 1994).

The three sets of interviews with each family were all digitally recorded and later transcribed. The GTM was carried out through manual coding, in that data were initially coded by reading through the transcripts several times while making notes, which were then sorted into themes and integrated into a theoretical framework. According to Charmaz (2000) this is part of the interpretive work in gaining a sense of the whole body of data, all interviews and all stories. Only after the core themes were established was selective coding applied using the computer program NVivo 8 for the writing up of the findings. This program proved especially helpful with managing the volume of data (150 interviews: 30 group and 120 individual interviews) in that it enabled specific searches using more than one code/theme simultaneously and according to the perspectives (e.g. fathers).

Using the GTM meant that the successive stages of research involved the concurrent collection and analysis of data informing the next stage or constant comparative analysis (Glaser & Strauss, 1967). Key grounded themes initially generated from the data were elaborated and modified as incoming data from the next stages were meticulously compared against them. The aim of this iterative research design was to refine themes and ideas, not to increase the size of the original sample (Charmaz, 2000) and led to the modification of the interview questions as the study progressed. After all of the interview data had been coded, a comparative analysis was conducted. During this stage of the analysis some codes were merged, while others emerged, were subdivided and/or redefined, which proved to be an organic process. After the comparative analysis was completed, all the data fitted into the theoretical framework of the main themes of family time and own time. Theoretical saturation was deemed achieved when the addition of new data fitted into themes already devised (Morse, 1995).

The analytical framework used combines the multiple perspectives of generation, gender and group dynamics, with three phases of time (pre-, on- and post-holiday) and the two dominant themes of family time and own time that resulted from the GTM process (see Figure 5.1). Together these form a cube with three axes: perspectives, temporality and themes

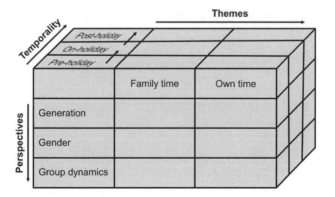

**Figure 5.1** Analytical framework for whole-family experiential dimensions

(for more detail see Schänzel, 2010). Temporality as a longitudinal element to family holidays was signified more by a continuation of the main themes and perspectives than distinctions between the stages. This made its overall importance less dominant and more constant than the other two dimensions. The dominant themes and perspectives are now illustrated with examples from the findings.

# An Illustration of Children, Fathers and Group Dynamics According to the Main Themes

Examples from the findings are used to illustrate generational, gender and group dynamic perspectives according to the main themes and are contextualised with finding from the literature. This allows some understandings of family group dynamics, and of individual family member perspectives, such as those of fathers and children, which are under-represented in tourism research. The main themes centre on the ideal of family togetherness in family time and the reality of also needing own time, and the negotiation of the internal dynamics between the two. Family time encapsulated the purposiveness of spending time together with the immediate and extended family and included idealised notions of change of routine, social connectedness and social identities. In contrast, own time encapsulated freedom from those family commitments to pursue own interests alone or with peers, which included comparisons with non-family holidays and previous family holidays. The relationship between family time and own time led to the internal family group dynamics of cooperation, compromise and conflict. The different perspectives of generation (children), gender (fathers) and group dynamics are used to illustrate the main themes (see Figure 5.1) with New Zealand birds as pseudonyms for family names.

## Children as an illustration of generational perspectives

The notion of *family time* as being fun was particularly prevalent in the voices of children and highlights the importance of including the generational perspective of children in the research process:

> Going out, having some time together and having fun. (Tui girl, 14, pre-holiday family interview)

> Seeing all the relatives and having fun with them as well, particularly my cousins. (Weka girl, 8, post-holiday family interview)

The emphasis on fun by children has been recognised (e.g. Carr, 2011; Gram, 2005; Hilbrecht et al., 2008) but gets often overlooked because the focus is on the parents. Fun for children reflected their self-interest and primary purpose of family holidaying and included connecting with relatives. Giving a voice to the children highlighted the social aspect of fun, which emphasises a social emotional process (Podilchak, 1991) in that children perceive fun as fundamentally interactive on holiday. This stresses the fact that holiday experiences for children have a stronger social dimension and are different from the individual focus of most tourism research. Children mainly desired active fun and sociality, whereas the parents' main purpose of holidaying was more deliberate, such as establishing social identities.

For children the notion of spending time with peers in their *own time* emerged from the findings. This could be time with siblings, or time with other children such as friends or cousins, or making new friends on holiday, which is linked to social reconnecting. The first was more related to deliberately connecting with relatives and known friends while the second was more incidental:

> We were spending a lot of time alone and doing stuff within the family and that was good but it was good to have a break from that and catch up with <friend> and chat together and do things together. (Hoiho boy, 11, post-holiday family interview)

> I met a girl called [name] and she came over to our motel and played stuff in Kerikeri. But now they went back to Australia but I got their email. She emailed me twice and I emailed her once. When we were in Kerikeri, me and [name] met because I was looking for a friend. (Goldfinch girl, 10, post-holiday family interview)

Peer time for younger children was more about making new friends, whereas for teenagers it was more about established friends or cousins. Peer time for the children was more important than for the parents, which was about spending time as a couple or with friends and relatives. Spending time with other children was considered by both parents and children to be an imperative for a good holiday, confirming a finding by Small (2002). In contrast, couple time was considered subsidiary to family time and less important. Including the perspectives of the children then adds a generational dimension to our understandings of family holiday experiences. This highlights differences, in that children seek fun and sociality as their primary purpose on holiday, which their parents do not.

## Fathers as an illustration of gender perspectives

It emerged that within *family time* fathers were expected to take on a more physically active role as entertainer of children, with a focus on facilitating fun with the children. This was particularly prevalent when visiting attractions and activities. The parental role of the father is illustrated by the Hoiho family, whose trip included a visit to the Rainbow's End theme park in Auckland. In the post-holiday family interview, the Hoiho father emphasised his active involvement in the theme park experience:

> I did a lot of rides with the children. I was not a spectator so I accompanied the children on those rides. So I enjoyed those days as well because the children were enjoying themselves and just for their own sake. They were quite fun too.

The on-holiday engagement of fathers in more active leisure behaviour with their children mirrors findings in the leisure literature (Kay, 2009). This reflected New Zealand men's involvement with their children through physical activity, which is comparable to Australian men (Harrington, 2009). In contrast, mothers preferred a more passive and emotional involvement with their children and generally saw theme parks as more of a sacrifice, valued because of the children's enjoyment rather than their own. The activities-based parenting of the fathers on holiday also meant that they were often the facilitators of the mothers' own time. This meant that fathers were entertaining the children partly to enable the mothers to pursue their individual interests, for example reading or shopping. This facilitation role was highlighted by the Hoiho father in his final individual interviews:

> I suppose at those campgrounds I would be happy to just sit in the chair and read but I realise that it is important for them [the children] particularly to be entertained and have fun with me and do these sort of activities when I would personally be just as happy sitting and reading because <wife> tends to spend time during the [school] term with dealing with the children while I am at work.

By including the voices of the fathers it emerged that an entertainment imperative exists for fathers that has largely been unreported due to a lack of research into fatherhood on holiday (Schänzel & Smith, 2011). Getting a break from the fatherhood discourse can then be considered secondary to the needs of mothers for their own time.

In their *own time*, fathers engaged in personal interests revolving more around independent physical and mental activities and challenges such as surf kayaking and Sudoku. Some of these activities fathers undertook only in the holidays, such as fishing and sailing:

> It is the sailing that is good sport. You try and make the boat go and just the challenge of making the boat work and sail and get where you want to go. (Kereru father, post-holiday individual interview)

Individually best day probably the day we went kayak surfing. That was the most exciting and fun day.... I suppose it was the most fun for me because it was the limit of what I can actually kayak surf.... It was definitely a challenge to actually try to keep the kayak under control and keep surfing and when I couldn't to just fall out and that was a heap of fun. (Hoiho father, post-holiday individual interview)

This differed from the mothers in the study, who sought out fewer physical activities and more restful relaxation in their own time. Including the fathers' voices thus managed to offer a different gendered perspective to that of the mothers' need for relaxation and a break from domestic responsibilities (see Deem, 1996; Small, 2005b). It emerged from the fathers' individual perspectives that men sought more physically challenging activities in their own time than women, which is unrecognised in the family tourism literature.

## Family group dynamics as an illustration of collective perspectives

In *family time*, the mention of car travel brought out family dynamics in that fathers mostly liked driving, mothers were more pragmatic and children resented it, as the following exchange in the Pukeko family group interview post-holiday demonstrated:

Father: 'It was a good drive, I enjoyed it.'
Mother: 'I thought it was beautiful.'
Boy 1: 'I thought it was horrible, boring and I hated it.'
Boy 2: 'The only reason why you [dad] like it is because you are driving and we are sitting in the back.'

Car travel highlighted how enforced family time over a prolonged time and in a confined space could lead to tensions, with parents acknowledging the stresses involved:

Travelling in the car for long times can be stressful. (Takahe father, pre-holiday family interview)

All the children reported not liking the journey, finding it boring, annoying and tedious:

Travelling in the car is boring. (Kakariki girl, 8, pre-holiday family interview)

Talking about enforced family time on car journeys within the family group revealed conflicts of interest or stresses which differed from the more positive portrayal of family bonding on long car journeys when relying wholly on parental perspectives (see Crompton, 1979; Lehto *et al.*, 2009). Including the voices of all family members then could reveal internal family dynamics or social tensions (see Small, 2005a) and highlight gender and generational differences on holiday.

Other examples of conflicts of interests that could arise were demonstrated by this exchange between the Takahe mother and her 12-year-old son at the final family interview:

> Mother: 'I didn't really enjoy walking on Westshore beach which is very notoriously dangerous and I told the kids and so <son> had to go and have a try and walk right by the waves.'
> Son: 'I wasn't anywhere near the waves. I was the whole room away from the waves. You were having a panic attack.'

What emerged was that safety concerns proved particularly taxing for the mothers, in that children wanted to pursue their interests but mothers were more anxious about their well-being. This resulted in a parent–child conflict over safety from risk and the freedom to take and explore risks (Carr, 2011). Generational differences in perceptions of danger were then played out in group dynamics and could highlight conflicts of interest.

The notion of requiring *own time* on holiday emerged almost exclusively in the individual interviews with all family members but provided valuable insights into group dynamics. Holidays are exemplified as times of prolonged togetherness but these can be found challenging compared with everyday life:

> Like I said before, you get to spend 24/7 with family and I don't normally. I am out the door to work and on the weekends we are off doing different activities. And I am a person who needs a bit of solitude. I don't actually enjoy living in somebody's pocket all the time. I am quite happy to go for a wander or go for a run in the morning or just a bit of time on my own. I think we are all like that but me in particular. I don't need someone around all the time. (Pukeko father, final individual interview)

Children also recognised their need for individual pursuits in their own time when asked about ideal family holidays:

> Having the family all together but still doing some things separate and having a big rest. Just like having fun ourselves. (Kereru boy, 10, pre-holiday individual interview)

This meant that for harmonious group dynamics a state of balance or homeostasis was needed between the more obligatory aspects of family time and the perceived freedom from commitments in own time. Including the children's voices highlighted again the important notion of social fun on holiday, while the fathers' voices stressed their need to pursue their own interests away from the family. This provides an understanding of family holidays that encapsulates the lived complexities of family life and moves away from the idealistic notions of family time discussed in Chapter 2. Rather than focusing on family togetherness, a more holistic and critical approach allows acknowledgement of the private needs for time away from the whole family, and is attentive to generational and gender differences. At a societal level, the orthodoxy of family time (Daly, 2001; Shaw, 2010) needs to incorporate these individual needs and thus to reflect a more realistic representation of holiday life than is presented in the media and academic literature.

## Conclusion

Against a background of weak methodological developments in family tourism and fragmented understandings of family holiday experiences, the application of the whole-family methodology is making original contributions. This is based on a more critical and holistic approach to research that allows for a more balanced representation between the individual perspectives of all the family members and the more collective perspective of the family group. It adds the role of the father, the emphasis placed by the children and the internal family group dynamics to understandings of the family holiday. Giving a voice to fathers within the context of the family has identified gender differences and highlighted the undervalued fathering role as main entertainer of the children and as facilitator of mothers' own interests. The gendered role of the father on holiday is more concerned with activity-based parenting. This echoes themes in the leisure literature on fathers and active involvement in their children's leisure (Kay, 2009) and represents a continuation of their fatherhood discourse on holiday.

The tourism context, however, extends our understanding of fatherhood, as holidays are concentrated time spent with the family, away from everyday school, leisure and work schedules. Including both group and individual perspectives in the research process gave the opportunity for participants to talk as both family members and individuals. This highlighted that the individual pursuits of fathers on holiday centre more on physical and mental activities and challenges. A focus solely on the fathers' role with the children on holiday without an understanding of their own pursuits away from the children would provide an incomplete understanding of the complexities and contradictions of fatherhood in tourism.

Giving a voice to the children has identified generational differences and highlighted the importance that children place on fun and sociality on holiday. Parents and children bring different purposes to the holiday environment, in that parents are more deliberate, whereas children's desires are more immediate. Fun for the children reflects their self-interest and is fundamentally perceived as interactive. Holidays for children are also perceived as opportunities to (re)affirm social relationships with peers, providing them with their own time away from the family. This stresses the fact that holiday experiences for children have a stronger social and personalised dimension than is acknowledged from a solely adult perspective. While family holidays provide opportunities for increased family interactions it also highlights the individual needs of children for time away from parental restrictions in the company of peers.

Giving a voice to the family group allowed insights into internal group dynamics and highlighted potential social tensions and conflicts that can arise on holiday. This differs from the ideal image of the happy family on holiday within the media and society at large (Carr, 2011) and introduces notions of negative family holiday experiences, which are largely unreported in the academic literature. The findings revealed that conflicts could arise during holidays because family members were less insulated from internal dynamics than they were at home. For example, more time is spent in shared spaces such as car journeys, which become enforced family times, and there are more opportunities for experiences that involve a level of risk or danger.

This highlights the fact that family holidays offer the only occasion for the whole family to be closely together for an extended time in an alien environment and without the distractions of other commitments, which can reveal gender and generational differences in interests and needs. Examining the experiences of all family members on holiday through a whole-family methodology then provides a social lens (Lashley et al., 2007) into family life outside the home. This chapter therefore demonstrates the wider contribution that tourism research can make to the social enquiry into fatherhood, childhood and contemporary family life dynamics.

## References

Anderson, J. (2001) Mothers on family activity holidays overseas. In S. Clough and J. White (eds), *Women's Leisure Experiences: Ages, Stages and Roles* (pp. 99–112). Eastbourne: Leisure Studies Association.

Blichfeldt, B.S. (2006) *A Nice Vacation* (IME Report 8/06). Esbjerg: University of Southern Denmark. Retrieved from http://static.sdu.dk/mediafiles//Files/Om_SDU/Institutter/Miljo/ime/rep/blichfeldt8.pdf.

Carr, N. (2011) *Children's and Families' Holiday Experiences*. London: Routledge.

Charmaz, K. (2000) Grounded theory: objectivist and constructivist methods. In N.K. Denzin and Y.S. Lincoln (eds), *Handbook of Qualitative Research* (2nd edition) (pp. 509–535). Thousand Oaks, CA: Sage.

Crompton, J.L. (1979) Motivations for pleasure vacation. *Annals of Tourism Research*, 6(4), 408–424.

Cullingford, C. (1995) Children's attitudes to holidays overseas. *Tourism Management*, 16(2), 121–127.

Daly, K. (2001) Deconstructing family time: from ideology to lived experience. *Journal of Marriage and Family*, 63(2), 283–294.

Davidson, P. (1996) The holiday and work experiences of women with young children. *Leisure Studies*, 15(2), 89–103.

Deem, R. (1996) Women, the city and holidays. *Leisure Studies*, 15(2), 105–119.

Denzin, N.K. and Lincoln, Y.S. (eds) (2000) *Handbook of Qualitative Research* (2nd edition). Thousand Oaks, CA: Sage.

Fagan, J. (2003) Editorial. *Fathering*, 1(1), 1.

Farrell, A. (2005) Ethics and research with children. In A. Farrell (ed.), *Ethical Research with Children* (pp. 1–14). New York: Open University Press.

Freeman, M. and Mathison, S. (2009) *Researching Children's Experiences*. New York: Guilford.

Glaser, B.G. and Strauss, A.L. (1967) *The Discovery of Grounded Theory*. Chicago, IL: Aldine de Gruyter.

Gram, M. (2005) Family holidays: a qualitative analysis of family holiday experiences. *Scandinavian Journal of Hospitality and Tourism*, 5(1), 2–22.

Greene, S. and Hogan, D. (2005) *Researching Children's Experience: Approaches and Methods*. London: Sage.

Gyimothy, S. (1999) Visitors' perceptions of holiday experiences and service providers: an exploratory study. *Journal of Travel and Tourism Marketing*, 8(2), 57–74.

Handel, G. (1991) Case study in family research. In J.R. Feagin, A.M. Orum and G. Sjoberg (eds), *A Case for the Case Study* (pp. 244–268). Chapel Hill, NC: University of North Carolina Press.

Handel, G. (1996) Family worlds and qualitative family research: emergence and prospects of whole-family methodology. *Marriage and Family Review*, 24(3/4), 335–348.

Harrington, M. (2006) Sport and leisure as contexts for fathering in Australian families. *Leisure Studies*, 25(2), 165–183.

Harrington, M. (2009) Sport mad, good dads: Australian fathering through leisure and sport practices. In T. Kay (ed.), *Fathering Through Sport and Leisure* (pp. 51–72). London: Routledge.

Hilbrecht, M., Shaw, S.M., Delamere, F.M. and Havitz, M.E. (2008) Experiences, perspectives, and meanings of family vacations for children. *Leisure/Loisir*, 32(2), 541–571.

Jamal, T. and Hollinshead, K. (2001) Tourism and the forbidden zone: the underserved power of qualitative inquiry. *Tourism Management*, 22(1), 63–82.

Johns, N. and Gyimothy, S. (2003) Postmodern family tourism at Legoland. *Scandinavian Journal of Hospitality and Tourism*, 3(1), 3–23.

Kay, T. (2006) Special issue. Fathering through leisure. *Leisure Studies*, 25(2), 125–256.

Kay, T. (ed.) (2009) *Fathering Through Sport and Leisure*. London: Routledge.

LaRossa, R., Bennett, L.A. and Gelles, R.J. (1994) Ethical dilemmas in qualitative family research. In G. Handel and G.G. Whitchurch (eds), *The Psychosocial Interior of the Family* (4th edition) (pp. 109–126). New York: Aldine de Gruyter.

Lashley, C., Lynch, P. and Morrison, A. (eds) (2007) *Hospitality: A Social Lens*. Oxford: Elsevier.

Lehto, X.Y., Choi, S., Lin, Y.-C. and MacDermid, S.M. (2009) Vacation and family functioning. *Annals of Tourism Research*, 36(3), 459–479.

Morse, J.M. (1995) The significance of saturation. *Qualitative Health Research*, 5(2), 147–149 (doi:10.1177/104973239500500201).

Obrador, P. (2012) The place of the family in tourism research: domesticity and thick sociality by the pool. *Annals of Tourism Research*, 39(1), 401–420.

Podilchak, W. (1991) Distinctions of fun, enjoyment and leisure. *Leisure Studies*, 10(2), 133–148.

Prentice, R., Witt, S.F. and Hamer, C. (1998) Tourism as experience: the case of heritage parks. *Annals of Tourism Research*, 25(1), 1–24.

Pritchard, M.P. and Havitz, M.E. (2006) Ratios of tourist experience: it was the best of times, it was the worst of times. *Tourism Analysis*, 10(3), 291–297.

Ryan, C. (2003) A new wave – or beached fathers! Gender issues in academic tourism literature – where is the dad? In R.W. Braithwaite and R.L. Braithwaite (eds), *CAUTHE Conference Proceedings*. Coffs Harbour: Southern Cross University.

Schänzel, H.A. (2008) The New Zealand family on holiday: values, realities and fun. In J. Fountain and K. Moore (eds), *Proceedings of the New Zealand Tourism and Hospitality Research Conference*. Canterbury, New Zealand: Lincoln University.

Schänzel, H.A. (2010) Whole-family research: towards a methodology in tourism for encompassing generation, gender, and group dynamic perspectives. *Tourism Analysis*, 15(5), 555–569.

Schänzel, H.A. and Smith, K.A. (2011) The absence of fatherhood: achieving true gender scholarship in family tourism research. *Annals of Leisure Research*, 14(2–3), 129–140.

Shaw, S.M. (2010) Diversity and ideology: changes in Canadian family life and implications for leisure. *World Leisure Journal*, 52(1), 4–13.

Shaw, S.M., Havitz, M.E. and Delemere, F.M. (2008) I decided to invest in my kids' memories: family vacations, memories, and the social construction of the family. *Tourism Culture and Communication*, 8(1), 13–26.

Small, J. (2002) Good and bad holiday experiences: women's and girls' perspectives. In M.B. Swain and J.H. Momsen (eds), *Gender/Tourism/Fun?* (pp. 24–37). Elmsford, NY: Cognizant Communication Corporation.

Small, J. (2005a) *Holiday Experiences of Women and Girls Over the Life-Course*. PhD thesis, University of Technology, Sydney, Australia.

Small, J. (2005b) Women's holidays: disruption of the motherhood myth. *Tourism Review International*, 9(2), 139–154.

Small, J. (2008) The absence of childhood in tourism studies. *Annals of Tourism Research,* 35(3), 772–789.

Sterry, P. and Beaumont, E. (2006) Methods for studying family visitors in art museums: a cross-disciplinary review of current research. *Museum Management and Curatorship*, 21(3), 222–239.

Such, E. (2009) Fatherhood, the morality of personal time and leisure-based parenting. In T. Kay (ed.), *Fathering Through Sport and Leisure* (pp. 73–87). London: Routledge.

Thompson, S.M. (1999) *Mother's Taxi: Sport and Women's Labor*. Albany, NY: State University of New York Press.

Travelhorizons (2009) Leisure Travel Profiles July. Retrieved 19 September 2011 from http://www.ustravel.org/research/domestic-research/travelhorizons.

# 6 VFR Travel: Why Marketing to Aunt Betty Matters

## Elisa Backer

## Introduction

Families often have particularly strong needs to travel to reconnect with friends and family. When there is the birth of a baby, family members typically want to visit to see the new arrival. Close friends will do likewise. Similarly, regular trips are often planned to observe significant milestones of the child as well as to ensure a bond forms with that child. Thus the very nature of having a family lends itself to visiting friends and relatives (VFR). Travel for births, birthdays, significant achievements, graduations, weddings and other special events is important for families.

These types of travel – celebrations of milestones and events – are forms of travel that are not as susceptible to economic downturns as leisure-based travel. When the economy tends towards recessionary conditions, people's confidence often declines. Purchases such as holidays can be forsaken, regarded as a luxury that is not necessary. However, the mind-set for many forms of VFR travel – funerals, weddings, graduations and reconnecting socially – is different. Some people may feel that they do not *need* a holiday; those same people may feel that they do *need* to be at their niece's wedding, their father's funeral, their daughter's graduation. Those people will often not question whether they should go. They may not even consider the best flight deals. The thinking underpinning VFR travel is different to leisure-based travel and so VFR travel may not be as vulnerable to changes in the exchange rate, economic conditions and seasonality.

Given the importance of VFR travel for family tourism and its economic stability, it is useful to consider the relative merit of tourism practitioners essentially 'marketing to Aunt Betty'. This chapter therefore discusses an essential aspect of family tourism. It begins by reviewing the literature and goes on to describe a study undertaken in the state of Victoria, Australia.

## Literature Review

Since 1998, the propensity for Australians to travel domestically for holidays has waned. In 2010 Australians took 6.4 million fewer domestic holidays than they did in 1998, which was an average annual decrease of 0.8%. Over that same period, Australians took almost double the number of international holidays, resulting in a 7% average annual growth rate. With an increased household income, more access to overseas markets, improved competition resulting in cheaper airfares and technological improvements, Australians are increasingly holidaying overseas. Coupled with this, a high exchange rate for the Australian dollar heightened the appeal of international travel.

However, not all travel is for holiday purposes. People also travel for other purposes, such as VFR. VFR travel is an important component of family tourism. As discussed in Chapter 9, families often struggle with the stress of travelling, especially when their children are young. As a result, many families with children at primary school travel to see friends and family as a way of having a break with the support available to ensure some form of leisure can be achieved by the parents.

In the Australian state of Victoria, almost half of its visitors are visiting friends and relatives (Backer, 2012). VFR travellers may be less sensitive to exchange rates and the destination is more fixed. As a result, VFR travel can actually provide destinations with a buffering effect against economic downturns. Economic conditions have also affected destinations outside Australia. In 2009 the global recession resulted in a 'steep decline in tourism worldwide' (Liu, 2009). Some countries have been particularly affected, in Europe as well as Asia (Liu, 2009).

The recessionary conditions stimulated a trend towards cheaper destinations and there has been a shift towards caravanning and camping (Liu, 2009). While the USA also suffered a significant drop in international tourism, it has not been as badly affected as some other countries, mainly because of its strong domestic tourism market (Liu, 2009). The link with VFR travel in recessionary conditions can also be seen in the USA. For example, an increased number of Americans were recorded travelling on the 2011 Thanksgiving holiday, 'giving the sluggish economy a small boost' (*People's Daily Online*, 2011). While Thanksgiving has traditionally been a holiday to celebrate the harvest in the USA and Canada, the modern celebration is 'where American families come together; even more than Christmas' (Baigrie, 2011). The increase in travel over Thanksgiving in America despite the decrease in tourism for the country highlights the point about VFR travel being less vulnerable to recessionary conditions compared with other forms of tourism.

New Zealand has also seen the strength of VFR of late, in comparison with other segments. While business travel fell by 5% and holiday arrivals fell by 2.2%, international VFR travel grew by 4.2% in 2008 (Angus &

Associates, 2011). VFR was also shown to remain strong in the UK (Key Note, 2010). Key Note (2010), a provider of market intelligence in the UK, claimed that 'another indication of the recession's impact is that activities which cost very little, such as visiting friends or relatives (VFR) … either remained stable or increased between 2008 and 2010'. VFR can be seen as less vulnerable and should also be recognised as an important economic contributor.

Highlighting its value to a local economy, VFR research in the Albury–Wodonga area of Australia, undertaken in 1994, indicated that VFR travel was of major economic importance. It was found to be worth between AU$27 and AU$52 million per annum and responsible for creating between 540 and 1135 full-time-equivalent jobs (McKercher, 1994).

The value of VFR travel has been highlighted through recent literature (Backer, 2007, 2010a, 2010b, 2011). While VFR travellers are often assumed to spend less than non-VFR travellers, research in seven contrasting destinations in Australia has shown that in some destinations this is not the case. In all seven destinations researched, VFRs outspent non-VFRs across a wide range of categories. While the categories varied across the destinations, often the high VFR spend was linked to retail shopping, groceries, entertainment and dining out.

As suggested above, VFR travel also has economic importance because it tends to have a stabilising effect on an economy and is less vulnerable to market fluctuations. King (1994: 175) presented data showing that between 1980 and 1990 'VFR travel grew by 87%, a higher figure than the one attributable to holiday travel of 69%'. He also pointed out that VFR travel 'experienced a further growth of 22% between 1990 and 1991 whilst outbound holiday numbers declined' (King, 1994: 175). Because of this, King (1996) believes that targeted VFR strategies may be appropriate during economic declines to help buffer against business downturns. He refers to the fact that during previous recessions VFR travel held up better than holiday travel in Australia's state of Victoria, particularly in Victoria's rural areas.

Furthermore, VFR travel is said to be less susceptible than other forms of tourism to seasonality issues (Asiedu, 2008; Bull, 1995; Denman, 1988; Hay, 1996; McKercher, 1994; Seaton & Palmer, 1997; Seaton & Tagg, 1995; Weaver & Lawton, 2010) and 'is most likely to fall outside the conventional tourism season' (Aseidu, 2008: 617). Therefore, the reduced seasonality aspect of VFR travel also compounds its stabilising effect. In fact, according to Seaton and Palmer (1996), VFR travel is not only spread more evenly throughout the year than other tourism segments, but may also peak in times that are traditionally low, off-season times. As seasonality can be a major problem in tourism (Baum & Lundtorp, 2001), this illustrates a major economic benefit of VFR travel, in that it may serve as an economic stabiliser (King, 1996; Lehto et al., 2001; McKercher, 1994; Seaton & Palmer,

1997). With VFR travel having been shown to be more resilient than other types of travel in Victoria, this chapter discusses why destinations should be marketing to 'Aunt Betty'.

Marketing to 'Aunt Betty' is rarely done. Despite VFR travel being a large (by size) form of tourism in most destinations, it is typically overlooked as a segment to market to. The reasons for this neglect have been put forward (Backer, 2010a) as being:

• perceived minor economic impact;
• definitional problems;
• discrepancies in official data;
• lack of lobbying;
• lack of coverage in tourism textbooks;
• perception that VFR travellers are difficult to influence;
• difficulties with measurement;
• VFR travel is not a 'sexy' market.

That final reason for neglect – that VFR travel is not a 'sexy' market – is important to consider. Typically, international marketing is regarded as prestigious and domestic tourism is seen as inferior to it (Pearce, 1993; Scheyvens, 2007). Even less prestigious is 'marketing to "Aunt Betty" [which] is not as glamorous' (Backer, 2010a: 340).

The eight reasons offered for why VFR travel has been neglected link in to why the sector has been overlooked by many operators in their marketing. Many tourism marketing bodies appear to believe that the investment returns on VFR marketing campaigns are greatly inferior to those from other campaigns (Morrison et al., 1995). One study surveyed destination marketing organisations (DMOs) to ascertain whether they specifically target VFR travellers in their marketing, or whether VFR travellers were 'lumped together with other groups of visitors' (Morrison et al., 2000: 106). The researchers concluded that a majority of tourism organisations did not specifically market to VFR travellers. This was in part due to the perceived disadvantages associated with VFR travel. VFR travellers were perceived to make little use of tourism products and commercial accommodation outlets, and to have levels of low expenditure on tourist products.

It is hardly surprising that minimal marketing specifically towards VFR travellers is undertaken, given its perceived secondary status in tourism. As little is known about VFR travel, not much effort seems to be placed on dedicating resources towards research in this area. As a result, operators have been traditionally disinclined to undertake dedicated VFR tourism campaigns. Few organisations have developed marketing activities focused on VFR travel. King (1996: 85) believes it is just as well that so little marketing has been done in the area of VFR travel, given the 'absence of adequate research', which may have caused the campaigns to 'miss their mark'.

Within this discussion concerning marketing, it is useful to highlight that much of the literature discussing VFR travel refers to it being a 'market' (Braunlich & Nadkarni, 1995; Denman, 1988; Hay, 1996; Lehto *et al.*, 2001; McKercher, 1994, 1995; Morrison *et al.*, 1995, 2000; Seaton, 1994; Seaton & Palmer, 1997; Seaton & Tagg, 1995; Yaman, 1996; Yuan *et al.*, 1995). However, in cases where VFR travellers are staying with friends or relatives there are no property rights being exchanged, and therefore VFR travel in those cases is not really a market. Visitors staying with friends and relatives do not tend to pay their host for their lodging and, as such, there has been no property exchange. The whole concept of a market involves exchange between buyers and sellers, who are connected by four flows. These flows are communication, products/services, money and information (Kotler *et al.*, 2006). Without the host acting as a seller and receiving money in exchange for goods (the accommodation), this form of tourism cannot be considered a market.

Nonetheless, VFR travellers do enter into market transactions; for instance, as they enter a theme park the seller is receiving something in return for the transaction. Those VFR travellers staying in commercial accommodation are also entering into market transactions. However, VFR travel cannot be categorised in its entirety as a market. The assertion that VFR travel is a worthwhile market segment cannot really be made, and in the broad manner in which it is made authors are only really borrowing the term. VFR travel is a market segment only for some organisations and operators. While VFR travellers may spend money and become involved in activities that involve market transactions, their accommodation, if they are staying with friends or relatives, is a form of non-marketised tourism. As such, the trip itself may involve both non-marketised and marketised activities.

Marketing specialists have developed a set of four criteria as appropriate determinants of whether a market segment should be considered feasible for targeting. The four criteria, all four of which must stand, are that the segment needs to be: identifiable and measurable; accessible; substantial; and actionable (Leiper, 2004). As outlined above, VFR travel is problematic to identify and measure and, as such, this market segment criterion can be difficult to satisfy. However, VFR travellers are accessible, primarily through the hosts (Backer, 2007, 2008, 2011). For some tourism operators, VFR travellers may be a part of their set of consumers, but they may not be a substantial part. Therefore, the third market segment criterion may be difficult to meet in many instances. In terms of being actionable, the marketing budget of many small tourism operators may be so limited that they would not be able to justify dedicating these resources to marketing to VFR travellers. In many cases, for those operators with few or no staff and a small operating budget, the difficulty of identifying these consumers and measuring their consumption would make marketing impractical. However, there may be a case to argue that VFR travellers are a market segment for certain operators and worthy of targeting.

Because VFR travel is large by size, it is of value to tourism regions. The issue of size and neglect was first mooted more than 20 years ago, when Jackson (1990) raised awareness of VFR travel by asking the question 'VFR tourism: is it underestimated?' in a seminal paper of that title. Over the past two decades, other researchers have added to the VFR literature. More recently, Jackson's important question was answered by Backer (2012), who demonstrated that official data cannot be used as a tool for measuring the size of VFR travel, and doing so will underestimate its size by at least 20%. It is useful to note that in that paper by Backer (2012), the terminology changed from 'VFR tourism' to 'VFR travel'. This distinction between travel and tourism is important. Definitions of tourism tend to share a number of characteristics. For instance, one common element is: 'it is primarily for leisure or recreation, although business is also important' (Hall, 2007: 11). This point is similarly addressed by Leiper (2004: 35), who states that 'being a tourist has three attributes. It requires travelling, visiting, and having a leisure experience.'

There can be people who travel for VFR purposes and/or who stay with friends or relatives whose trip has no leisure component whatsoever. There may be some individuals who would not be considered to be tourists under many tourism definitions. They may be travelling to attend a funeral, to care for a sick relative or to undertake an obligatory en route visit. They are travellers, they are spending money, but they may not be tourists.

Consideration of the notion of travel rather than tourism can be particularly important in the context of an economic downturn, because tourism can be affected to a greater extent than travel. Consumers' expectations regarding the future affect spending on non-essential items such as holidays. Those people who have optimistic expectations tend to spend more on discretionary goods and services than those who have pessimistic expectations (Van Raaij, 1991). Therefore, consumers are more likely to consume more when they feel confident about their own future economic and financial situations (Gelper et al., 2007). More specifically, the demand for business travel can be affected by the economy and level of economic development (Njegovan, 2005; Swarbrooke & Horner, 2001).

In appreciating that official data are not able to measure all VFR travel, observing the proportion of people staying with friends and relatives does provide an indicator regarding travel behaviour. This may be particularly so during economic downturns.

## Method

The aim of this research was to investigate the numbers of domestic travellers staying with friends and relatives across the regions within the Australian state of Victoria. Secondary data from Tourism Research Australia (TRA) were used. TRA produced a wide range of data for the nation, as well as at the state and regional levels. Data were derived from the two main survey instruments used by TRA – the National Visitor Survey and the International Visitor Survey.

In Australia there are 83 tourism regions, as defined by TRA. The available TRA tourism profile data for 2008–2009 and 2009–2010 were examined for the state of Victoria. Regional tourism profiles prior to 2008–2009 are not available. Each region within the state of Victoria was then considered, to ascertain whether the general pattern of declining domestic travel in Australia was also evident in terms of people staying with friends and relatives in Victoria. There were 17 regions in Victoria in which there were data available across the two years that had a sample size high enough to be considered valid and publishable. The data from those 17 regions were analysed.

## Research Findings

As revealed in Table 6.1, the number of visitors who were staying with friends and relatives in the state of Victoria increased from 2008–2009 to 2009–2010. The length of stay did not change. In 12 out of the 17 regions (71%) the number of visitors increased. For some of those regions, the increases were considerable. High Country recorded the highest growth rate in VFR numbers (31.7%), followed by Bendigo (24.8%) and Geelong (20.2%).

An examination of population growth rate data (Australian Bureau of Statistics, 2011) did not reveal any linkage between regions that were growing fastest and VFR growth rates. In fact, Ballarat is experiencing one of the highest population growth rates in Victoria but had one of the lowest growth rate increases in VFR numbers. Populations in Bendigo and Geelong are growing slower than Ballarat yet their VFR numbers grew much faster than Ballarat. Therefore, while there is a relationship between population and VFR (i.e. the more residents, the more people coming to visit those residents), there was no relationship between the growth of populations and VFR travellers.

While Victoria as a state did not see any change in the average length of stay for VFRs, there were changes at a regional level in most areas. Ballarat recorded a modest VFR growth rate of 4.8% but the average length of stay increased 11.1%. Many of the other regions also saw an increase in the average length of stay of VFRs, while four regions did not see any changes and some saw declines.

The region that saw the greatest decline in VFR travel – in terms of both visitor numbers and average length of stay – was Murray East. However, this is one region that cannot be solely assessed in terms of the economic conditions since it was one of the regions devastated by the bushfires in February 2009. As a region heavily reliant on its river for visitation, it is still suffering from the post-bushfire damage. The Department of Primary

**Table 6.1** Numbers of domestic visitors staying with friends and relatives in Victoria 2008–2009 and 2009–2010, and length of stay

| | 2008–2009 | | 2009–2010 | | Growth rate (%) |
|---|---|---|---|---|---|
| | No. of visitors | Mean length of stay | No. of visitors | Mean length of stay | |
| Victoria (state figures) | 6,128,000 | 3.1 | 6,290,000 | 3.1 | 2.6 |
| Ballarat | 188,000 | 2.7 | 197,000 | 3.0 | 4.8 |
| Gippsland | 409,000 | 2.4 | 354,000 | 2.6 | −13.5 |
| Geelong | 382,000 | 2.7 | 459,000 | 3.0 | 20.2 |
| Bendigo | 290,000 | 2.0 | 362,000 | 2.4 | 24.8 |
| Lakes | 116,000 | 3.4 | 125,000 | 2.9 | 7.8 |
| Melbourne | 2,497,000 | 3.4 | 2,546,000 | 3.3 | 2.0 |
| Mallee | 162,000 | 3.3 | 175,000 | 4.0 | 8.0 |
| Melbourne East | 206,000 | 2.5 | 229,000 | 2.5 | 11.2 |
| Western region | 389,000 | 2.8 | 472,000 | 2.8 | 21.3 |
| Western Grampians | 110,000 | 2.7 | 111,000 | 3.0 | 0.9 |
| Central Highlands | 53,000 | 2.4 | 51,000 | 3.3 | −3.7 |
| Peninsula | 510,000 | 2.9 | 407,000 | 3.0 | −20.2 |
| Murray East | 99,000 | 3.9 | 60,000 | 2.8 | −39.4 |
| Central Murray | 151,000 | 3.1 | 171,000 | 3.1 | 13.2 |
| Philip Island | 217,000 | 2.9 | 231,000 | 2.4 | 6.5 |
| Goulburn | 173,000 | 2.5 | 169,000 | 2.5 | −2.4 |
| High Country | 202,000 | 3.1 | 266,000 | 2.9 | 31.7 |

*Source*: Adapted from Tourism Research Australia (2010, 2011)

Industries stocked 35,000 Murray cod fingerlings in the Goulburn River in September 2011 to try to encourage tourists back to enjoy the recreational fishing (Department of Primary Industries, 2011) since it is still facing difficulties.

Various factors could have affected other regions in the state of Victoria over the past few years, given the severity of the bushfires across the state in early 2009. Families whose homes were lost in the fires would not have been in a position to host friends and family for some time.

However, looking at the state-level data, there was an overall 2.6% growth in the number of people staying with friends and family. Yet there were fewer people staying in hotels, motels and serviced apartments (a drop from 5,660,000 to 5,497,000) and a drop in the average length of stay (from 2.4 to 2.3). There was also an increase in caravanning and camping during that time, which could be linked to selection of cheaper accommodation because of the recession. This was also seen in the UK (Liu, 2009).

## Implications

Despite a decade-long trend of domestic travel declining in Australia, VFR travel, in Victoria at least, is more resilient. When an international conference was dedicated to VFR travel in the mid-1990s (held at Victoria University in Melbourne), King (1996) highlighted that VFR had stood up well in Victoria despite recessionary conditions. It has similarly been shown that VFR travel has withstood the recessionary tourism downturn in other countries. While only two years' worth of official data at regional profile levels were available for this research, it does show growth in the VFR sector in Victoria despite the recessionary conditions over the period. This trend has also been revealed in other destinations outside Australia.

Thus, VFR may be a viable marketing opportunity for tourism destinations and tourism operators. While marketing to 'Aunt Betty' lacks glamour, it does have merit. This may be particularly appropriate in economic downturns, when some people will forgo the family holiday. However, the mind-set towards reconnecting socially is different. Travel to meet a new-born baby, attend a funeral, a wedding, anniversary, a birthday celebration, a graduation, a christening, or a celebration of Christmas as a family is unlikely to be considered a luxury. Such events are more likely to be considered an essential part of functioning and connecting as a family.

Families have needs to reconnect socially regardless of economic conditions. As a result, travel is less likely to diminish than are holidays per se. People's desire to purchase and to travel is affected by confidence. So, despite a general trend away from domestic tourism in Australia, people still travel to connect with friends and relatives. Family and friends are always important.

## Conclusion

For many destinations VFR travel is a large (by size) and valuable part of tourism. While marketing to VFR travellers has been traditionally ignored, marketing to VFR travellers should be regarded as an opportunity and a potential market segment for some operators and promotional bodies. This could be particularly the case in recessionary conditions, as it can create a buffer against economic downturn.

In the USA, travel reached a record level in 2011 for the Thanksgiving celebration, despite a general downwards trend in tourism for the country. Similarly, combating a trend against domestic travel in Australia, Victoria recorded an increase in the numbers of visitors staying with friends and relatives. Staying with friends and relatives, as with caravanning and camping, increased in Victoria. During the same period, the use of hotels, motels and apartments declined.

Travel to reconnect with friends and family is particularly important for families because celebrations and special occasions cannot be done alone. People rely on close friends and family to support celebrations in life. At various times of the year, families are compelled to travel because tradition dictates this. In Western countries, travel at Christmas time is important and many people will travel long distances at great expense to reconnect socially with family. In America and Canada family will also come together for Thanksgiving. A modernisation of a tradition based on celebrating the harvest, it is now seen by some as more important for family connection than Christmas. Easter is also often about family togetherness. Easter school holidays provide the opportunity to travel.

Time is of course only one element necessary for tourism to take place. The tourist's pre-trip psychological process contains seven elements – needs, information, expectations, motivation, time, money and the absence of other constraints (Leiper, 2004). However, it is easier to fulfil those conditions – the motivations and means – with VFR travel than with non-VFR travel. Money can be saved by staying with family or friends and redirected into other areas of the local economy. The motivation to travel is heightened by family occasions. Information is made more accessible by having family or friends to assist. Needs are created as a state of deprivation otherwise exists (not being connected as a family in key times).

Because families need to reconnect socially for various events and at various times of the year, travel typically occurs frequently for families visiting relatives and friends. VFR travel is therefore less vulnerable to seasonality and economic conditions. VFR travel grew in the 1990s in Victoria despite the economic conditions. The official data reviewed for this study has shown this same pattern. VFR thus remains an important part of family travel and an important part of strengthening destinations against economic downturns. Based on the size and economic significance of VFR travel to many destinations, marketing to 'Aunt Betty' may be a way in which destinations can buffer against economic downturns in the future.

## References

Angus & Associates (2011) Need to investigate VFR travel. Retrieved 28 November 2011 from http://www.angusassociates.co.nz/need-investigate-vfr.html.

Asiedu, A. (2008) Participants' characteristics and economic benefits of visiting friends and relatives (VFR) tourism – an international survey of the literature with implications for Ghana. *International Journal of Tourism Research*, 10(6), 609–621.

Australian Bureau of Statistics (2011) *Regional Population Growth, Australia*. Canberra: ABS.

Backer, E. (2007) VFR travel – an examination of the expenditures of VFR travellers and their hosts. *Current Issues in Tourism*, 10(4), 366–377.

Backer, E. (2008) VFR travellers – visiting the destination or visiting the hosts? *Asian Journal of Tourism and Hospitality Research*, 2(2), 60–70.

Backer, E. (2010a) Opportunities for commercial accommodation in VFR. *International Journal of Tourism Research*, 12(4), 334–354.

Backer, E. (2010b) *VFR Travel: An Assessment of VFR Versus Non-VFR Travellers*. PhD thesis, Southern Cross University, Lismore, NSW.

Backer, E. (2011) VFR travelers: how long are they staying? *Tourism Review International*, 14(2), 61–70.

Backer, E. (2012) VFR travel: it is underestimated. *Tourism Management*, 33(1), 74–79.

Baigrie, K. (2011) Celebrating Thanksgiving. *The Chronicle* (Toowoomba), 25 November, 23–25. Retrieved 28 November 2011 from http://www.thechronicle.com.au/story/2011/11/25/celebrating-thanksgiving.

Baum, T. and Lundtorp, S. (2001) *Seasonality in Tourism*. Oxford: Pergamon.

Braunlich, C. and Nadkarni, N. (1995) The importance of the VFR market to the hotel industry. *Journal of Tourism Studies*, 6(1), 38–47.

Bull, A. (1995) *The Economics of Travel and Tourism* (2nd edition). Melbourne: Longman.

Denman, R. (1988) *A Response to the VFR Market*. London: English Tourist Board.

Department of Primary Industries (2011) Murray cod stocking a tourism boost for North East. Media release, 5 September. *About Us*. Retrieved 28 November 2011 from http://www.dpi.vic.gov.au/about-us/news/media-releases/category/fisheries/murray-cod-stocking-a-tourism-boost-for-north-east.

Gelper, S., Lemmens, A. and Croux, C. (2007) Consumer sentiment and consumer spending: decomposing the Granger casuality relationship in the time domain. *Applied Economics*, 39(1), 1–11.

Hall, C.M. (2007) *Introduction to Tourism in Australia* (5th edition). Frenchs Forest: Pearson Education.

Hay, B. (1996) An insight into the European experience: a case study on domestic VFR tourism within the UK. In H. Yaman (ed.), *VFR Tourism: Issues and Implications. Proceedings from the Conference Held at Victoria University of Technology* (pp. 52–66). Melbourne: Victoria University of Technology.

Jackson, R. (1990) VFR tourism: is it underestimated? *Journal of Tourism Studies*, 1(2), 10–17.

Key Note (2010) Recession alters consumer's choice of leisure activities. Press release, 15 November. Retrieved 28 November 2011 from http://www.keynote.co.uk/media-centre/in-the-news/display/recession-alters-consumers-choice-of-leisure-activities/?articleId=513.

King, B. (1994) What is ethnic tourism? An Australian perspective. *Tourism Management*, 15(3), 173–176.

King, B. (1996) VFR – a future research agenda. In H. Yaman (ed.), *VFR Tourism: Issues and Implications Proceedings from the Conference Held at Victoria University Conference, Victoria, Australia* (pp. 85–89). Melbourne: Victoria University of Technology.

Kotler, P., Bowen, J. and Makens, J. (2006) *Marketing for Hospitality and Tourism* (4th edition). Cranbury, NJ: Pearson Education.

Lehto, X.Y., Morrison, A.M. and O'Leary, J.T. (2001) Does the visiting friends and relatives typology make a difference? A study of the international VFR market to the United States. *Journal of Travel Research*, 40(2), 201–212.

Leiper, N. (2004) *Tourism Management* (3rd edition). Frenchs Forest: Pearson Education.

Liu, L. (2009) Global travel takes a dive. *Bloomberg Businessweek*, 4 August. Retrieved 28 November 2011 from http://www.businessweek.com/print/globalbiz/content/aug2009/gb2009084_138150.htm.

McKercher, B. (1994) *Report on a Study of Host Involvement in VFR Travel to Albury Wodonga*. Wodonga: Tourism Albury Wodonga.

McKercher, B. (1995) An examination of host involvement in VFR travel. *Proceedings from the National Tourism and Hospitality Conference 1995* (pp. 246–255). Melbourne: Council for Australian University Tourism and Hospitality Education.

Morrison, A.M., Hsieh, S. and O'Leary, J. (1995) Segmenting the visiting friends and relatives market by holiday activity participation. *Journal of Tourism Studies*, 6(1), 48–63.

Morrison, A., Woods, B., Pearce, P., Moscardo, G. and Sung, H. (2000) Marketing to the visiting friends and relatives segment: an international analysis. *Journal of Vacation Marketing*, 6(2), 102–118.

Njegovan, N. (2005) A leading indicator approach to predicting short-term shifts in demand for business travel by air to and from the UK. *Journal of Forecasting*, 24(6), 421–432.

Pearce, D. (1993) Domestic tourism travel patterns in New Zealand. *GeoJournal*, 29(3), 225–232.

*People's Daily Online* (2011) Record number of Americans travel in Thanksgiving since recession. *People's Daily Online* (Beijing), 25 November. Retrieved 28 November 2011 from http://english.peopledaily.com.cn/90777/7655865.html.

Scheyvens, R. (2007) Poor cousins no more: valuing the development potential of domestic and diaspora tourism. *Progress in Development Studies*, 7(4), 307–325.

Seaton, A. (1994) Are relatives friends? Reassessing the VFR category in segmenting tourism markets. In A. Seaton (ed.), *Tourism: The State of the Art* (pp. 316–321). Chichester: Wiley.

Seaton, A. and Palmer, C. (1996) The structure of domestic VFR tourism in the UK 1989–1993, and what it tells us about the VFR category. In H.R. Yaman (ed.), *VFR Tourism: Issues and Implications* (pp. 26–50). Melbourne: Victoria University of Technology.

Seaton, A. and Palmer, C. (1997) Understanding VFR tourism behaviour: the first five years of the United Kingdom tourism survey. *Tourism Management*, 18(6), 345–355.

Seaton, A.V. and Tagg, S. (1995) Disaggregating friends and relatives in VFR tourism research: the Northern Ireland evidence 1991–1993. *Journal of Tourism Studies*, 6(1), 6–18.

Swarbrooke, J. and Horner, S. (2001) *Business Travel and Tourism*. Oxford: Butterworth–Heinemann.

Tourism Research Australia (2010) *Regional Tourism Profiles 2008/09*. Canberra: TRA.

Tourism Research Australia (2011) *Regional Tourism Profiles 2009/10*. Canberra: TRA.

Van Raaij, W.F. (1991) The formation and use of expectations in consumer decision making. In T.S. Robertson and H.H. Kassarjian (eds), *Handbook of Consumer Behavior* (pp. 401–418). Englewood Cliffs, NJ: Prentice-Hall.

Weaver, D. and Lawton, L. (2010) *Tourism Management* (4th edition). Milton: Wiley.

Yaman, H. (1996) VFR tourism: issues and implications. In *VFR Tourism: Issues and Implications, Proceedings from the Conference Held at Victoria University of Technology, Victoria University of Technology, Victoria*. Melbourne: Victoria University of Technology.

Yuan, T., Fridgen, J., Hsieh, S. and O'Leary, J. (1995) Visiting friends and relatives travel market: the Dutch case. *Journal of Tourism Studies*, 6(1), 19–26.

# 7   The Value of Social Tourism for Disadvantaged Families

## Lynn Minnaert

## Introduction

In popular Western culture, as exemplified in movies and television adver-tisements, the family is stereotypically presented as a smiling, supportive, nuclear unit. Although alternative family types have become more prolific and accepted in recent decades, it seems the concept of the nuclear family, based on the relationship between a man and a woman legally bound together through marriage, sharing a common residence (Muncie & Sapsford, 1995), still holds a strong appeal. The stereotypical family as depicted in the media is affluent, travels the world and all members regard each other with affection and are supportive of each other (Dallos & Sapsford, 1995).

Real families rarely live up to all or even most of the stereotype (Dallos & Sapsford, 1995). Non-nuclear family types, such as lone-parent families, families with single-sex parents and reconstituted or blended families are on the rise (UK National Statistics, 2007). There is an increasing lack of trust in the institution of the family to play a role in the social integration of individuals: the family, 'by many accounts, is becoming less cohesive, less embedded in the community, and hence less able to provide the necessary connections, normative control, and civic training that is required to prepare children for productive adult roles as workers, family members and citizens' (Furstenberg & Kaplan, 2007: 219).

Families are also not universally affluent and well travelled. This chapter focuses on disadvantaged families, as defined by the UK Index of Multiple Deprivation. The Index determines disadvantage in terms of deficiencies in six 'dimensions': 'income, employment, health deprivation and disability, education and training, housing and geographical access to services' (Miller, 2003: 5). Disadvantage is often a combination of these: low education levels, for example, may lead to unemployment, resulting in a low income. Individuals on low incomes are more likely to live in poor housing and areas with fewer services.

Low travel horizons, or a person's fear of travelling outside their own environment, is also connected to social exclusion. Mohan (2002: 66) illustrates this with the example of marginal owners-occupiers in Swindon, who, 'facing severe pressure on household budgets, found that their everyday lives were concentrated around their homes, which had almost become prisons'. Different studies report that, on average, unemployed people (one of the groups more liable to be socially excluded) spend 51–52% of their waking day at home. Television is the major leisure pursuit, consuming two to three hours a day as a main activity and another hour or two alongside other activities (Glyptis, 1989). This suggests low involvement in social leisure activities and indicates isolation. Leary also describes the psychological effects of social exclusion and 'links the concept to social anxiety, jealousy, loneliness, depression and low self-esteem' (Leary, 1990: 221).

Cohen and MacCartney (2007) highlight four ways in which families can be linked with inequality:

(1) Families may reflect inequalities. Poverty, for example, may lead to people having to live with their extended family. Single parents in many cases may be forced to share their living space with others, or to live with their relatives at least temporarily, in which case the lone-parent family becomes part of a wider extended family (Dallos & Sapsford, 1995).
(2) Families may contain and reproduce inequalities. The division of labour and resources within the family often privileges men. Larson *et al.* (1997), for example, highlight that the term 'family leisure' is often an oxymoron for women, as they generally take on caring and supporting roles even during leisure times.
(3) Unequal outcomes may result from different family forms. Lone-parent families, for example, are particularly exposed to poverty because of the necessary trade-off between earning and childcare (Walker & Collins, 2007).
(4) Family relationships may offer responses to inequality and hardship. For example, good family relationships are linked to better educational performance and greater family resilience.

If good family relationships can indeed offer responses to inequality and hardship, then this function is of particular importance to disadvantaged families. This chapter examines the value of social tourism as a potential measure to increase the social and family capital of the family as a unit, and of individual family members.

## Disadvantaged Families, Tourism and Leisure

Zabriskie and McCormick (2001) report that researchers have examined recreation and leisure patterns in families for many decades and have consistently reported relationships between family leisure involvement and positive family outcomes. Leisure allows families to bond and communicate, through the development of collective interests and a family identity. The leisure patterns of families can be divided into two types:

(1) *Core family leisure patterns.* These are everyday, low cost and often home based. Examples are watching television together, playing board games or having a barbecue in the garden. These activities involve little planning and limited novelty or risk.
(2) *Balance family leisure patterns.* These refer to activities that require greater investment of resources and that are usually not home based, like family tourism. They mostly occur less frequently than core family leisure patterns but may be of longer duration. (Zabriskie & McCormick, 2001)

Both patterns can contribute to greater family cohesion, but balance family leisure patterns have one additional benefit: 'the nature of these types of activities tends to facilitate the development of adaptive skills and the ability to learn and change.... The adaptive skills that are developed and practiced in this context of family leisure may be readily transferred to other areas of family life' (Zabriskie & McCormick, 2001: 284). This means that family holidays, compared with home-based leisure pursuits, allow the family to develop new skills: the holiday presents the family with 'new and unexpected stimuli from the outside environment, which provide the input and challenge necessary for families to learn and progress as an evolving system' (Zabriskie & McCormick, 2001: 284).

Families who are unable to take holidays are thus excluded from these learning opportunities. Disadvantaged families in particular may lack the financial means to participate in tourism, yet to be resilient in the face of disadvantage and change their situation they can be seen as being the most in need of the learning opportunities a holiday can provide. In several (mainly European) countries, social tourism initiatives encourage the participation of those who would otherwise be excluded from tourism.

Minnaert *et al.* (2007, 2009) define *social tourism* as 'tourism with an added moral value, of which the primary objective is to benefit the host or the visitor in the tourism exchange'. In practice, social tourism for disadvantaged families usually refers to budget-friendly holidays in their own country, or in some cases day trips to theme parks, museums and attractions, that are funded or made available at highly reduced rates, by charities or agencies in the public sector.

According to the European Economic and Social Committee (EESC), social tourism initiatives are (co-)funded by the public sector – via either direct grants or public–private partnerships – in several countries and regions of mainland Europe (France, Belgium, Spain, Portugal). The main justification for the provision of social holidays via the public sector is the notion, supported by a number of European institutions, that everyone has the right to basic tourism provision (EESC, 2006) and the assumption that 'social tourism clearly promotes integration, greater knowledge and personal development' (EESC, 2006: 76). In the UK and the USA social tourism is not usually part of public policy and is mostly provided via charitable bodies.

## Social and Family Capital in the Disadvantaged Family

The concepts of social and family capital may be useful to theoretically evaluate the social integration, greater knowledge and personal development that are claimed to be the outcomes of social tourism by the EESC (2006).

Disadvantage and social exclusion may be caused by a deficiency in *social capital*. Coleman describes social capital as the benefits people (he refers to 'actors') accrue through their relationships with others. He contrasts social capital with two other forms of capital: physical capital (machines, tools, productive equipment) and human capital (generally the product of training). If physical capital is wholly tangible, being embodied in observable material form, and human capital is less tangible, being embodied in the skills and knowledge acquired by an individual, social capital is still less tangible, for it exists in the *'relations* among persons' (Coleman, 1998: 100, original emphasis). Coleman defines social capital by its function: 'it facilitates certain actions of actors – either persons or corporate actors – within the social structure. Like other forms of capital, social capital is productive, making possible the achievement of certain ends that in its absence would not be possible' (Coleman, 1998: 98). Individuals or social groups, in other words, benefit from ties and relationships with others – the ties are mutually beneficial, and through cooperation the different 'actors' achieve goals that they may not have been able to achieve in isolation. Although there are a variety of definitions of the concept, a consensus is growing that social capital stands for the ability of actors to secure benefits by virtue of their membership of social networks or other social structures (Portes, 1998).

According to Coleman (1998), there are three forms of social capital. Firstly, there is the form that consists mainly of obligations, expectations and the trustworthiness of structures. Personal relationships can foster trust and cooperation between people, resulting in mutual benefits. Connected to this form is the second one: norms and effective sanctions. This refers to social rules and the punishment of unacceptable behaviour. The third and last form of social capital are information channels, as a network of close contacts can provide access to any information each of these contacts possesses.

As with any form of capital, social capital has positive but also negative uses. As stated above, one of the forms of social capital is norms and sanctions, based on obligations and the need for trustworthy structures in a network. More than once the question has then been asked whether social capital is at war with liberty and tolerance (Putnam, 2000). This has to do with the concept of 'closure', which means 'the existence of sufficient ties between a certain number of people to guarantee the observance of norms' (Portes, 1998: 6). Closure is a form of social control and a reliable frame for the judgement of actions within a certain group. Close social control might, on the one hand, guarantee the smooth functioning of the network, but, on the other, it may also imply conformity. To integrate with a certain group, its members might have to assimilate, and 'deviant' individuals may not be allowed access to the group. Closure thus protects the interests of the insiders of a group, but can also reduce the chances of outsiders to be allowed into it. This illustrates the link between social capital, closure and social exclusion, and even the link between social exclusion, poverty and social capital. Putnam argues that 'precisely because poor people (by definition) have little economic capital and face formidable obstacles in acquiring human capital (that is: education), social capital is disproportionately important to their welfare' (Putnam, 2000: 318). Their exclusion might thus have greater consequences, as they often lack the other forms of capital to form the valuable connections. Not only their psychological well-being is affected; economists have developed an impressive body of research which suggests that 'social ties can influence who gets a job, a bonus, a promotion and other employment benefits' (Putnam, 2000: 319). This means that social networks are often absent for people who need them the most: the unemployed, the excluded, the poor and so on.

In recent studies, mainly in the field of education and learning, the terms 'family capital' and 'family-based social capital' have been used to define the nature and value of social capital within the family. Parcel and Dufur (2001: 882) describe the concept as 'the bonds between parents and children that are useful in promoting child socialization. [It] reflects the time and attention parents spend in interaction with children, in monitoring their activities, and in promoting child well-being, including academic achievement.' As such, it refers to parental resources used in the socialisation process. These parental resources are distinguished from 'parental financial capital such as family financial resources, and from human capital such as parental years of schooling' (Parcel & Dufur, 2001: 883). This means that families on low incomes or parents with limited schooling are not necessarily low on family capital. Family capital is determined by the stability of the family, on the one hand, and the social contacts of the parents, on the other hand. Family capital 'is greater when the family system is characterized by time-closure; when the parents' commitment to each other is long term, children benefit from the stability of the union. In addition, children benefit from continued exposure to the social connections parents have with others outside the family group, such as neighbours, school personnel or work colleagues' (Parcel & Dufur, 2001: 882–883).

For socially excluded families, both stability within the family unit and social contacts can be particularly problematic. In families where the family capital is particularly low, the children's academic development is likely to be poor. Two studies by Marjoribanks have shown that 'family environmental contexts are moderately to largely associated with children's academic performances and adolescents' aspirations' (Marjoribanks, 1998: 328).

Although mainly used in the context of education and learning, the concept of family capital is not only useful to describe children's development. The level of family capital can also affect the resilience of the family as a whole, and thus influence (being part of social capital) each member of that family. Belsey describes the concept of family capital, from this angle, as having three dimensions: 'relations and the family network; family resources (knowledge, skills and material resources); and resilience. Resilience has much in common with the more widely understood concept of social capital, which, when applied to the family, includes one or a combination of the following: a sense of personal security, religious affiliation/practice, and social and moral points of reference' (Belsey, 2003: 3). In his study the value of family capital was examined for families confronted with AIDS. Being confronted with AIDS can rapidly diminish family capital: 'family members may react to the disclosure of the HIV status with anger and rejection ..., the bonds of trust and affection [can be] severely strained both within and beyond the family as a result of discrimination and stigmatization' (Belsey, 2003: 6). The report goes on to say that both for the well-being of the family itself, and to optimise its functioning in society, a focus on family policy is required. 'The overall objective of family policy is to promote, protect and support the integrity and functioning of the family by ensuring that family capital can be accumulated and strengthened' (Belsey, 2003: 10).

## Benefits of Social Tourism

Although social tourism is a long-established practice in many European countries, research evidence on the subject in English is relatively recent. This section reviews evidence from three recent studies in the UK, Belgium and Ireland, and highlights how social tourism can increase both family capital and social capital. It also explores how balanced family leisure patterns can lead to the development of new skills, potentially resulting in lasting behaviour change.

Multiple studies have shown that social tourism can contribute to an increase in *family capital* (McCabe, 2009; Minnaert, 2008; Minnaert *et al.*, 2009; Minnaert *et al.*, 2010). In each of these studies, social tourism beneficiaries reported that the holiday allowed the family members to spend quality time together away from the problems and the routine of the home environment. In McCabe's (2009) study, this was evaluated as the second biggest benefit of the holiday, reported by 76% of the surveyed social tourism beneficiaries. On holiday, families may engage in new activities, or do things together they would not do at home. In many cases, this resulted in improvements in family relations: between the parents and the children, the adults as a couple or between siblings. In some cases, the holiday was also used to allow the children to adjust to new family members or a new family structure (McCabe, 2009).

The effect of the holiday on the well-being of the children is both an important motivation and an often-reported outcome (Minnaert, 2008; Minnaert et al., 2010). It was reported that the ability to go on a holiday allowed many children to gain confidence, make new friends and feel more integrated into school life after the experience. Many parents commented how on the first day of school, for example, the children would often be asked to draw a picture or say a few words about their holidays. In many cases, however, the children of low-income or disadvantaged families have not been away, even on a day trip, and may feel a particular sense of exclusion. The holiday experience in these cases can be a source of pride and happy memories after the experience. In McCabe's (2009) study, the 'opportunity for fun and happy memories for the children' was evaluated as the most important benefit of the holiday, reported by 80% of the social tourism beneficiaries. Parents also often emphasised that the inability to afford a holiday resulted in feelings of shame and embarrassment for them, illustrating that 'poverty can seem like personal failure in a society that views success in terms of conspicuous consumption' (Walker & Collins, 2007: 208).

Even though family holidays can be a source of stress and conflict, and many families have arguments on holiday, in the study by Minnaert et al. (2010) the holiday was often reported to result in lasting improvements in the relationships between family members. After the holiday, many parents, for example, reported that they spent more time with their children, played with them more, or communicated with them better. One example was that of a single father who noted a big improvement in the communication with his teenage son after the holiday:

> It's a lot better yeah. He's certainly opened up more, at one time he wouldn't speak to anybody, like when you'd say, how was work. But now he's like 'I am doing this today', 'I am doing that today'. He's looking forward to go to college, and everything seems to be falling into place. He's happy now. (Minnaert et al., 2010: 135)

Another participant, who had a daughter with behavioural problems, reported a similar improvement:

> I am spending quite a lot of time with my little one now, quality time. Maybe it's just sitting down at home doing a puzzle, or sitting in the garden having biscuits together, at home. Or going out in the weekend, we had a good time in the weekend. And I didn't do that. But I have

started taking her out and stuff. I didn't realize how good it would be, to have time together, just as a family, or just me and her. (Minnaert *et al.*, 2010: 135)

Social tourism has equally been shown to lead to increases in *social capital* (McCabe, 2009; Minnaert, 2008; Minnaert *et al.*, 2009, 2010). As social isolation is a common problem for disadvantaged families, holidays can be particularly valuable where they lead to an expansion of social networks or a strengthening of social ties. Minnaert *et al.* (2009) found that group holidays were particularly useful for this purpose, as they encourage intense contact with other holidaymakers, often from similar geographical and social backgrounds. After holidays, many adults keep in touch via telephone or pay each other visits. Minnaert *et al.* (2010) include examples of similar impacts of group holidays on disadvantaged children in Dublin. One striking finding from that study concerned the extent to which the children's geographical and social worlds were very limited, with little exposure to different areas, people and lifestyles. In contrast with their normally limited social worlds, on holiday children encountered and engaged with children from other areas. The importance of making new friends and reconnecting with friends made on previous holidays emerged strongly. Often, the new friends lived in relative proximity, yet it was only through the intervention of the holiday that children managed to attain this modest broadening of their social worlds. McCabe (2009) reports on focus groups with children who have participated in social tourism: although they had generally not been on group holidays, the children still mentioned improved social contacts in relation to playing with cousins or other children.

Minnaert *et al.* (2009) found that where families travelled as a unit, and not as part of a group holiday, most participants did not build strong personal ties with other holidaymakers. However, their social capital could increase in other ways. Rather than expanding their membership of social networks, they often increased their involvement in social structures, most commonly the support organisation that facilitated and supported the holiday application. In many cases the participants proved more engaged or open to the support programme, or more confident in seeking help from the support staff. One of the support workers in that study testified:

Afterwards they might come to a group session or they might bring their child to stay and play. They might even not have been confident enough to talk to you before, but then afterwards they are. (Minnaert *et al.*, 2009: 326)

These findings highlight that social tourism can lead to increases in social capital in a variety of ways: some respondents met new people on holiday they stayed in touch with afterwards; others strengthened their ties with fellow travellers (often members of the extended family); others still made more intensive use of the support options offered by social organisations. In each of these cases, the social tourism beneficiaries increased the 'stock of good will created through shared norms and a sense of common membership upon which individuals may draw in their efforts to achieve collective or personal objectives' (Furstenberg & Kaplan, 2007: 221).

Above, it was highlighted that participation in tourism (balance family leisure patterns) may lead to the development of adaptive skills and the *ability to learn and change* (Zabriskie & McCormick, 2001). The potential of social tourism to encourage behaviour change that outlasts the duration of the holiday was a particular research theme of Minnaert *et al.*'s (2009) study. Coleman (1998: 98) describes social capital as 'productive, making possible the achievement of certain ends that in its absence would not be possible'. If this is indeed the case, then an increase in social capital could have a transformative effect. Minnaert *et al.* (2009) found that the holiday had given many respondents the time to reflect on their lives and identify areas where a change was desirable. With the help of their new social networks and the support of the social support organisation, some of the respondents were able to make positive changes to their families' lives. The research findings made clear that this benefit did not develop immediately after the holiday – at first, the escape from routine is often seen as one of the most important benefits of the holiday. Being able to leave the worries and financial problems at home and concentrate on more positive things offered many participants an opportunity to change their perspective.

A second round of fieldwork, involving 30 of the original 40 respondents, highlighted the impacts of social tourism six months after the tourism experience. A number of respondents showed more marked behaviour change. Social support organisations often play a vital role in facilitating this behaviour change. However, it is the holiday that is seen as the key motivational factor behind it. Most support opportunities the organisa-tions offer, for example, were already available before the holiday, but the participants did not take them up until after their holiday. Several social tourism beneficiaries, for instance, reported enrolling on courses (often related to parenting or childcare) or seeking individual counselling. The two respondents in work in the study both changed jobs after the holiday. Three respondents changed their views on debt and financial management and started budgeting better. Their support worker stated:

I know [she] had terrible trouble the year before last at Christmas time, she had no money, she was depressed. But this year seems to have been a complete turn-around, they have budgeted, it wasn't huge amounts, but budgeting for the holiday has started the ball rolling with them. (Minnaert *et al.*, 2009: 329)

## Conclusion

This chapter has explored the value of family tourism as a facilitator for the expansion of social and family capital in disadvantaged families. It has highlighted that all families (not only the nuclear, affluent and well travelled stereotype of the family often portrayed in Western popular media) can build affectional ties and resilience through participation in leisure and recreation. 'Balance family leisure patterns', which include family tourism experiences, play a particular role here, as they allow opportunities for learning and behaviour change. Disadvantaged families, which are at greater risk of being low on social and family capital, can particularly benefit from these experiences; however, due to financial restraints, many are not able to participate in tourism.

Social tourism initiatives have been shown in a range of studies to bring a variety of potential benefits for disadvantaged families. They offer opportunities to strengthen family relationships and to increase social networks, and can provide the motivational impetus for behaviour change. Successful social tourism initiatives thus have the potential to achieve a wide range of social outcomes. As such, an argument exists for them to be integrated in social policy as motivational or integrational measures. Where social tourism is already provided by the public sector, these schemes are often run as social enterprises or public–private partnerships, which limits the associated public spending. Moreover, social tourism initiatives are increasingly used in Europe as vehicles for the stimulation or regeneration of destinations (for a more in-depth discussion see Minnaert et al., 2011). The integration of social tourism initiatives in the policy domain can thus be seen to have a clear social and economic rationale.

In current times, when 'the fear of social disintegration is rampant' (Furstenberg & Kaplan, 2007: 218), the role of the family holiday may need to be reassessed. Perceiving tourism as a potential catalyst of social benefits goes against its typical depiction as a frivolous and hedonist activity. In the UK, the Conservative Party has developed a strong political discourse around 'broken Britain' and a central element in this discourse is the 'broken family', addressed in 2007 by the Social Justice Policy Group. The report of the Social Justice Policy Group (2007) refers to policy goals as increasing well-being, encouraging family cohesion and improving mental health. Yet at no point is tourism, or leisure, mentioned in this report. The role of tourism in social integration is still largely overlooked in the political and even the academic sphere. This chapter has highlighted that family leisure and tourism, instead of a frivolous activity, can be seen as a central building block for the creation and strengthening of family capital – a function that is of particular importance to disadvantaged families.

# References

Belsey, M. (2003) *AIDS and the Family: Policy Options for a Crisis in Family Capital*. New York: United Nations Department of Economic and Social Affairs.

Cohen, P. and MacCartney, D. (2007) Inequality and the family. In J. Scott, J. Treas and M. Richards (eds), *The Blackwell Companion to the Sociology of Families* (pp. 181–192). Malden, MA: Backwell.

Coleman, J. (1998) Social capital in the creation of human capital. *American Journal of Sociology*, 94 (supplement), 95–120.

Dallos, R. and Sapsford, R. (1995) Patterns of diversity and lived realities. In J. Muncie, M. Wetherell, M. Langan, R. Dallos and A. Cochrane (eds), *Understanding the Family* (pp. 125–170). London: Sage.

EESC (2006) *Opinion of the Economic and Social Committee on Social Tourism in Europe*. Brussels: European Economic and Social Committee.

Furstenberg, F. and Kaplan, S. (2007) Social capital and the family. In J. Scott, J. Treas and M. Richards (eds), *The Blackwell Companion to the Sociology of Families* (pp. 218–232). Malden, MA: Backwell.

Glyptis, S. (1989) *Leisure and unemployment*. Open University Press, Milton Keynes.

Larson, R., Gillman, S. and Richards, M. (1997) Divergent experiences of family leisure: fathers, mothers and young adolescents. *Journal of Leisure Research*, 29(1), 78–97.

Leary, M. (1990) Responses to social exclusion: social anxiety, jealousy, loneliness, depression, and low self-esteem. *Journal of Social and Clinical Psychology*, 9(2), 221–229.

Marjoribanks, K. (1998) Family capital, children's individual attributes, and adolescents' aspirations: a follow-up analysis. *Journal of Psychology*, 132(3), 328–336.

McCabe, S. (2009) Who needs a holiday? Evaluating social tourism. *Annals of Tourism Research*, 36(4), 667–688.

Miller, J. (2003) *Travel Chances and Social Exclusion*. Resource paper delivered at the 10th International Conference on Travel Behaviour Research, 'Moving Through Nets: The Physical and Social Dimensions of Travel', Lucerne, 10–14 August.

Minnaert, L. for Tourism Flanders (2008) *Holidays Are for Everyone. Research into the Effects and the Importance of Holidays for People Living in Poverty*. Brussels: Tourism Flanders. Retrieved 1 March 2012 from http://www.holidayparticipation.be/downloads/tourism_research_notebook.pdf.

Minnaert, L., Maitland, R. and Miller, G. (2007) Social tourism and its ethical foundations. *Tourism Culture and Communication*, 7(12), 7–17.

Minnaert, L., Maitland, R. and Miller, G. (2009) Tourism and social policy – the value of social tourism. *Annals of Tourism Research*, 36(2), 316–334.

Minnaert, L., Maitland, R. and Miller, G. (2011) Editorial. What is social tourism? *Current Issues in Tourism*, 5 (special issue on social tourism), 403–415.

Minnaert, L., Quinn, B., Griffen K. and Stacey, J. (2010) Social tourism for low-income groups: benefits in a UK and Irish context. In S. Cole and N. Morgan (eds), *Tourism and Inequality* (pp. 126–142). Wallingford: CABI.

Mohan, J. (2002) Geographies of welfare and social exclusion: dimensions, consequences and methods. *Progress in Human Geography*, 26(1), 65–75.

Muncie, J. and Sapsford, R. (1995) Issues in the study of the family. In J. Muncie, M. Wetherell, M. Langan, R. Dallos and A. Cochrane (eds), *Understanding the Family* (pp. 7–38). London: Sage.

Parcel, T. and Dufur, M. (2001) Capital at home and at school: effects on student achievement. *Social Forces*, 79(3), 881–912.

Portes, A. (1998) Social capital: its origins and applications in modern sociology. *Annual Review of Sociology*, 24(1), 1–24.

Putnam, R. (2000) *Bowling Alone. The Collapse and Revival of American Community*. New York: Simon and Schuster.

Social Justice Policy Group (2007) *Breakthrough Britain: Family Breakdown.* London: Centre for Social Justice.

UK National Statistics (2007) *Focus on Families.* London: Office for National Statistics. Retrieved 1 March 2012 from http://www.ons.gov.uk/ons/rel/family-demography/focus-on-families/2007/index.html.

Walker, R. and Collins, C. (2007) Families of the poor. In J. Scott, J. Treas and M. Richards (eds), *The Blackwell Companion to the Sociology of Families* (pp. 193–217). Malden, MA: Backwell.

Zabriskie, R. and McCormick, B. (2001) The influences of family leisure patterns on perceptions of family functioning. *Family Relations*, 50(3), 281–289.

# 8 The Stress of the Family Holiday

## Elisa Backer and Heike Schänzel

## Introduction

A holiday is by definition a time that is 'free': free from work and from producing things for the profit of others; holidays are 'good times' (Inglis, 2000). Holidays are commonly understood as a means to rest and recover from the stress and demands of everyday life (Valtonen & Veijola, 2010). Compared with home and daily routines, holidays involve leisure, 'anti-structure', and are liberating, at least in the daydream/fantasy version (Urry, 1996, cited in Gram, 2005). Many people elect to take a holiday for the purposes of rest and relaxation (Leiper, 2004), with 70% of people citing the reduction of stress as their main reason (Plog, 2005). However, as Urry (1996) notes, there is the ideal and there is the reality of holidays. Holidays with children are different from holidays without them and this is acknowledged in some studies of family holidays, where holidays are not all harmony but also involve conflicts at times (Gram, 2005; Johns & Gyimothy, 2002; Schänzel, 2010). Parents and children have different needs and interests regarding holidays, leading to tensions and added stresses.

The societal pressures on parents to have a 'happy holiday' are significant and are bound to idealised notions of contemporary parenting (Carr, 2011). As discussed in Chapter 2, a dominant ideology of parenting has emerged that increasingly perceives holidays as opportunities for 'quality family time' or 'purposive leisure time' away from everyday distractions. However, there is scant literature on the work involved in and the difficulties with organising and facilitating positive family experiences (Shaw, 2008). Therefore, the sources of stress remain under-researched and unacknowledged. This chapter seeks to establish the range of possible stress factors in the context of the family holiday and their relative significance.

Given the significance of accommodation as an influence on satisfaction with holiday experiences, this research specifically considers the extent to which numerous forms of accommodation add to or relieve stress and what responses accommodation providers could make to alleviate some of the stressors. The research sought to examine the relative significance of the following factors in adding to or relieving stress associated with taking a family holiday: type of accommodation and facilities provided in addition to work commitments of parent/s and life-stage of families.

## Literature Review

Families travelling with children represent one of the largest markets in tourism and yet tourism research has rarely taken notice of children's and families' holiday experiences (Carr, 2011; Obrador, 2012). Family holidays can be deemed to be a more 'mundane' and trivial type of tourism (Bærenholdt *et al.*, 2004). Despite the economic significance of family tourism, this is a marginalised research area (Schänzel *et al.*, 2005). Previous research has been mainly market and consumer driven (Lehto *et al.*, 2009), with a lack of research into experiential dimensions or family group dynamics. The predominance of tourism research that focuses on the individual and em-phasises detachment has effectively de-socialised tourist subjects, rendering such research approaches unsuitable for families (Obrador, 2012). This has resulted in mainly individual interpretations of group behaviour not inclusive of sociality (Schänzel, 2010).

Relatively little attention has been paid to the meaning of family holiday experiences for parents (Blichfeldt, 2006; Carr, 2011; Shaw *et al.*, 2008) or the family group (Gram, 2005), and few studies have investigated the family holiday experiences of children (Blichfeldt *et al.*, 2011; Carr, 2011; Hilbrecht *et al.*, 2008; Small, 2008). There have been studies of family holiday experiences that are mainly informed by a feminist perspective and thus focused on mothers (Anderson, 2001; Davidson, 1996; Deem, 1996b; Small, 2005). Conversely, research on the holiday experiences of fathers is only just emerging (Schänzel & Smith, 2011).

When family group dynamics are considered it emerges that a relation-ship exists between time together or family time and pursuing own interests or own time, and this can involve conflict (Schänzel, 2010). In fact, Gram (2005) has pointed out that holidays present conflicts in that parents seek relaxation and children seek activities, which makes the ideal of togetherness hard to achieve. This is highlighted by Jepsen and Blichfeldt's (2005) study at a caravan site where children were kept busy with activities which allowed adults to be passive and was thus found conducive to family togetherness.

There is considerable literature on the positive contributions of family leisure to family cohesion, family interaction and overall satisfaction with family life (Orthner & Mancini, 1990; Reilly, 2002/2003). Similarly, research has indicated that family holidays are associated with bonding, togetherness and quality family time (Carr, 2011; Gram, 2005; Schänzel, 2008; Shaw *et al.*,

2008) and have a beneficial effect on well-being (Gilbert & Abdullah, 2004); research has also looked at the social value of holidays for disadvantaged families (McCabe, 2009; Minnaert *et al.*, 2009).

A realisation exists among researchers that 'family leisure' has an underlying ideological notion that reflects a romanticised version of family life (Harrington, 2001; Hilbrecht *et al.*, 2008). This idealisation of family leisure can have negative consequences for parents through increased feelings of guilt and stress, especially among mothers, as the ideal of family togetherness can be difficult to achieve (Shaw, 2001). Several studies have found that mothers report a less positive leisure experience than fathers (e.g. Freysinger, 1994; Wearing, 1993). There is increasing research evidence that family leisure activities may not always be a positive experience for all family members (Larson *et al.*, 1997; Shaw & Dawson, 2001). Acknowledgment of both the benefits and the difficulties of family leisure can lead to a more realistic view of this valued aspect of family life (Shaw & Dawson, 2003/2004).

Within the substantial literature addressing women's leisure (e.g. Cyba, 1992; Kay, 2001; Shaw, 1985) two key issues appear: (1) women's experiences of time tend to be much more fragmented than those of many men, and (2) women tend to be the facilitators of others' leisure, and only secondarily the recipients of leisure themselves (Kinnaird & Hall, 1996), which means that family leisure becomes a source of both satisfaction and frustration for women (Clough, 2001). It also means that women participate significantly less in physically active leisure than men (Miller & Brown, 2005). These issues are associated with the 'ethic of care' in relation to women's leisure (Bialeschki, 1994; Henderson & Allen, 1991). Gilligan's research has shown that women's greater concerns for social responsibility and relationships place a constraint upon their lives as others are often placed before themselves (Gilligan, 1982). Women often receive double messages about the value of individuality and achievement, and also the need to be in connection with others (Chodorow, 1989), and thus lack autonomy compared with men (Wearing & Wearing, 1988).

Tourism research on family holiday experiences from the mother's perspective provides a partial insight into tensions and stresses within the family group on holiday. Recognising a general absence of gender research in the tourism literature, researchers in the 1990s examined impacts on host women, gendered guest–host relationships, employment of women in tourism and, to a lesser extent, women as tourists (e.g. Kinnaird & Hall, 1994; Sinclair, 1997; Swain, 1995). The female emphasis of socialising and interactions with others is highlighted by Chaplin (1999), compared with the male emphasis on action and self. Selänniemi (2002) concluded that women more often experience their holiday through relationships, while men seem more likely to let go into a liminoid float, free of everyday demands.

Other tourism studies informed by a feminist research perspective are focused on mothers' family holiday experiences. For example, Cerullo and

Ewen (1984) looked at American family camping holidays and confirmed earlier findings of women bearing the main domestic and caring responsibilities. Illustrations of family holidays as potentially stressful times, particularly for women, can be found in New Zealand because domestic holidays traditionally occur directly after the celebration of Christmas, which women usually plan, organise and orchestrate (Fitzgerald, 1993; Richmond & Tolich, 2000). This is supported by other tourism researchers (Anderson, 2001; Di Leonardo, 1992; Small, 2002), who have highlighted the never-ending physical and emotional work of motherhood, both at home and when travelling. In ensuring the enjoyment of others, women sacrifice their own holiday time to plan activities that will create lasting memories (Davidson, 1996) and feel dissatisfied when conflicts and difficulties exist between family members on holiday (Deem, 1996b). Those studies identify a relationship between an 'ethic of care' and motherhood and women's family holiday experiences.

Family holidays are enjoyed by women when they provide opportunities to nurture relationships and allow for a reduction in the pace and standards of work. The notion of women performing the bulk of tasks while on holiday, and especially in activities that reveal a caring ethic, is common throughout feminist leisure and tourism literature. Thus, holidays cannot be described as an escape from work when others (e.g. children) are involved. For many women the continuation of domestic and caring responsibilities is merely transposed from home to another location (Bella, 1992; Deem, 1996a; Small, 2005). Instead of a break from home, holidays for women contain obligation, work, social disapproval and responsibility (McCormack, 1998). Rosenblatt and Russell (1975) alluded to potential problems in family travel as families are typically better insulated from interpersonal problems at home than on holiday. While family holidays are seen as providing the opportunity for both revitalisation and family bonding, there is also the opportunity for serious interpersonal difficulties. However, the notion of families spending happy periods together is a persistent marketing image and has long been part of the 'mythology of tourism' (Seaton & Tagg, 1995).

It appears there is a disjunction between the ideal of happy family holidays and the realities that apply to mothers as much as fathers. Strong ideological notions of how parents ought to behave underpin much family leisure (Shaw, 2010) and extend to holiday behaviour. Blichfeldt (2006) found that providing new experiences (such as holidays) is considered a critical element of good parenting. There are cultural standards of putting children first whereby the character and achievements of children are linked to the moral worth of parents (Coakley, 2006).

Fathers today are expected to be more intimate and to have greater involvement with their children (Kay, 2009). This is deeply embedded in the social discourse about being a good father (Daly, 1996), but the ideology of being a 'good mother' is still pervasive (Miller & Brown, 2005). Also, there are strong cultural constraints on expressing dissatisfaction with family holidays (Deem, 1996b), which can lead to guilt for mothers and blame when there is conflict between family members (Davidson, 1996; Small, 2005).

Facilitating family leisure is seen as an obligatory aspect of parental responsibility (Shaw, 2008), yet the achievement of family leisure, as argued in Chapter 2, is perceived as a personal problem rather than a societal dilemma. Rather than gender per se, it is the presence and absence of children and partners that has an impact on travel behaviour (Freysinger & Ray, 1994; Lin & Lehto, 2006).

Women are found to report more negative holiday experiences than men, due to the women having feelings of responsibility for others (Crawford *et al.*, 1992). However, recent research into fathers' holiday experiences reveals that fathers can take primary responsibility as entertainer of the children and facilitator of mothers' own interests (Schänzel & Smith, 2011), roles which have been little acknowledged previously. In effect, freedom from family obligations to achieve a good holiday experience is sought not just by mothers (Davidson, 1996; Small, 2005), but also fathers (Schänzel & Smith, 2011). Thus both mothers and fathers are constrained on holiday and more research is needed on the social dynamics present and possible societal influences.

The limited research on family tourism that has included children's perspectives highlights some generational differences in experience, and even conflict (Carr, 2006, 2011; Schänzel, 2010). In fact, as Carr (2006) highlights, family holidays are among those products that have the potential to cause the most family conflict. Children generally express more immediate goals of having fun with others on holiday (Gram, 2005; Hilbrecht *et al.*, 2008) rather than any purposive notions of togetherness. Yet very few studies focus on the difficulties of facilitating family fun (Churchill *et al.*, 2007) because social interaction and fun are seen as inferior to other tourism experiences. As reported in Chapter 5, children on holiday seek fun and sociality with family but also with their peers as part of gaining freedom from parental restrictions. Holidays, then, are as much about family time as they are about time to pursue own interests either alone or with peers and a balance is needed to avoid conflicts or tensions. This chapter is about the stress factors associated with family holidaying and thus adds to the limited research on negative tourism experiences within families.

## Method

According to the Global Organization for Stress (2011), holidays are helpful in reducing stress levels and 'you can feel totally relaxed'. Reducing stress was found to be the main reason why people took a holiday in a study by Plog (2005). Other basic things, such as spending time with a spouse and having no schedules, rated most highly, while learning about local history

**Table 8.1** Reasons for taking a holiday in America, 2003

| Reason | % | Reason | % |
| --- | --- | --- | --- |
| Get rid of stress | 70 | Have time for friends | 23 |
| Time with spouse | 60 | Learn history/culture | 23 |
| Enjoy no schedules | 59 | Important part of life | 21 |
| See/do new things | 56 | Romantic time | 21 |
| I feel alive/energetic | 33 | Like solitude/isolation | 16 |
| Gain perspective | 31 | Enjoy being outdoors | 14 |
| Like being waited on | 24 | Enjoy physical tests | 10 |

*Source*: Plog (2005)

and culture, being outdoors, romantic time and enjoying physical tests were least common (Table 8.1).

The aim of the present research was broadly to explore whether taking a holiday assists in reducing stress or adds to it for a family. This study also aimed to ascertain whether families would report similar reasons for holidaying as Plog (2005) found.

An online survey was selected for undertaking the research. The survey was designed to take about 10 minutes to complete. Primary schools in the regional Victorian city of Ballarat (about 100 kilometres from the state capital, Melbourne, Australia) were contacted and asked if they would be prepared to circulate the web address and an invitation to participate in this research via the school newsletter and/or notice board. The URL was also circulated through major employers, media and through the snowball technique. It was determined that access through the school system was the best way to contact a broad range of families, in common with previous studies (e.g. Carr, 2006; Schänzel, 2010).

The most common stated reason for taking a holiday has been found to be 'to reduce stress', with 70% of people identifying this reason (Plog, 2005). However, anecdotal evidence indicates that for families, particularly larger families with young children, holidays may create rather than reduce stress. Thus, the aim of the research was to find out whether taking a family holiday confirms or disconfirms the primary stated reason for taking holidays, that is, to relieve stress.

Research on family tourism is a marginalised area. Despite the size of the market the research on family tourism has struggled to take account of the family dynamics that choreograph tourism practices (Obrador, 2012). Research to date has focused on family holidays as mainly associated with bonding, togetherness and quality family time (Carr, 2011; Gram, 2005; Schänzel, 2008). The present research aimed to contribute to both theory and practice by establishing whether stress can accompany the family holiday experience. It also explored a range of other factors.

## Results

There were 20 questions in the survey. All except the last question required an answer in order to proceed through the online survey. The first question asked respondents to identify their gender. The vast majority of respondents were female (88%). Respondents were then asked to indicate their family situation. Virtually all respondents (96%) indicated that they were part of a two-parent family. Only 4% were single-parent families. This bias reflects a major difficulty associated with collecting data from fathers, as identified by Carr (2006).

The third question asked respondents to select an option that described the work demands in their household. The majority (56%) of responses revealed that households comprised a father who worked full time and a mother who worked part time or casually. Twenty percent of respondents stated that their household comprised two parents working full time. The third most popular response was that the father worked full time and the mother was not in the workforce (10%). Mothers working full time with a father who worked part time or casually comprised 6% of the responses. As such, 82% of responses indicated that both parents worked.

Question 4 asked respondents to state the number of dependent children they had living with them full time. The number ranged from one up to four. The mean number of children was 2.46. The median was 2, with 36% of respondents indicating that they had two children living with them. Only 11% of respondents indicated that they had only one child, which was the same proportion of responses for having four children. Twenty-nine percent of respondents stated that they had three dependent children living with them.

The fifth question in the survey asked for the ages of the respondents' children. Ranges were offered for selection: 0–4; 5–9; 10–14; 15–18; and 19+. The majority of children were in the 5–9 age range (72%), which reflects a natural bias due to the authors targeting primary schools. The second most popular choice was 0–4 (40%), followed by 10–14 (34%).

The sixth question asked respondents to state how many of their children went on their last holiday with them. The mean number of children accompanying the respondent was 2.4, indicating a slight variation from the average number of dependent children as revealed in question 4. Responses showed some minor variation from question 4, since question 4

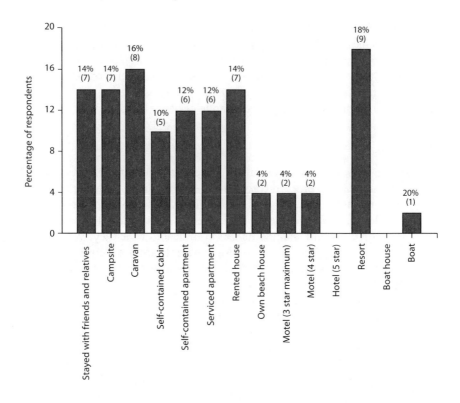

**Figure 8.1** Accommodation stayed in during most recent holiday. Percentage of respondents who indicated the type of accommodation in response to the question 'Thinking about your most recent family holiday, what type of accommodation did you stay in? (NB: If you stayed in multiple forms of accommodation on your last holiday, please select as many as apply)'

enquired about dependent children living with the respondent. While most responses were identical to those for question 4, in some cases an additional child accompanied the family who was no longer living at home; in other cases a child did not accompany the family despite being a dependant and still living at home.

Question 7 asked respondents to identify what type of accommodation they stayed in on their last holiday (Figure 8.1). Responses were very broad and covered most types of accommodation. The only options that received no selections were boat house and five-star hotels. The single most popular choice was resorts (18%).

Question 7 did allow specific separation of each type of accommodation. For example, it allowed for a distinction between self-contained apartments and serviced apartments. Serviced apartments, self-contained apartments and rented/holiday houses are essentially substitutes – all offering similar attributes. If combined, 38% of respondents elected these forms of accommodation. Caravanning, self-contained cabins and campsites were also a popular type of accommodation (40% if aggregated). Staying with friends and relatives was also a popular form of accommodation (14%).

The eighth question asked respondents how often someone in their travel party cooked dinner while on their last holiday. Almost two-thirds (64%) of respondents cooked either every night or most nights. Only 18% of respondents did not cook dinner at all while on their most recent holiday.

Question 9 asked respondents to explain why they had selected the accommodation they had identified previously in the survey. As open-ended responses were used for this question, each answer was unique. However, some common themes were evident. Cost came through as a strong theme, for example 'cheapest accommodation for 6 people'. The other strong theme that was evident was space, for example 'it was self-contained and had at least three bedrooms' and 'all inclusive package. Four children could stay and eat free'.

Question 10 was 'Thinking about your most recent family holiday, what were your reasons for taking that holiday?' This was another open-ended question and, as such, attracted a range of unique responses. However, some common themes emerged. One central theme was that the holiday was to reunite as a family. For example, one respondent stated the holiday was for 'time away from work as a family'. Similarly, another respondent stated it was an 'annual family holiday with other family members'. Another claimed it was 'to relax and spend time together as a family', while another stated 'relax, get some exercise and spend time together as a family'. The other theme that emerged related to needing a break, for example 'we needed something different' and 'needed a break and had too much leave owing from work'. Similarly, other respondents said the holiday was 'to get away from normal life at home' and represented a 'break away from [the] farm where there are constant interruptions even on occasional day[s] off'.

Question 11 asked 'When did you take your most recent family holiday?' Three broad categories emerged. The largest category was the previous Christmas–New Year period (about six months prior to the survey). The next largest category was between 18 months and 3 years ago. The third largest response was that the last holiday was in the Easter period that had recently passed.

For question 12, respondents were asked 'Has your choice of accommodation type been influenced by previous holiday experiences? If so, please explain.' The responses were evenly split between 'yes' and 'no'. Interesting explanations were provided by respondents. Some demonstrated a high

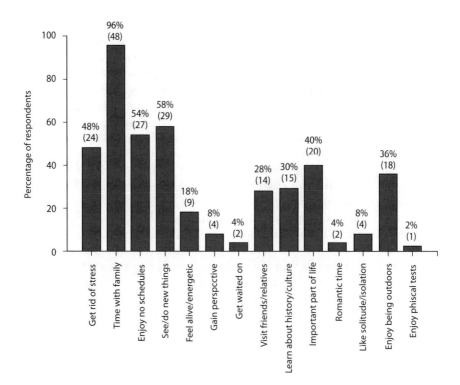

**Figure 8.2** Reasons for taking a family holiday. Percentage of respondents who indicated the reason in response to the question 'Which of the following reasons were important to you in taking your most recent family holiday? (Select as many as apply)'

degree of repeat visitation, such as 'yes, stayed in same house 6 years in a row'. Others showed a preference for a particular style of accommodation based on past experiences (rather than actually booking the exact same place each time). Some comments included 'yes, resort style suits us' and 'yes, we will always want 2–3 bedroom accommodations for a family of 5–7'. Similarly, 'yes, it was more desirable to spend more time in independent accommodation' and also 'yes got over camping. Too small, noisy, wet. Sharing bathrooms. Moved on.'

Question 13 asked 'Which of the following reasons were important to you in taking your most recent family holiday?' Respondents could select as many options as were applicable. Spending time with the family was an important reason for almost all respondents (Figure 8.2). Other commonly

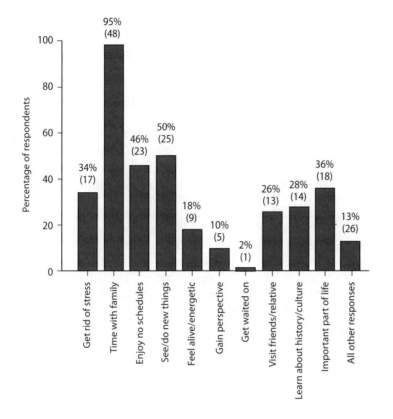

**Figure 8.3** Reasons for taking a holiday that were achieved. Percentage of respondents who indicated the reason in response to the question 'Thinking about your most recent family holiday, which reasons for taking that holiday were actually achieved? (Select as many as apply)'

mentioned reasons included to see/do new things, enjoy no schedules and get rid of stress.

Question 14 was specifically designed to follow on from the previous question, to establish whether the reasons for taking the holiday were achieved. Most of the intended reasons were achieved to a similar capacity (Figure 8.3). The main difference was that although almost half (48%) of respondents claimed they took a holiday to get rid of stress, only around one-third (34%) claimed that this was achieved.

The issue of experience was considered further in question 15, which asked 'What types of things impacted negatively on your level of stress whilst on your most recent family holiday (consider both preparing for that trip as well as during that trip and explain in detail)؟' Some of the responses involved matters that would be stressful for anyone planning a holiday – such as 'weather and travel time' and 'worrying about the cost/money'. However, many responses were specific to families, such as 'packing was stressful, ensuring there were plenty of down time activities for the children'.

Many of the responses to question 15 were linked to the accommodation facilities, such as 'not having all our stuff we normally have at home. Things in the house not child safe/friendly, i.e. the oven or doors etc.' Similarly, 'blinds in the bedrooms let light through, making it extremely hard for a two year old to have naps and sleep past 5:30 a.m. The outside noise was constant, traffic, humming of heaters/air conditioners, music etc.' Another respondent claimed 'sharing the one room was stressful especially in the evenings when we wanted a bit of a reprieve from the kids'. Another example was 'our son had a reaction to food and vomited four times, all over himself and me. I had two loads of washing and couldn't get access to the advertised washing machine, so spent what was meant to be a relaxing night prior to a wedding hand washing clothes in a tiny bathroom'. There were also discussions about dirty cooking appliances and cutlery, lack of facilities, getting the wrong room, dusty bedding, a dirty microwave, dusty room, and no response from the enquiries number listed for the venue.

Accommodation facilities were a likely contributor to stress for some respondents, with some finding facilities inadequate. Question 16 was 'How well did the facilities at your accommodation on your last family holiday cater for the size and shape of your family؟' The most commonly stated area of inadequacy was drying facilities (Figure 8.4).

The issue of stress was considered further in question 17: 'Thinking about your most recent family holiday, did you feel less stressed, more stressed, or the same when you returned؟' There were five options to select: much less stressed, slightly less stressed, stress level unchanged, slightly more stressed, much more stressed. For 36% of respondents, their stress levels were either unchanged (16%) or had increased (20%) after going on their last family holiday.

Question 18 was 'In thinking about all your past family holiday experiences, describe your best family holiday and explain why it was the best'. The responses varied widely, with a range of destinations mentioned. However, sometimes the destination was not mentioned and the only focus was on the weather, or the stage the children were at that seemed to be why the holiday was a success – with no relationship to the destination. Several respondents spoke of a stay in luxury accommodation being their best holiday. For example, one respondent said 'our holiday to the Sunshine Coast in March was fantastic as it was in a large luxury home. We will do this again with our family as it was great accommodation.' Another said, 'we spent a bit more on accommodation so even though we stayed in most nights while the kids slept, it felt like a luxury because we got to lounge

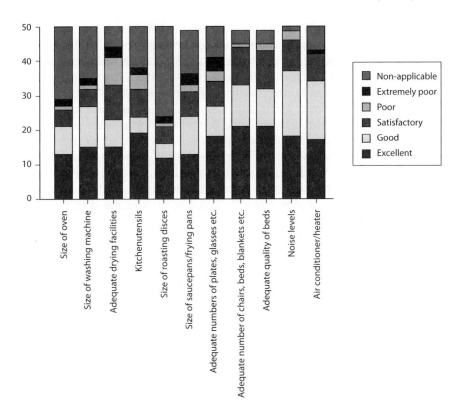

**Figure 8.4** Standard of facilities in accommodation. Numbers of respondents who rated the facilities in categories from extremely poor to excellent in response to the question 'How well did the facilities at your accommodation on your last family holiday cater for the size and shape of your family? (NB: If you stayed in multiple types of accommodation on your last holiday, please select the one you stayed in for the most nights)'

around a gorgeous apartment'. Similarly, another person stated a 'five star apartment … just amazing'.

Some respondents were unable to identify their best holiday, as they had 'only been on one family holiday'. Others claimed that their best holiday was without their children or without a young child – for example 'the one where we left our youngest with my parents' or 'weekend away when only had one child'. A 'staycation' was also mentioned: 'if we stay at home we usually have the best time. We can do short day trips. My kids hate spending time in the car for longer than 30 minutes.'

The following question was 'In thinking about all your past family holiday experiences, describe your worst family holiday and explain why it was the worst'. Some respondents were unable to nominate a worst holiday. Some holiday experiences were affected by poor weather. Other respondents indicated that their accommodation had caused their holiday experience to be poor – for example, 'stayed in a hotel room. All in the one room. Kids wouldn't go to sleep. No backyard, etc. No locks on doors so kids kept escaping. No kitchen so had to eat all the time in the onsite restaurant. Very stressful!' Another example was 'poor or unclean accommodation' and respondents often referred to children being awake very early or not sleeping properly due to lack of blinds, noise, or poor-quality beds. Others stated that it the facilities were inadequate for the size of the family it added too much household work. For example, 'where the accommodation was deficient in too many things … it adds to the household chores instead of a holiday being about relaxing it is more work'.

The final question was 'Are there any other comments you would like to make?' Almost half of the respondents made a comment. Some mentioned stress, such as 'I think family holidays with young kids are very stressful unless there is some support for the parents and opportunities for parents to have some time to themselves'. Another response was 'travelling with young children, especially toddlers, can be more trouble that it is worth which is why we have not taken long holidays'. And similarly, 'a wise friend once told me once you have kids they are no longer called holidays but "time-away". I now agree.'

## Discussion

Holiday experiences are greatly affected by the presence or absence of children (Freysinger & Ray, 1994; Lin & Lehto, 2006). Freedom from typical family obligations is sought by mothers (Davidson, 1996; Small, 2005) as well as fathers (Schänzel & Smith, 2011). Rest and relaxation are a common holiday purpose for many people (Leiper, 2004) and 70% of people state that reducing stress is their main reason for going on a holiday (Plog, 2005). Despite this, family holidays are among those things that can cause the most family conflict (Carr, 2006).

This study has revealed that family holidays can add to stress in some cases. While almost half (48%) of the respondents stated that reducing stress was one of their reasons for taking a holiday, it was not necessarily achieved. Only around one-third (34%) of respondents found that the holiday had the desired effect of reducing stress. At times, contributors to the stress were variables such as the weather. Often the sheer orchestration of packing for a family and dealing with the needs of children while en route added stress to the travel experience. Yet, of significance here, at times the creation of stresses and the cause of negative holiday experiences were accommodation facilities not being suitable. Where laundry facilities were promoted in the brochure, they were sometimes inadequate or at other times not present. The effort involved in doing multiple loads of washing due to a small machine or hand washing instead of machine washing, or trying to dry clothes with no drying facilities added stress and discomfort. This increased household chores instead of the holiday being an opportunity to relax.

Of note, respondents provided very different reasons for taking a holiday compared with the findings from Plog (2005). While reducing stress was the most common reason found in Plog's (2005) research, with 70% of people stating that reason, only 48% of respondents in this study identified reducing stress as a reason. Instead, spending time with family was the primary driver, with almost all respondents stating that reason, confirming the definition of a family holiday given in Chapter 1. Enjoying no schedules and seeing/doing new things had similar response levels in both the present research and Plog's study. However, while Plog (2005) found that 33% of people stated they wanted to feel alive/energetic, only 18% of respondents in this study selected this option.

**Table 8.2** Reasons for taking a holiday: Comparison of Plog's (2005) findings and the present study

| Reason | % (Plog, 2005) | % (this study) |
|---|---|---|
| Get rid of stress | 70 | 48 |
| Time with spouse/family | 60 | 95 |
| Enjoy no schedules | 59 | 54 |
| See/do new things | 56 | 58 |
| I feel alive/energetic | 33 | 18 |
| Gain perspective | 31 | 8 |
| Like being waited on | 24 | 4 |
| Have time for friends/visit friends or relatives | 23 | 28 |
| Learn history/culture | 23 | 40 |
| Important part of life | 21 | 30 |
| Romantic time | 21 | 4 |
| Like solitude/isolation | 16 | 8 |
| Enjoy being outdoors | 14 | 36 |
| Enjoy physical tests | 10 | 2 |

*Source*: Plog (2005)

Other differences could be seen with the 'gain perspective' and 'like being waited on' options. These received low responses in this study (8% and 4% respectively) but were higher in Plog's (2005) research (31% and 24% respectively). The full comparison is outlined in Table 8.2.

## Conclusion

Stress levels are for many parents unchanged or worsened by a holiday. Parents are often among those most in need of a holiday, yet in some cases they are not experiencing the benefits that holidaying can bring to others. What is of significance is that the cause or at least a contributor to stress is often the simple things missing from the accommodation. Respondents spoke of major angst arising from having no blinds in a child's bedroom, preventing the child from being able to have an afternoon nap. As the lack of the afternoon nap resulted in irritable behaviour from the child, the child became a poor companion for the parents and led to a loss of enjoyment of the holiday.

At other times, cooking utensils were inadequate for a family, despite brochures advertising the accommodation as being suited to families. In one instance only a small saucepan was available and therefore the parents had to cook two dinners instead of one. Small washing machines resulted in more loads of washing. A lack of facilities to dry clothes was awkward and created angst. Other stories included the dining table having only four seats in a three-bedroom apartment designed to sleep six people. Other sources of stress arose from the parents requesting accommodation with no stairs yet having an apartment with stairs, which was considered a hazard for young children. Where requests for a laundry were not addressed it meant that parents were washing in a hand basin for an entire family. These examples added to people's workload of household chores that are not typically considered relaxing. In some cases, then, the holiday resulted in an increase in unpleasant tasks, not a relaxing and enjoyable experience.

This research adds to our understanding of the diverse needs of families, particularly those families with pre-school children. Specific requirements to ensure young children's sleep routines are maintained are considered essential for those families. This family stage can be identified as family life cycle (FLC) stage III, which is an area discussed in Chapter 12. Accommodation developers are most likely not in the FLC stage III, resulting in those small but essential design components being forgotten. Realising the stress impact that relatively minor shortcomings of accommodation can have on the family holiday can lead to change. Only by catering to the varied needs of families can the long-term future of these businesses be ensured. The costs of ensuring a relatively stress-free holiday experience can be considered minor compared with the costs of families not returning or poor word of mouth and poor word-of-mouse (i.e. negative consumer comments made online). There is a need for operators to be made aware of the findings from this study. In many cases the cause of stress arose from small expenses in terms of the cost of fitting out an apartment. At times the frustrations developed from the simplest things missing, such as cheap drying racks for clothes or window blinds.

This study has added to the literature exploring family holidays and has shown that families' reasons for taking holidays differ from those of general holidaying individuals. As a result, operators specifically targeting families as their market need to be mindful of their specific needs, in order to ensure the holiday experience is a positive one, which may also increase repeat visitation.

This study was limited by its small sample size and, as such, further research to explore these issues with a larger sample would add to our understanding of stress factors for families on holiday.

## Acknowledgement

The authors would like to acknowledge the contribution by Dr Mary Hollick to this research.

## References

Anderson, J. (2001) Mothers on family activity holidays overseas. In S. Clough and J. White (eds), *Women's Leisure Experiences: Ages, Stages and Roles* (pp. 99–112). Eastbourne: Leisure Studies Association.

Bærenholdt, J.O., Haldrup, M., Larsen, J. and Urry, J. (2004) *Performing Tourist Places*. Aldershot: Ashgate.

Bella, L. (1992) *The Christmas Imperative: Leisure, Family, and Women's Work*. Halifax, Nova Scotia: Fernwood Publishing.

Bialeschki, M.D. (1994) Re-entering leisure: transition within the role of motherhood. *Journal of Leisure Research*, 26(1), 57–74.

Blichfeldt, B.S. (2006) *A Nice Vacation* (IME Report 8/06). Esbjerg: University of Southern Denmark. Retrieved 9 June 2011 from http://static.sdu.dk/mediafiles//Files/Om_SDU/Institutter/Miljo/ime/rep/blichfeldt8.pdf.

Blichfeldt, B.S., Pedersen, B.M.I., Johansen, A. and Hansen, L. (2011) Tweens on holidays. In-situ decision-making from children's perspective. *Scandinavian Journal of Hospitality and Tourism*, 11(2), 135–149.

Carr, N. (2006) A comparison of adolescents' and parents' holiday motivations and desires. *Tourism and Hospitality Research*, 6(2), 129–142.

Carr, N. (2011) *Children's and Families' Holiday Experiences*. London: Routledge.

Cerullo, M. and Ewen, P. (1984) The American family goes camping: gender, family, and the politics of space. *Antipode*, 16(3), 35–46.

Chaplin, D. (1999) Back to the cave or playing away? Gender roles in home-from-home environments. *Journal of Consumer Studies and Home Economics*, 23(3), 181–189.

Chodorow, N. (1989) *Feminism and Psychoanalytic Theory*. New Haven, CT: Yale University Press.

Churchill, S.L., Clark, V.L.P., Prochaska-Cue, K., Creswell, J.W. and Ontai-Grzebik, L. (2007) How rural low-income families have fun: a grounded theory study. *Journal of Leisure Research*, 39(2), 271–294.

Clough, S. (2001) A juggling act: women balancing work, family and leisure. In S. Clough and J. White (eds), *Women's Leisure Experiences: Ages, Stages and Roles* (pp. 129–138). Eastbourne: Leisure Studies Association.

Coakley, J. (2006) The good father: parental expectations and youth sports. *Leisure Studies*, 25(2), 153–163.

Crawford, J., Kippax, S., Onyx, J., Gault, U. and Benton, P. (1992) *Emotion and Gender: Constructing Meaning from Memory*. London: Sage.

Cyba, E. (1992) Women's attitudes towards leisure and family. *Society and Leisure*, 15(1), 79–94.

Daly, K. (1996) Spending time with the kids: meanings of family time for fathers. *Family Relations*, 45(4), 466–476.

Davidson, P. (1996) The holiday and work experiences of women with young children. *Leisure Studies*, 15(2), 89–103.

Deem, R. (1996a) No time for a rest? *Time and Society*, 5(1), 5–25.

Deem, R. (1996b) Women, the city and holidays. *Leisure Studies*, 15(2), 105–119.

Di Leonardo, M. (1992) The female world of cards and holidays: women, families, and the work of kinship. In B. Thorne and M. Yalom (eds), *Rethinking the Family: Some Feminist Questions* (pp. 246–261). Boston, MA: Northeastern University Press.

Fitzgerald, C.H. (1993) *Getting Away from It All? An Exploration into New Zealand Women's Experience of Christmas Holidays*. Unpublished masters thesis, Victoria University, Wellington, New Zealand.

Freysinger, V.J. (1994) Leisure with children and parental satisfaction: further evidence of a sex difference in the experience of adult roles and leisure. *Journal of Leisure Research*, 26(3), 212–226.

Freysinger, V.J. and Ray, R.O. (1994) The activity involvement of women and men in young and middle adulthood: a panel study. *Leisure Sciences*, 16(3), 193–217.

Gilbert, D. and Abdullah, J. (2004) Holidaytaking and the sense of well-being. *Annals of Tourism Research*, 31(1), 103–121.

Gilligan, C. (1982) *In a Different Voice: Psychological Theory and Women's Development*. Cambridge, MA: Harvard University Press.

Global Organization for Stress (2011) *Stress Solutions for the World*. Retrieved 9 June 2011 from http://www.gostress.com/stress-question-do-vacations-solve-stress.

Gram, M. (2005) Family holidays. A qualitative analysis of family holiday experiences. *Scandinavian Journal of Hospitality and Tourism*, 5(1), 2–22.

Harrington, M. (2001) Gendered time: leisure in family life. In K.J. Daly (ed.), *Minding the Time in Family Experience: Emerging Perspectives and Issues* (vol. 3, pp. 343–382). Oxford: Elsevier Science.

Henderson, K.A. and Allen, K.R. (1991) The ethic of care: leisure possibilities and constraints for women. *Society and Leisure*, 14(1), 97–113.

Hilbrecht, M., Shaw, S.M., Delamere, F.M. and Havitz, M.E. (2008) Experiences, perspectives, and meanings of family vacations for children. *Leisure/Loisir*, 32(2), 541–571.

Inglis, F. (2000) *The Delicious History of the Holiday*. London: Routledge.

Jepsen, A.L. and Blichfeldt, B.S. (2005) Freed from experience: why people spend their vacations at a nearby caravan site. Symposium conducted at the 18th Scandinavian Academy of Management (NFF) Conference, Århus, Denmark, August.

Johns, N. and Gyimothy, S. (2002) Mythologies of a theme park: an icon of modern family life. *Journal of Vacation Marketing*, 8(4), 320–331.

Kay, T. (2001) New women, same old leisure: the upholding of gender stereotypes and leisure disadvantage in contemporary dual-earner households. In S. Clough and J.

White (eds), *Women's Leisure Experiences: Ages, Stages and Roles* (pp. 113–128). Eastbourne: Leisure Studies Association.

Kay, T. (ed.) (2009) *Fathering Through Sport and Leisure*. London: Routledge.

Kinnaird, V. and Hall, D. (eds) (1994) *Tourism: A Gendered Analysis*. Chichester: Wiley.

Kinnaird, V. and Hall, D. (1996) Understanding tourism processes: a gender-aware framework. *Tourism Management*, 17(2), 95–102.

Larson, R.W., Gillman, S.A. and Richards, M.H. (1997) Divergent experiences of family leisure: fathers, mothers, and young adolescents. *Journal of Leisure Research*, 29(1), 78–97.

Lehto, X.Y., Choi, S., Lin, Y.-C. and MacDermid, S.M. (2009) Vacation and family functioning. *Annals of Tourism Research*, 36(3), 459–479.

Leiper, N. (2004) *Tourism Management* (3rd edition). Sydney: Pearson.

Lin, Y.-C. and Lehto, X.Y. (2006) A study of female travelers' needs trajectory and family life cycle. *Journal of Hospitality and Leisure Marketing*, 15(1), 65–88.

McCabe, S. (2009) Who needs a holiday? Evaluating social tourism. *Annals of Tourism Research*, 36(4), 667–688.

McCormack, C. (1998) Memories bridge the gap between theory and practice in women's leisure research. *Annals of Leisure Research*, 1(1), 37–49.

Miller, Y. and Brown, W. (2005) Determinants of active leisure for women with young children – an 'ethic of care' prevails. *Leisure Sciences*, 27(5), 405–420.

Minnaert, L., Maitland, R. and Miller, G. (2009) Tourism and social policy: the value of social tourism. *Annals of Tourism Research*, 36(2), 316–334.

Obrador, P. (2012) The place of the family in tourism research: domesticity and thick sociality by the pool. *Annals of Tourism Research*, 39(1), 401–420.

Orthner, D.K. and Mancini, J.A. (1990) Leisure impacts on family interaction and cohesion. *Journal of Leisure Research*, 22(2), 125–137.

Plog, S. (2005) *Targeting Segments: More Important Than Ever in the Travel Industry*. In W. Teobald (ed.), *Global Tourism* (3rd edition) (pp. 271–293). Sydney: Elsevier.

Reilly, R.C. (2002/2003) Family volunteering: making a difference together. *Leisure/Loisir*, 27(3–4), 305–332.

Richmond, E.H. and Tolich, M. (2000) The third shift: task allocation and ultimate responsibility on family camping holidays. *New Zealand Sociology*, 15(2), 284–303.

Rosenblatt, P.C. and Russell, M.G. (1975) The social psychology of potential problems in family vacation travel. *Family Coordinator*, 24(2), 209–215.

Schänzel, H.A. (2008) The New Zealand family on holiday: values, realities and fun. In J. Fountain and K. Moore (eds), *Proceedings to the New Zealand Tourism and Hospitality Research Conference*. Canterbury, New Zealand: Lincoln University.

Schänzel, H.A. (2010) Whole-family research: towards a methodology in tourism for encompassing generation, gender, and group dynamic perspectives. *Tourism Analysis*, 15(5), 555–569.

Schänzel, H.A. and Smith, K.A. (2011) The absence of fatherhood: achieving true gender scholarship in family tourism research. *Annals of Leisure Research*, 14(2–3), 129–140.

Schänzel, H.A., Smith, K.A. and Weaver, A. (2005) Family holidays: a research review and application to New Zealand. *Annals of Leisure Research*, 8(2–3), 105–123.

Seaton, A.V. and Tagg, S. (1995) The family vacation in Europe: paedonomic aspects of choices and satisfactions. *Journal of Travel and Tourism Marketing*, 4(1), 1–21.

Selänniemi, T. (2002) Couples on holiday: (en)gendered or endangered experiences? In M.B. Swain and J.H. Momsen (eds), *Gender/Tourism/Fun(?)* (pp. 15–23). Elmsford, NY: Cognizant Communication Corporation.

Shaw, S.M. (1985) Gender and leisure: inequality in the distribution of leisure time. *Journal of Leisure Research*, 17(4), 266–282.

Shaw, S.M. (2001) The family leisure dilemma: insights from research with Canadian families. *World Leisure*, 43(4), 53–62.

Shaw, S.M. (2008) Family leisure and changing ideologies of parenthood. *Sociology Compass*, 2(2), 688–703.

Shaw, S.M. (2010) Diversity and ideology: changes in Canadian family life and implications for leisure. *World Leisure Journal*, 52(1), 4–13.

Shaw, S.M. and Dawson, D. (2001) Purposive leisure: examining parental discourses on family activities. *Leisure Sciences*, 23(4), 217–231.

Shaw, S.M. and Dawson, D. (2003/2004) Contradictory aspects of family leisure: idealization versus experience. *Leisure/Loisir*, 28(3/4), 179–201.

Shaw, S.M., Havitz, M.E. and Delamere, F.M. (2008) I decided to invest in my kids' memories: family vacations, memories, and the social construction of the family. *Tourism Culture and Communication*, 8(1), 13–26.

Sinclair, M.T. (ed.) (1997) *Gender, Work and Tourism*. London: Routledge.

Small, J. (2002) Good and bad holiday experiences: women's and girls' perspectives. In M.B. Swain and J.H. Momsen (eds), *Gender/Tourism/Fun?* (pp. 24–37). Elmsford, NY: Cognizant Communication Corporation.

Small, J. (2005) Women's holidays: disruption of the motherhood myth. *Tourism Review International*, 9(2), 139–154.

Small, J. (2008) The absence of childhood in tourism studies. *Annals of Tourism Research*, 35(3), 772–789.

Swain, M.B. (1995) Gender in tourism. *Annals of Tourism Research*, 22(2), 247–266.

Urry, J. (1996) *The Tourist Gaze: Leisure and Travel in Contemporary Societies*. London: Sage.

Valtonen, A. and Veijola, S. (2010) Sleep in tourism. *Annals of Tourism Research*, 38(1), 175–192.

Wearing, B. (1993) The family that plays together stays together: or does it? Leisure and mothers. *World Leisure and Recreation*, 35(3), 25–29.

Wearing, B. and Wearing, S. (1988) 'All in a day's leisure': gender and the concept of leisure. *Leisure Studies*, 7(2), 111–123.

# 9 Gay and Lesbian Families and Tourism

## Howard Hughes and Carol Southall

## Introduction

The academic interest in tourism of gay men and lesbian women has not yet extended to studies of families in this context (Guaracino, 2007; Hughes, 2006; Waitt & Markwell, 2006). This may be because studies in this field are relatively new and have focused on more obvious dimensions. It is also the case that 'family' has not usually been a concept applied to gay and lesbian people.

There is a lack of academic studies of the gay and lesbian family and tourism. This chapter therefore has the limited objective of reviewing the nature of the gay or lesbian family and drawing upon this to derive implications for the travel experiences of gay and lesbian people. The gay or lesbian 'family' exists in the context of societies where there is a heterosexual norm of family. Gay or lesbian relationships are complex and diverse but can, nonetheless, be interpreted as families, especially where there are children parented by gay or lesbian persons. They do, though, tend to be judged, usually negatively, by that heterosexual norm and this gives rise to particular issues in holiday decision-making.

## Families

The 'family' is conventionally regarded, at core, as two, different-sex, partners who have children as the biological product of their relationship. Invariably these partners have undertaken a formal affirmation of their relationship – usually marriage. There is a presumption of a special relationship wherein the partners have 'rights' relating to each other and to children (Demo & Allen, 1996); particular roles are assumed, with men undertaking 'instrumental' and women more 'expressive' activities. Such a structural–functional family model implicitly ensures commitment, stability and the transmission of common values to following generations (Demo & Allen, 1996).

Marriage is, though, becoming less esteemed and popular in 'Western' societies, which are experiencing a new era of 'de-traditionalisation' and 'individualisation' (Duncan & Smith, 2006). Traditional social structures, including family, are declining, to be replaced by a concern for 'the self' (Duncan & Phillips, 2008). 'Non-traditional families such as divorced, step-families and single parents are now the norm ... [and] the term "family" no longer fits with traditional perceptions of a married couple with children' (Jenkins et al., 2009: 28). The individualisation view is that friends are increasingly at the core of new, more fluid relationships as 'families of choice'; gay men and lesbian women are regarded as the epitome of this.

Connection with and commitment to others do, however, remain a strong value, though not necessarily in the traditional form. Cohabitation is widely regarded as an equally acceptable form of relationship as marriage (only 19% of respondents to the 2006 British Social Attitudes Survey disagreed) (Duncan & Phillips, 2008). In practice, 'family' remains highly regarded in terms of reliability and dependability, and most people still feel some obligation to it. Generally, while there is more flexibility and choice about relationships, certain social bonds remain strong.

## Same-Sex Families

The different-sex two-partner relationship sanctioned by a legal (and often religious) ceremony does not correspond with non-heterosexual life. Legal recognition of same-sex partnerships is only a recent occurrence – as in the form of marriage in five US states, including Massachusetts (since 2004). Elsewhere in the world, same-sex marriages are legal in only a small number of countries, such as Spain, Canada, The Netherlands, Argentina and South Africa. Legal recognition of other forms such as civil partnerships in UK is more widespread (18 countries in 2010) but not universal.

Same-sex relationships have therefore developed without legal or social sanction and in an unrestricted and largely unique way (Adam, 2006). There has been no 'guidance' as to how same-sex individuals should or could relate to each other, other than from gay or lesbian cultures. Criminalisation of same-sex sexual activity (until liberalisation in the mid-20th century) and continuing discrimination and disapproval have restricted the overt development of relationships and have influenced their form (Hughes, 2006).

Gay and lesbian people have long formed same-sex relationships that operated as family, regardless of the lack of legal or religious sanction. Many have identified 'family' more with a network of friends – 'families of choice' – than with families of origin (Nardi, 1992; Weeks et al., 1999). This is particularly likely where they have experienced rejection by their own blood families. They may extend to 'families' centred on political or social change or healthcare (Demo & Allen, 1996; Oswald, 2002). Relationships that differ from the heterosexual norm may be purposely chosen and valued, combining a degree of commitment with flexibility in the relationship (Adam, 2004; Weeks *et al.*, 1999). Given the lack of formal legal arrangements, relationships may be entered and exited casually, though evidence for this is unclear (Patterson, 2000).

Despite relationships that do not ostensibly match heterosexual family and marriage, same-sex couples have lived in ways similar to those of heterosexual couples – renting or owning homes jointly and making financial provision for partners. Income is commonly pooled for household expenses, though in a UK study 'total' pooling was less than for comparable heterosexual couples (Burns *et al.*, 2006; Morgan Centre, 2006). Same-sex partnerships are claimed to be more egalitarian, as relationships are more freely chosen. There may also be a desire not to mimic heterosexual relationships, with their inherent power imbalance (Carrington, 1999; Weeks *et al.*, 1999).

Assertions about 'difference' continue to be regarded as sufficient to deny gay and lesbian people rights equal to those enjoyed by heterosexual people. It may be, though, that the denial itself has contributed to the behavioural pattern; permitting same-sex marriage or partnerships may lead to changes in behaviour (King & Bartlett, 2006). Opposition may also derive from dislike of homosexuality per se. Opposition to the legal recognition of same-sex partnerships is frequently expressed in terms of marriage being only between a man and woman, as evidenced by, for instance, the US Defense of Marriage Act 1996. Invariably marriage is conflated with the issue of raising children, in the belief that one entails the other. Gay and lesbian marriage or legally recognised partnerships have generated extreme negative views, some of which may be the outcome of deeply felt religious beliefs (see, for example, Chrisafis, 2005; Congregation for the Doctrine of the Faith, 2003; Green, 2010; Wynne-Jones, 2009; Towlerroad, 2010).

There is, though, increasing public support for some form of legal recognition: a poll conducted in the UK in 2009 showed that 61% of respondents agreed that 'gay couples should have an equal right to get married, not just to have civil partnerships' (Populus, 2009). Similarly, there was support in another survey for the view that same-sex partnerships can be as committed as men and women (63% agreed) (Duncan & Phillips, 2008).

The provision for civil partnerships in the UK (from 2005) was welcomed by same-sex couples in one study, not only for conferring legal rights but also as a sign of acceptance and 'normalisation' (Mitchell *et al.*, 2009). In another UK study, couples welcomed the opportunity to express commitment (and gain legal rights) but, at the same time, live their lives without reference to heterosexual norms (Morgan Centre, 2006). Legal recognition may lead to greater stability of relationships. It has been argued that marriage itself has a positive effect on health. This, combined with the greater acceptance of same-sex couples, may have a significant effect on the well-being of gay and lesbian people (King & Bartlett, 2006).

It is evident that it is impossible to identify a typical gay or lesbian family – they fit no one simple model and not only are they diverse but the members of each may not be fixed. Some relationships are, though, similar to those traditionally associated with heterosexual persons. There may be change in the nature of the gay or lesbian family as legal recognition of partnerships becomes more widespread, though lingering societal disapproval will itself continue to influence relationships in negative ways.

## Children in Same-Sex Families

In addition to gay and lesbian families comprising single individuals or same-sex couples, there may be families that include children. There is a considerable diversity within such families, including single or two (or more) parents and children biologically related to at least one parent and children who are adopted or fostered. Parents may be gay or lesbian or either, but with a heterosexual partner; a gay man may father a lesbian woman's child and the child may live and be parented by either or both or with other gay or lesbian individuals. Insemination and surrogacy may be significant for some couples, though many children raised by a lesbian parent, in particular, will be the biological child from a previous heterosexual relationship. One US author refers to a 'gayby' boom – an increased visibility of children raised by same-sex parents (Garner, 2005).

Although there is support for gay and lesbian marriage or civil partnerships, gay or lesbian families with children are not accepted as readily. A UK poll in 2009 showed only under half agreed that gay or lesbian couples should have equal adoption rights to heterosexual couples (Populus, 2009). Only 36% and 31%, in another survey, agreed that lesbian or gay male couples (respectively) were as good parents as men and women couples (Duncan & Phillips, 2008). The argument is often couched in terms of a child's 'need' for two parents of different genders and anything other than this is not 'natural'. Some US states do not allow adoption by same-sex couples and there are many challenges to the desire of lesbian couples to access medical services for insemination. US courts have been reluctant to grant custody of children to gay or lesbian parents in divorce cases (Biblarz & Savci, 2010a; Patterson, 2006). UK legislation in 2007 meant that adoption and fostering agencies could not turn down gay or lesbian couples on the basis of their sexuality alone. A Roman Catholic agency (unsuccessfully) resisted this and commented that 'what is best for children is that they be brought up by married couples' (Caldwell, 2009).

Arguments have been articulated in terms of 'damage' caused to a child by having same-sex parents. Claims of damage include children experiencing stress, ridicule and harassment and, as they lack role models for each sex, they would be at least confused about relationships, if not more likely to be homosexual themselves. Criticism has also included possible corruption and child abuse (Akersten, 2010; Blake, 2009). Some commentators have observed that children may be regarded by gay or lesbian people as a 'trophy' or the 'ultimate gay accessory' to acquire, without consideration of the responsibilities or competences required, when everything else – house, car, holidays etc. – has been acquired (Blake, 2009; Moorhead, 2010). Gay men themselves, in a US study, expressed ambivalence about parenting (Stacey, 2006). As homosexuality becomes more accepted the number of gay fathers may fall, as most gay fathers became fathers when in heterosexual marriages.

It is only recently that studies of children in gay or lesbian families have been undertaken and judgements previously have often been unfounded contentions. Recent studies conclude that a two-parent family may provide 'good' emotional and material support for a child regardless of whether parents are of the same or different sex (Biblarz & Stacey, 2010). Parenting skills are not gender specific and family dynamics and processes are more influential than family structure in child development (Scottish Government, 2009; Short et al., 2007). Both lesbian and gay couples undertake the parenting process in 'gender flexible' ways, negotiate responsibility and generally adopt more equal roles (Biblarz & Stacey, 2010).

Studies have shown that lesbian parent couples are strongly committed to the notion of motherhood and to each other and parenting skills are as good as if not better than in equivalent heterosexual couples (Biblarz & Savci, 2010). There have been fewer studies of gay parent families and such families were less likely to include biological children. The strengths that gay fathers demonstrated were, in part, attributed to resilience in overcoming obstacles to becoming parents (Biblarz & Savci, 2010).

Children in gay or lesbian families are similar to children in heterosexual families in respect of psychological development and well-being, relations with others and behaviour. They are also generally more well balanced, tolerant and open minded, are less likely to identify particular genders with specific traits or responsibilities and demonstrate higher levels of competence (by social and academic measures) than equivalent children in heterosexual families (Gartrell & Bos, 2010).

Some problems faced by children have, however, been identified. Children of gay or lesbian parents, in a UK study, celebrated their families as 'special and different' but acknowledged that others – children and adults – could be hurtful in their comments and actions (Guasp, 2010). A UK study comparing children in families with same-sex and different-sex parents concluded that children of same-sex parents were less likely to seek support for 'victimisation' at school (Rivers et al., 2008). In one US study, children (now in their 20s and 30s) of gay or lesbian parents were 'comfortable' with their family but felt rejection because of society's view that their family was in some sense 'wrong' and damaging (Garner, 2005).

Children who denied the nature of their family did so more from concern about others' reactions than from negative feelings about parents (Garner, 2005). A study of gay father families concluded that adolescent children were less likely to disclose the nature of the family than were the parents (Demo & Allen, 1996). Children of gay or lesbian parents may fear identification of themselves as gay or lesbian and conceal the nature of the family (Bozett, 1987). There is, though, no evidence that children of same-sex couples are more likely to have homosexual feelings (Garner, 2005).

The presence of children adds to the diversity of gay and lesbian families. Parents may be of the same or different sex and children may be biological, adopted or fostered. Such families, although as 'good' as other families, do face particular issues with public acceptance. There does appear, nonetheless, to be an increased visibility of such families and possibly an increasing desire on the part of some gay and (especially) lesbian people to parent children.

## Market Size

Given the diversity and non-institutionalisation of gay or lesbian families, it is difficult to obtain an indication of market size or potential. Gay men, in particular, have been regarded as having particularly high discretionary incomes and leisure time and identified as a growing and profitable market to target for many consumer products and services (Guaracino, 2007; Hughes, 2006).

The number of gay or lesbian people is not, though, known with certainty; one review of estimates of the extent of homosexuality in North America showed they ranged from 0.2% to 37% of national populations (Banks, 2003). In a national UK household survey, 1.5% of adults identified themselves as gay, lesbian or bisexual (Office for National Statistics, 2010a); the survey asked about people's sexual identity and not sexual attraction or sexual behaviour. Higher proportions reported in other studies may be the result of having included responses about these matters (Joloza *et al.*, 2010). The UK government had earlier estimated that 5% of the population (over 16) in Britain was gay, lesbian or bisexual (Department of Trade and Industry, 2003).

The number of gay and lesbian people who live as couples was estimated in the UK national census of 2001. This was a crude estimate, in that the census identified same-sex couples who lived in the same household and did not identify sexual identity; nor did it take account of any same-sex 'couples' or partners who did not live together. It was reported that 78,000 individuals in England and Wales co-habited in a same-sex relationship (about 0.3% of co-residential couples) (BBC News, 2004; Duncan & Phillips, 2008). The advent of civil partnerships for same-sex couples in the UK since 2005 gives an indication of what may be conventionally labelled 'family'. In the four years 2005–2009, just over 40,000 partnerships (mostly male) had been formed (Office for National Statistics, 2010b).

The number of same-sex couples was also identified in the USA national census of 2000; they accounted for 594,000 households (less than 1% of all households), of which the majority were male (Sears *et al.*, 2005). Notwithstanding the hazards of interpreting these couples as having gay or lesbian sexual identity, the US census gives further detail of the characteristics and 'family' composition of the households. They were more likely to be in employment than married couples and more likely to have both persons employed. They also had higher educational qualifications and were more likely to live in urban areas.

The UK Labour Force Survey also provided data about same-sex couples. It was estimated they were about 0.2% of the working population and were typically younger and had achieved higher levels of education than other couples (Arabsheibani *et al.*, 2006). In an earlier paper, they were identified as being likely to live in cities and to be in professional, managerial and intermediate occupations (Arabsheibani *et al.*, 2004). These characteristics suggest further caution about the representative nature of the data.

Difficulties in determining numbers of gay and lesbian people and families are reflected in estimates of the number of children in these families. Numbers of children are derived from the same sources, with all their inherent shortcomings. Nearly 40% of the US same-sex couples (aged 22–55) were raising children – mostly in female households; they were 'less affluent, [and] more racially and ethnically diverse' than different-sex couples with children (Sears *et al.*, 2005: 2). It was estimated that 270,313 children lived in same-sex couple households in the USA in 2005 and nearly twice as many again had a single gay or lesbian parent (Gartrell & Bos, 2010). In the UK there was at least one dependent child in the household of 8.6% of gay/lesbian respondents and 30% of bisexual respondents – without indication of whether single or couples (Office for National Statistics, 2010a). Whether these children were biologically related to respondents is not known but adoption by same-sex couples has been possible in the UK since 2005 (and by single gay or lesbian people before that). Over the period 2007–2008, 170 children were adopted in Britain by same-sex couples (Baron, 2010). It was estimated that even before legalisation, 5% of adopted children were living with a gay or lesbian couple (*London Evening Standard*, 2007). It is estimated, too, that 4% of all adopted children in the USA are raised by gay or lesbian parents (Craft, 2010).

There is considerable uncertainty about the number of gay and lesbian people and added uncertainty about the nature and structure of their relationships. Further problems arise in determining numbers of children parented by gay or lesbian people and the nature of their family structure. It would appear, however, that both the number in formally recognised relationships and the number who are parenting are relatively low. Parents may well typically be single and female.

# Implications for Tourism

The concept of 'family' as applied to gay men and lesbian women is as amorphous as it now is in heterosexual relationships. Gay men and lesbian women have not usually been regarded as having family other than in the sense of their own parents and siblings. The reluctance of many societies to accept homosexuality has resulted in gay men or lesbian women creating their own families – often a network of friends. Members of the families of origin may, though, continue to play important and committed support roles, leading to extended families or dual families.

Gay men and lesbian women have entered into partnerships prior to any legal recognition and have lived as families. Family life practices and roles may not always have mirrored those in heterosexual families, even in legally recognised same-sex partnerships. The presence of children gives rise to further variations of the gay and lesbian family. There are indisputably a number of gay or lesbian families which include children and it is evident that there is no single 'model' of the gay or lesbian family. There does, though, seem to be some justification for identifying a number of market segments – at the least, singles, partners and those with and those without children. It is almost impossible to identify a typical family and, as such, development and marketing of holiday products for this market will be difficult. Families with children face particular issues in public acceptance and this will be reflected in holiday requirements.

The market for gay men and lesbian women without children is currently recognised as a desirable and profitable segment and is targeted by a number of destinations and suppliers, including airlines, hotels and tour operators (Guaracino, 2007; Hughes, 2006). Gay men and, to a lesser extent, lesbian women are identified as being well off in terms of both income and leisure time. Gay men in particular have been targeted, with an emphasis on beach and sun holidays products for younger males, though cities have also been positioned for this market. There is a greater diversity of products – such as activity and adventure holidays and cruises – on offer in the USA, where the market size is greater. There are relatively few holiday products targeted at lesbian women; there is limited evidence of their holiday preferences but what there is suggests a demand for 'quieter' destinations and types of holiday than are preferred by men. Marriage and similar arrangements have led to the development of gay and lesbian honeymoon holiday products. Most gay and lesbian people appear to remain single or in relationships that are not legally recognised. There is not, in the immediate future, likely to be a significant change in this 'without children' market.

Consideration of holiday motivations and requirements, holiday and destination choice issues and the decision process is likely to be complex. Those relating to a single gay or lesbian person holidaying alone or with friends are likely to be different from those relating to a gay or lesbian couple with children. For many gay and lesbian persons, travel is an opportunity to escape the constraints of heteronormative society and to be oneself; it gives the opportunity to meet other gay and lesbian persons and validate identity (Hughes, 2006). The single person may also be seeking new relationships (including sexual). Sexual contact may remain a factor even for partners. The sexual dimension is usually regarded as less important for women, though establishing relationships may still be significant.

Particular issues may be common, however, to all gay and lesbian tourists. Gay-friendliness has been widely identified as a key element in destination and supplier choice, as it means that the risks of 'discomfort, discrimination and physical attack' are minimised (Hughes, 2002: 303). These issues are likely to be applicable to all forms of gay and lesbian family, especially given the considerable resistance to and disapproval of gay or lesbian persons having child-rearing roles. Understanding and acceptance of (if not empathy with) gay or lesbian parenthood will be key in choices.

For children who are comfortable with their home situation and who live in an accepting local community it would be important to avoid holiday experiences that conflict with these. A child experiencing harassment and stress from society labelling such families as unnatural would be anxious to escape from these and to avoid further disapproval on holiday. On holiday, the nature of the family is exposed to a new audience and is exposed more openly than in many 'at home' situations. Even where a gay-friendly place and hotel are chosen, there is always the possibility of problems arising from fellow holidaymakers. Desired destinations and suppliers would need to be both child-friendly and gay-friendly. Such characteristics may not be evident even in destinations or accommodation that are popular with gay and lesbian tourists. There may be a tension between the requirements of gay and lesbian tourists without children and those with – many gay men and, to a lesser extent, lesbian women may not wish to be in a family environment when on holiday, and vice versa. The outcome may be a desire, of families with children, for holidays in less popular places, where a degree of privacy may reduce the likelihood of overt disapproval or, at least, of discomfort. There may be a preference for holidays that are more small-scale, patronised by holidaymakers who are more likely to be accepting of gay and lesbian families. This could include adventure or educational holidays, cultural trips and alternative tourism.

Families will seek an environment that is 'strengthening' and supportive and which raises self-esteem. Meeting similar families on holiday may be a means of reassuring children of the 'normality' of their situation. An online survey of gay/lesbian parents undertaken by Rainbow Family Holidays, a small-scale UK specialist holiday organiser, showed that the overwhelming majority wished to holiday with other gay or lesbian families (Businesswire, 2009). It may even be a case of seeking some form of 'private' holiday that is confined to gay or lesbian parents and children. This can be achieved, for instance, on cruises, holiday clubs and at dedicated hotel or holiday village complexes. Camping is claimed to be popular with lesbian parents, in part for the privacy it enables. Mainstream destinations may be avoided and there may be a preference to holiday in familiar environments. Many parents will be single with relatively low incomes and those who are couples will have lower discretionary incomes than the 'non-parent' market already targeted by the tourist industry.

There is little evidence of the tourist industry offering a product targeted at gay or lesbian families with children. This may be because of a reluctance to approach this relatively controversial market but also because the market is relatively small and lacks the discretionary purchasing power of gay and lesbian singles or couples without children. In the USA, however, R Family Vacations has offered, since 2004, holidays for gay and lesbian families with children, with a particular object of facilitating children meeting other children in similar family units. The company has done this through a cruise ship product offer. Another US holiday company, Olivia, which specialises in holidays (especially cruises) for lesbian women also introduced a family vacation in the form of a resort vacation at Club Med near West Palm Beach in 2003.

Holidays, as high-risk, high-involvement and shared experiences are, in studies of heterosexual families, characterised by collective responsibility for choice and joint decision-making (Bronner & deHoog, 2008; Kozak, 2010; Mottiar & Quinn, 2004). Such shared activity is more evident for holidays than it is for most other products consumed by families (Belch & Willis, 2002). For gay or lesbian families, the lack of gender roles may lead to the decision-making being even more egalitarian. The direct influence of children (in heterosexual families) is limited in most aspects of holiday decision-making (Wang et al., 2004). It may be that egalitarian ideals extend to the child in gay or lesbian families and there may be a wish to include the child because of particular difficulties they may face on holiday.

The benefits of holidays as identified for heterosexual families – improving and maintaining relationships and, during planning stages, facilitating communication – are equally applicable to gay and lesbian families (Lehto et al., 2009). These may be particularly relevant given the stresses and tensions that characterise the lives of many gay and lesbian families. Benefits of holidays have been expressed, in particular, with respect to 'disadvantaged' (usually low-income) families (McCabe, 2009; Minnaert et al., 2009). While gay and lesbian families are not necessarily disadvantaged in the same way, holidays do have the potential to benefit relationships and to contribute to a sense of 'being like others' which may have particular significance for children of gay or lesbian families.

# Conclusion

There has been a long history of gay and lesbian persons travelling in order to escape restrictive environments, to meet similar others and confirm their identity. The tourism industry (at least in North America and Western Europe) has increasingly recognised that there is a growing and profitable market with respect to gay and lesbian persons without children, though much of the product offer is based on sun and sea. While a number of relatively small specialist operators have appeared (and disappeared) targeting the gay men's market in particular, it is significant that Thomson Holidays (part of the TUI group), a large 'mainstream' operator, now has a portfolio of holidays, labelled 'Freedom', designed for gay and lesbian holidaymakers. There are, too, a large number of destinations – cities such as San Francisco and Philadelphia (USA), Manchester and Brighton (UK), Sydney (Australia) and Cape Town (South Africa) as well as countries such as Switzerland and individual hotels and airlines (such as American Airlines and SAS) that have targeted the gay and lesbian market.

The emphasis in such holiday development and promotion has been gay-friendliness of carrier, accommodation and destination. It has meant an acknowledgement of the desire of the gay and lesbian traveller for 'gay space', which includes nightlife – bars and clubs frequented primarily by gay and lesbian persons.

Gay or lesbian families with children have not, with the odd exception, been recognised by the industry. Whatever the reasons the industry may have for not engaging with this market, it may also simply be a lack of awareness of the market and of its particular requirements – an environment that is supportive and which does not expose families to negative experiences. While understanding and acceptance will be key factors in any holiday choice, it will not necessarily be the same product that singles or couples desire. There may indeed be antagonism on the part of other gay and lesbian persons towards the gay and lesbian family with children. For such families, gay space in terms of nightlife is unlikely to be such an important factor.

Holidays for gay and lesbian persons have been characterised as yielding benefits of escape, rest and relaxation, as well as opportunities for relationship development and for having identity confirmed by being with similar others; the last latter issue takes on a more significant aspect in holiday decisions for families with children. The holiday experience has positive influences on gay and lesbian persons, influences beyond those associated with the rest of the population. Progress in 'safe' and appropriate opportunities for gay or lesbian families with children to holiday is likely to contribute further positive effects on family dynamics and on children's development.

# Further Research

There is limited (but increasing) research relating to the nature of the gay and lesbian family per se; studies that examine their tourism needs, patterns and impacts are correspondingly limited in number and scope. There is a growing research literature focusing on tourism by gay and lesbian people without children but there are many issues that remain to be explored even in this area. Studies have largely examined reasons why people go on holiday, satisfactions sought, activities undertaken and destinations visited. Other significant areas yet to be studied include social and economic impact and residents' attitudes and reactions. A number of commercial providers have identified the gay and lesbian market as one which they can target for holidays (especially all-inclusive holidays). Research has not, however, examined the rationale behind the decisions of such providers or the form of marketing strategies adopted. Supply-side research has been remarkably absent (as it has in much of tourism studies).

Although 'family' remains an imprecise concept in gay and lesbian studies, it is evident that there has long been a family construct – in the form of families of choice (often friends) as well as in the more conventional form of partners. This concept is being consolidated by an increased (but still geographically limited) legalisation of gay or lesbian partnerships. The family construct, however, has not been acknowledged in studies to date – in particular, the influence of families of choice and partners in decision processes.

Further, studies have not yet encompassed the concept of the family with children. This remains a completely open book with regard to potential for research. There is, initially, a major gap in knowledge about the structure of and processes in such families. This may be a gap for non-tourist researchers to fill but, nonetheless, there is scope for small-scale qualitative studies based on families (that may not be 'typical') which give insight to requirements and perceived satisfactions of the holiday. Such studies could also identify any difficulties faced in identifying satisfactory destinations and forms of holiday. They could also examine decision processes, identifying key decision-makers and determine how 'family' might influence destination choice. The significance of the holiday for families with children (in terms of relationships and self-esteem in particular) is another area of research that could be explored.

# References

Adam, B. (2004) Care, intimacy and same-sex partnership in the 21st century. *Current Sociology*, 52(2), 265–279.
Adam, B. (2006) Relationship innovation in male couples. *Sexualities*, 9(1), 5–26.
Akersten, M. (2010) Family First's anti-gay anger (9 August). Retrieved 16 August 2010 from http://www.samesame.com.au/news/local/5726/Family-Firsts-anti-gay-anger.htm.

Arabsheibani, R., Marin, A. and Wadsworth, J. (2004) In the pink: homosexual–heterosexual wage differentials in the UK. *International Journal of Manpower*, 25(3–4), 343–354.

Arabsheibani, R., Marin, A. and Wadsworth, J. (2006) Gay pay in the UK. *CentrePiece*, summer, 17–19.

Banks, C. (2003) *The Cost of Homophobia: Literature Review on the Human Impact of Homophobia in Canada*. Saskatoon: Gay and Lesbian Health Services of Saskatoon.

Baron, N. (2010) Pink pound loses its glow as more gay couples become parents. *Observer*, 25 April. Retrieved 10 August 2010 from http://www.guardian.co.uk/money/2010/apr/25/pink-pound-gay-couples-parents.

BBC News (2004) Brighton 'has most gay couples' (3 February). Retrieved 10 August 2010 from http://news.bbc.co.uk/1/hi/england/3456635.stm.

Belch, M. and Willis, L. (2002) Family decision at the turn of the century: has the changing structure of households impacted the family decision-making process? *Journal of Consumer Behaviour*, 2(2), 111–124.

Biblarz, T. and Savci, E. (2010) Lesbian, gay, bisexual and transgender families. *Journal of Marriage and Family*, 72(3), 480–497.

Biblarz, T. and Stacey, J. (2010) How does the gender of parents matter? *Journal of Marriage and Family*, 72(1), 3–22.

Blake, J. (2009) 'Gayby boom': children of gay couples speak out (29 June). Retrieved 10 August 2010 from http://edition.cnn.com/2009/LIVING/wayoflife/06/28/gayby.

Bozett, F. (1987) *Gay and Lesbian Parents*. New York: Praeger.

Bronner, F. and de Hoog, R. (2008) Agreement and disagreement in family vacation decision-making. *Tourism Management*, 29(5), 967–979.

Burns, M., Burgoyne, C. and Clarke, V. (2006) Financial affairs? Money management in same-sex relationships. Paper presented at the Congress of International Association for Research in Economic Psychology and the Society for Advancement of Behavioural Economics, Paris, July.

Businesswire (2009) 69% of gay families prefer to holiday without heterosexuals according to a survey by Rainbow Family Holidays. Retrieved 9 December 2010 from http://www.businesswire.com/news/home/20091209005532/en/69-Gay-Families-Prefer-Holiday-Heterosexuals-Survey.

Caldwell, S. (2009) Gay rights law halts catholic adoptions. *MailOnline*, 19 June. Retrieved 9 December 2010 from http://www.dailymail.co.uk/news/article-1194320/Gay-rights-law-halts-Catholic-adoptions.html.

Carrington, C. (1999) *No Place Like Home: Relationships and Family Life Among Lesbians and Gay Men*. Chicago, IL: University of Chicago Press.

Chrisafis, A. (2005) DUP hits at Trimble adviser's gay marriage. *Guardian*, 1 February. Retrieved 22 October 2008 from http://www.guardian.co.uk/uk/2005/feb/01/gayrights.northernireland.

Congregation of the Doctrine of the Faith (2003) *Considerations Regarding Proposals to Give Legal Recognition to Unions Between Homosexual Persons*. Rome: Vatican.

Craft, C. (2010) How many children have gay parents in the US? Retrieved 16 August 2010 from http://adoption.about.com/od/gaylesbian/f/gayparents.htm.

Demo, D. and Allen, K. (1996) Diversity within lesbian and gay families: challenges and implications for family theory and research. *Journal of Social and Personal Relationships*, 13(3), 415–434.

Department of Trade and Industry (Women and Equality Unit) (2003) *Civil Partnership: A Framework for the Legal Recognition of Same-Sex Couples*. London: Department of Trade and Industry.

Duncan, S. and Phillips, M. (2008) New families? Traditions and change in modern relationships. In A. Park, J. Curtice, K. Thomson, M. Phillips and E. Clery (eds), *British Social Attitudes: The 24th Report* (pp. 1–28). London: Sage.

Duncan, S. and Smith, D. (2006) Individualisation versus the geography of 'new' families. *Contemporary Social Science*, 1(2), 167–189.

Garner, A. (2005) *Families Like Mine: Children of Gay Parents Tell It Like It Is.* New York: Harper.

Gartrell, N. and Bos, H. (2010) US National Longitudinal Lesbian Family Study: psychological adjustment of 17-year-old adolescents. *Pediatrics*, 126(1), 28–36.

Green, S. (2010) Homosexuals adulterating marriage. Press release from Christian Voice, 30 June. Retrieved 16 August 2010 from http://www.repentuk.com/Press/press160.html.

Guaracino, J. (2007) *Gay and Lesbian Tourism: The Essential Guide for Marketing.* Oxford: Butterworth–Heinemann.

Guasp, A. (2010) *Different Families: The Experiences of Children with Lesbian and Gay Parents.* London: Stonewall.

Hughes, H. (2002) Gay men's holiday destination choice: a case of risk and avoidance. *International Journal of Tourism Research*, 4(4), 299–312.

Hughes, H. (2006) *Pink Tourism: Holidays of Gay Men and Lesbians.* Wallingford: CABI.

Jenkins, S., Pereira, I. and Evans, N. (2009) *Families in Britain: The Impact of Changing Family Structures and What the Public Think.* London: Ipsos/MORI and Policy Exchange.

Joloza, T., Evans, J. and O'Brien, R. (2010) *Measuring Sexual Identity: An Evaluation Report.* Newport: Office for National Statistics.

King, M. and Bartlett, A. (2006) What same-sex civil partnerships may mean for health. *Journal of Epidemiology and Community Health*, 60(1), 188–191.

Kozak, M. (2010) Holiday taking decisions – the role of spouses. *Tourism Management*, 31(4), 489–494.

Lehto, X.Y., Choi, S., Lin, Y-C. and MacDermid, S.M. (2009) Vacation and family functioning. *Annals of Tourism Research*, 36(3), 459–479.

*London Evening Standard* (2007) Rise in adopted children living with gay couples. *London Evening Standard*, 19 January. Retrieved 10 August 2010 from http://www.thisislondon.co.uk/news/rise-in-adopted-children-living-with-gay-couples-7187272.html.

McCabe, S. (2009) Who needs a holiday? Evaluating social tourism. *Annals of Tourism Research*, 36(4), 667–688.

Minnaert, L., Maitland, R. and Miller, G. (2009) Tourism and social policy: the value of social tourism. *Annals of Tourism Research*, 36(2), 316–334.

Mitchell, M., Dickens, S. and O'Connor, W. (2009) *Same-Sex Couples and the Impact of Legislative Changes.* London: prepared for Economic and Social Research Council by National Centre for Social Research.

Moorhead, J. (2010) I'm dad, he's daddy. *Guardian*, 17 July. Retrieved 17 July 2010 from http://www.guardian.co.uk/lifeandstyle/2010/jul/17/gay-fathers-drewitt-barlow.

Morgan Centre for the Study of Relationships and Personal Life (2006) *Gay and Lesbian 'Marriage': An Exploration of the Meanings and Significance of Legitimising Same-Sex Relationships.* Manchester: University of Manchester (School of Social Sciences).

Mottiar, Z. and Quinn, D. (2004) Couple dynamics in household tourism decision making: women as the gatekeepers? *Journal of Vacation Marketing*, 10(2), 149–160.

Nardi, P. (1992) That's what friends are for: friends as family in the gay and lesbian community. In K. Plummer (ed.), *Modern Homosexualities: Fragments of Lesbian and Gay Experience* (pp. 108–120). London: Routledge.

Office for National Statistics (2010a) *New ONS Integrated Household Survey: Experimental Statistics. Statistical Bulletin: September 2010.* Newport: ONS.

Office for National Statistics (2010b) Civil partnerships: formation numbers continue to fall. Retrieved 2 December 2010 from http://www.statistics.gov.uk.

Oswald, R. (2002) Resilience within the family networks of lesbians and gay men: intentionality and redefinition. *Journal of Marriage and Family*, 64(2), 374–383.

Patterson, C. (2000) Family relationships of lesbians and gay men. *Journal of Marriage and Family*, 62(4), 1052–1069.

Patterson, C.J. (2006) Children of lesbian and gay parents. *Current Directions in Psychological Science*, 15(5), 241–244.

Populus (2009) *The Times* 'Gay Britain' poll. *The Times*, 10 June 2009. Retrieved 17 August 2010 from http://www.populus.co.uk/uploads/download_pdf-100609-The-Times-The-Times-Gay-Britain-Poll.pdf.

Rivers, I., Poteat, V. and Noret, N. (2008) Victimisation, social support and psychosocial functioning among children of same-sex and opposite-sex couples in the United Kingdom. *Developmental Psychology*, 44(1), 127–134.

Scottish Government (Social Research: Equalities) (2009) *The Experiences of Children with Lesbian and Gay Parents – An Initial Scoping Review of Evidence*. Edinburgh: Scottish Government.

Sears, R., Gates, G. and Rubenstein, W. (2005) *Same-Sex Couples and Same-Sex Couples Raising Children in the United States: Data from Census 2000*. Los Angeles, CA: Williams Project on Sexual Orientation Law and Public Policy, UCLA School of Law.

Short, E., Riggs, D., Perlesz, A., Brown, R. and Kane, G. (2007) *Lesbian, Gay, Bisexual and Transgender Parented Families: A Literature Review Prepared for the Australian Psychological Society*. Melbourne: Australian Psychological Society.

Stacey, J. (2006) Gay parenthood and the decline of paternity as we knew it. *Sexualities*, 9(1), 27–55.

Towleroad (2010) Florida AG Bill McCullum wants gay foster parents outlawed (9 August). Retrieved 16 August 2010 from http://www.towleroad.com/2010/08/florida-ag-bill-mccollum-wants-gay-foster-parents-outlawed-i-do-not-think-we-should-have-homosexuals.html.

Waitt, G. and Markwell, K. (2006) *Gay Tourism: Culture and Context*. Binghamton, NY: Haworth Hospitality Press.

Wang, K-C., Hsieh, A-T., Yeh, Y-C. and Tsai, C-W. (2004) Who is the decision-maker: the parents or the child in group package tours? *Tourism Management*, 25(2), 183–194.

Weeks, J., Heaphy, B. and Donovan, C. (1999) Partners by choice: equality, power and commitment in non-heterosexual relationships. In G. Allan (ed.), *The Sociology of the Family* (pp. 111–128). London: Blackwell.

Wynne-Jones, J. (2009) Change and repent, bishop tells gays. *Telegraph*, 4 July. Retrieved 6 July 2009 from http://www.telegraph.co.uk/news/religion/5744559/Change-and-repent-bishop-tells-gays.html.

# Part 3
# The Futures of Family Tourism

# 10 Consumer Kids and Tourists – Creatively Marketing a City to Young Tourists

## Sally Webster

## Introduction

Tourism marketing, especially destination marketing, must constantly reinvent itself to ensure that tourist numbers increase. Therefore it is surprising that little has been done (outside of family holiday packages and theme parks) to specifically target young tourists, 8–14-year-olds, as a niche market (Seaton & Bennett, 1996). This age group can have enormous influence over their parents regarding where the family will spend its holidays and what they will do (Weaver & Lawton, 2006).

Young people are an important target group for destination marketing because they are the current and future consumer, and can also influence adult spending habits (Beder, 1998), including where families go on holidays (Thornton et al., 1997) . Destination marketing organisations (DMOs) often ignore young consumers or young tourists when developing marketing campaigns (Nanda et al., 2006). This is despite families being one of the biggest travel cohorts.

Even though young people have consumer influence and future spending power, there is limited research into the consumer habits of young tourists (Blichfeldt et al., 2011). The majority of research focuses on the role of the adult or the parents as the decision-makers regarding where the family will travel to. It should be noted too that there is a paucity of research into family holidays and how families select destinations. Perhaps this could explain the reluctance that DMOs demonstrate to researching and targeting the young tourist (Nanda et al., 2006).

This chapter discusses why it is important for DMOs to target young people or 'tweens', that is, those aged 8–14 years. Further, this chapter considers ways of reaching the tween market through creative tourism that encourages activity and engagement – key factors when capturing young consumers.

## The Young Consumer – Who Has the Buying Influence?

Cedric Cullingford expressed his concern that tourism operators were neglecting the young consumer, one he described as a powerful consumer. He explained that 'as future tourists, and as a potentially important influence, their views of their experiences are significant' (Cullingford, 1995: 121). Even though this was raised nearly 20 years ago, Cullingford's comments as he presented them in his 1995 paper 'Children's attitudes to holidays overseas' remain relevant. Cullingford's authority in this area is recognised by Thornton et al. (1997), who reflect on Cullingford's observations in their paper 'Tourist group holiday decision-making and behaviour: the influence of children', as well as in the more recent analysis by Blichfeldt et al. (2011).

As Cullingford emphasised, young people need to be targeted as a niche market for, being the current and future tourist, they will assist in supporting long-term tourism. To understand how to target this consumer market effectively, the Sutherland and Thompson (2001) consumer-based framework, which focuses on four sub-groups, is used as a theoretical concept for the present discussion. This is:

- pester power – children/teenagers who 'pester' and nag time-poor adults, who feel guilty about not providing more time for their children and succumb to the pressure – or give in – in order to keep the peace (both actions reinforce these behaviour patterns);
- influencers – children/teenagers who loudly or quietly convince and coerce adults and their peers to buy;
- current market – children/teenagers who have their own cash and buying ability (children now tend to receive higher amounts of pocket money and some teenagers receive an income);
- future market – children/teenagers who are cultivated 'now' by consumer industries with a view to being a future buyer.

Understanding young people's consumer behaviour characteristics, even broadly, supports strategies and approaches that could be adopted by DMOs to market to young tourists and their families in a way that will engage them (Quester et al., 2011).

## Young People as the Current Consumers

Even though it is accepted that young people or tweens are the current as well as the future tourist, there is a general assumption by many tourism operators that tweens do not have the buying power and that is why there has been a reluctance to target them as a niche audience (Cullingford, 1995). This attitude by some tourism operators, especially by many employed at

DMOs, is contrary to those in the fashion, toys, food and entertainment industries. For many industries, operators make it their business to understand the buying behaviour of young consumers and how to reach them and sell to them (Brooks, 2008; Mayo & Nairn, 2009). Marketers working in consumer-based industries, perhaps with the exception of many DMOs, have long understood the buying power of this age group. They know that young people are clever at getting what they want. They can identify how this age group behave in order to influence their parents' buying patterns. Children of all ages are known to drop hints, hassle, coerce, manipulate and even use guilt until they convince adults, in particular parents, grandparents and other family members, to give them what they are after (Schor, 2005; Thornton *et al.*, 1997).

This chapter takes a primary focus on the role of young tourists as the influencers and persuaders of their parents when families are selecting holidays. However, before discussing this, it is important also to reflect on the buying power of young consumers – either through their own purchasing power or their ability to influence adults to spend.

The Future Laboratory, an international trend forecaster, dedicated issue 14 of its *Viewpoint* magazine (2004) solely to the buying power of young people whom it describes as 'sunshine teens', a term that reflects the brightness this group can bring to retail business. The Future Laboratory revealed that in the USA alone 'teens (only) spend $160 billion annually and influence $800 billion of adult spending'. Schor defines this purchasing power as 'kid-fluence', explaining the 'more children shop, the more voice they have in parental purchases' (Schor, 2005: 23). Schor (2005) details how industry analysts in the USA had 'calculated that by 2004, total advertising and marketing expenditures directed at children [in the USA] reached $15 billion, a stunning rise from the mere $100 million in television advertising spent in 1983' (Schor, 2005: 21). Advertisers would not be spending on media advertising if they were not achieving the financial returns.

Schor stated that this advertising exposure to 'children aged four to twelve directly influenced $330 billion of adult purchasing in 2004 [in the USA] and "evoked" another $340 billion' (Schor, 2005: 23). In the UK, the spending power of children aged up to 19 years at around the same time period (2005) may appear more modest, approximately £12 billion; however, this 'spend' was 'from their own pocket money or part-time jobs' (Mayo & Nairn, 2009: 5) and not their buying through pester power or influence. While the financial results focus on differing age groups, all in all they highlight a formidable purchasing power and it is only increasing (Beder, 1998). Schor (2005) claims that children's buying power was growing at 20% per year in the USA, and there is evidence to suggest this is not country specific or culture specific, with similar patterns in the UK, mainland Europe, India and Asia (Lindstrom, 2004). It is no surprise that young consumers are described as 'sunshine'.

## Young Consumers Can Influence Spending

As Sutherland and Thompson (2001) explain through the sub-group framework, young people are effective at influencing and pestering adults into purchasing on their behalf. This skill in persuading adults was highlighted in VisitBritain's *Families Research* published in 2006, which investigated how young people persuade parents where to holiday. The research claimed that family holidays account for at least a third of all holiday trips in the UK and the key influencer on where the family visits is made either directly or indirectly by the children.

The National Trust, a major tourism organisation in the UK, experienced a similar pattern and believed that children had some influence on which National Trust sights the family visited (National Trust, 2010). As this was anecdotal, the Trust engaged the Market Research Group at Bournemouth University to investigate the issue, and the results indicated that the children influenced in more than 50% of all visits (John Bracktsone, 2007, personal communication). While both sets of market analysis specifically focused on short holidays in Britain, the findings can also be considered for other destinations when developing marketing strategies, particularly destination campaigns for the family holiday. These results reflect what Weaver and Lawton (2006: 175) describe as 'an interesting factor in the [destination] decision-making process, since they [young people] do not usually have much of an actual say, but exercise a strong influence over their parents'.

Similar findings were realised through research undertaken by both Australia's National Capital Authority and the University of Canberra's Centre for Tourism (in the National Capital Educational Tourism Project). Their findings revealed that 40% of students (aged 8–14) visiting the Australian capital, Canberra, for educational purposes returned to the city for a family holiday within two years. As the children enthusiastically discuss their initial school visit with their parents, this influences a family holiday return trip (Ritchie & Uzabeaga, 2005).

## The Young Traveller – Why the Need to Target Them

While some tourism operators may not believe that young people can influence major purchases, such as holidays or cars, there is evidence that they do (Lindstrom, 2004; Schor, 2005). This is supported by Thornton *et al.*, who contend that the tourism industry has traditionally believed that if young people do have influence in this area it is only in 'making small-scale choices and none in major resource-binding (expensive) and infrequent purchases, such as holidays' (Ekstrom *et al.*, 1986, as cited in Thornton *et al.*, 1997: 289.)

Thornton *et al.* take this point further by adding: 'this possibility of children being active participants, or negotiators, in family decisions has mostly been ignored' (Thornton *et al.*, 1997: 289). They reinforce this by citing Cullingford:

> Children are not the target audience for the tourist industry as a whole, especially when it comes to travel abroad for a major holiday. It is generally assumed that they submit to whatever choices their parents make, and that they have little secondary influence on their parents' particular choice of holiday destination. (Cullingford, 1995: 121)

From the market analysis undertaken in Britain it does appear that some areas of tourism are now understanding the influence of children and teenagers on family travel. Both VisitBritain (2006) and the National Trust (2010) state that their change in marketing tactics was due to responsiveness to market demands.

While Cullingford (1995) claimed that the tourism industry is reluctant to market to young consumers, there also appears to be reluctance by many organisations to research what marketing activities young consumers relate to and what motivates them. This reluctance could be misguided, in that 'in tourism research, few researchers have identified children as having an active role in decision-making' (Thornton *et al.*, 1997: 289) or it could be a way to avoid the ethical and moral considerations that arise when surveying young people (or, as many marketing professionals describe them, as 'children'). As Belch *et al.*, (2012) discuss, not only are there government regulations placed on the marketing communications industry on how it communicates to young people, but, due to parental and other social pressures, along with ethics, most industry associations have developed their own set of rigorous guidelines for advertising and marketing to young consumers.

If the tourism industry wants to encourage return visitation and establish longer-term strategies for the future tourists, it needs to begin considering young people as a key target audience. There are restrictions on the marketing communications industry in how it communicates with young people (Neal *et al.*, 2000) and it is acknowledged there are limited data on their buying power for family holidays (Nanda *et al.*, 2006). However, this does not mean that DMOs should avoid developing marketing strategies specifically for this audience. As Bronner and de Hoog explain, 'knowledge about family decision dynamics has not yet evolved to the extent that coherent marketing communications have been developed' (Su *et al.*, 2003, as cited in Bronner & de Hoog, 2008: 978). Nanda *et al.* maintain that the 'traditional thinking that children are not the target audience for travel products should be reconsidered because children are no longer submissive to whatever choices their parents make' (Nanda *et al.*, 2006: 118).

The challenge, then, is to suggest ways that DMOs could strategically develop destination marketing specifically for a young audience, aged, say, 8–16 years, especially as there is limited literature published in this area that can identify the issues which would then enable marketers to develop solutions. As Pike (2005) explains, there is very little research anyway into destination branding, so this creates challenges for DMOs to be pragmatic and strategic when developing marketing campaigns based on how the consumer relates and connects with destinations. The research into a general audience is limited. However, there is even less literature on niche target audiences, such as family tourism and how young tourists connect with a destination. There has been little examination of young tourists' travel intentions and what type of destination marketing activities are effective in capturing them (Bronner & de Hoog, 2008; Nanda *et al.*, 2006).

Any marketing approaches to be considered need to take into account how young people respond to messages. As Neal *et al.* (2000) explain, young people, aged 8–16, have the ability to understand messages and can cognitively digest them with logic or, as Brooks suggests, the 'younger we are, the more we absorb' and 'our children and their imaginations are like sponges that absorb information flowing around them' (Brooks, 2008: 8–9). Lindstrom (2004) maintains it is critical that young consumers are appealed to through their senses and their creativity, in a genuine and informative approach. They can quickly decipher marketing messages and determine if they are sincere.

For this reason the Future Laboratory explained in the *Independent* newspaper (Demetriou, 2004) that 'Sunshine Teens particularly like brands, but remain cynical about advertising'. One option when trying to reach them is to involve them in the marketing activity, to provide them with an experiential approach, a tactic successfully used by marketers in the children's consumer product industry (Schor, 2005). Creativity and experiencing this ('experiential' as defined by Belch *et al.*, 2012) is an approach that appeals to a young audience, especially if packaged into stories (Kavaratzis & Ashworth, 2005).

Anna Clark, author of *History's Children: History Wars in the Classroom* (2008), expressed it in a media interview as 'they don't just want the message, they want to think it themselves, too' (Guilliatt, 2008). Clark detailed in *History's Children* that young people want to be more engaged about history, culture and the location where history took place. She surveyed 34 schools across Australia, interviewing 182 students, 43 teachers and 20 curriculum officials. This was the first time a qualitative survey with in-depth analysis had been undertaken on this topic in Australia. The findings that are featured in *History's Children* indicate that students do not want to learn about history and culture through rote textbook learning, nor by teacher monologue or overhead projections, but via experiential learning. They want to read about a place, its history and culture, as well as experience it by visiting it. This is a premise that could be used by DMOs when marketing to the younger tourist.

# What Do Young Tourists Want From Their Travels?

In 2009, a qualitative survey of young tourists in Barcelona was undertaken by the author to identify their motivation to travel when holidaying with their families. Barcelona was selected as it is a city that boasts approximately 11 million visitors a year, with about 40% of these being families (Barcelona Turisme, 2006, 2007). In total, 25 young tourists and their families were surveyed to understand how young people are influenced by a culture when they travel to a particular destination. The aim was to consider the motivations of young tourists in relation to destination selection, cultural understanding and how their experiences on their holiday affect their motivation to undertake further travel. The respondents were from a range of developed countries: Italy (seven), Germany (two), France, England, Portugal, Czech Republic, Switzerland (two), Turkey, the USA (two), Canada, Singapore (three) and Australia (three). Not surprisingly, the majority were from Europe, because of the travel distances.

Of the 25 young people surveyed, 24 said they wanted to learn more about Barcelona and its culture, and that this influenced why their family selected Barcelona as the destination. All families explained that their children were eager to learn and that travelling supported this. The parents had a desire for their children to experience and explore cultures other than their own, and their children wanted this as well. All the families surveyed travelled at least once a year to a destination outside their home country, with the majority travelling more than annually.

The parent or parents accompanying the young tourists emphasised three things:

(1) Their children wanted travel information and material that were developed specifically for them, yet they could find little either during the holiday planning stages or while in country that was designed and produced for a young audience. This meant they had to absorb the information and translate it for their children. They all claimed this took away from the experience for their children to explore and discover for themselves.
(2) When their children had learnt about the destination, they enjoyed the holiday experience more, as they felt a stronger understanding of and connection to the culture and place.
(3) Each time they travelled with their children it unleashed an enthusiasm for all the family to learn more about other places and other cultures, even places they were not visiting.

This survey, while only a snapshot, reinforced the results from the National Capital Educational Tourism Project (Ritchie & Uzabeaga, 2005) and the research by Gmelch, described in *Tourists and Tourism* (2004), which canvassed the motivations of different tourists and what they are trying to achieve from their travels. Gmelch (2004) found that parents want their children not only to have a positive holiday experience but also to also learn from their travels. Gmelch highlighted that 'a seldom mentioned motivation to travel is the desire of parents to interest their children in the world around them: many family trips are undertaken to expose children to interesting and significant places – historical, cultural, and natural' (Gmelch, 2004: 9). Parents want and expect destination information to be developed specifically for a young audience, but in keeping with society's pressures that this be produced appropriately, such as emphasising cultural education.

To provide an indication of the size of the family traveller cohort, the United Nations World Tourism Organization (UNWTO) revealed in its 2011 'Tourism highlights' that 51% of all international tourist arrivals (or 480 million arrivals, including for example business tourists) were those travelling for leisure, recreation and holidays. This did not include those who were combining a trip that included visiting friends or family, even though it is believed that many in this category would be undertaking a family holiday. This was an additional 27%. If family holidays account for about 40% of the international tourist arrivals as suggested by many DMOs, this demonstrates how substantial this cohort is as a tourist market and the potential power of children, as many of them can influence their parents' buying (Lindstrom, 2004; Schor, 2005).

Tourism researcher Priscilla Boniface (1995) recommends that when marketing tourism to young people and educating them about tourist destinations and cultural sights it is vital to consider the messages from their perspective. Boniface (1995) maintains if cultural tourism is to be promoted successfully to a young audience there must be an understanding that they are a specific target audience and the marketing material must be developed in a way that speaks to them, engages and is appropriate. She explains that too often information aimed at a young audience is delivered more for the adult and is developed in a language appropriate for an adult audience.

The traditional promotional approaches used in destination marketing, such as brochures, posters and slogans, are less effective when it comes to marketing a destination to a young audience (Smith, 2007). Their 'educational and curiosity motives' (Boniface & Cooper, 2001: 356) must be considered as otherwise they do not engage or they simply just switch off (Sutherland & Thompson, 2001). The Future Laboratory (2004) expressed it clearly by stressing that young people are very cynical about up-front advertising and marketing materials. Therefore, they need to be reached in different and possibly more creative ways than the conventional marketing products that might appeal to their parents and other adults.

# Supporting Young Tourists Through Creative Tourism

Generally, creative activities, for example centred on art, music, literature, architecture, food, theatre, have an ability to convey character, culture and even heritage in a way that conventional tourism activities cannot. And, if reaching a young audience is critical as they are the current tourist as well as the future tourist, then creatively marketing a destination is a way to connect and engage with them.

Creative tourism is a relatively new concept within the tourism industry that in simple terms uses the creative industries to promote tourism and travel to a destination. Creative industries include, but are not limited to, art, music, architecture, literature, dance, fashion, design, cultural learning and heritage. The United Nations Educational, Scientific and Cultural Organization (UNESCO, 2006) developed a working definition of 'creative tourism' as 'travel directed towards an engaged and authentic experience, with *participative* learning in the arts, heritage, or special character of a place. It provides a connection with those who reside in this place and create this living culture.'

There are many successful examples of creative tourism that have arisen due to local entrepreneurship or as a direct result of urban planning initiatives. One example is Germany's Bayreuth Festival, an event that encourages classical music lovers to visit the town through participation at concerts. Another example is Bilbao in Spain. In Bilbao, Metropolis (an international association of urban planning and city redevelopment) was engaged to advise on how to rejuvenate a depressed town into one that is a showcase of cultural activities and heritage – and specifically to attract tourists. By working with Metropolis, the city was successful in securing a Guggenheim Museum, which was designed by internationally acclaimed architect Frank Gehry. Creative tourism was a key factor in revitalising the city of Bilbao into an energetic and creative city with a distinct character (Bilbao Metropoli-30, 1997).

These successful examples of creative tourism have been developed specifically for adults. Young people who can and do influence families on where they holiday should also be considered when developing creative tourism approaches.

Barcelona, likewise, could be considered to be the embodiment of creative tourism, with its showcase of art, sculpture, music, design, and distinct Catalan culture. Tourism marketing in Barcelona has traditionally focused on increasing business tourism, in particular ways to expand the large-scale, international event industry, which is highly profitable (Barcelona Turisme, 2007). There has been limited targeted marketing to promote Barcelona as a holiday destination. This also means there has been almost no marketing to young travellers, even though families along with business travellers are the biggest tourist cohorts visiting Barcelona. Barcelona consistently ranks as the leading tourist destination in Spain, and is the reason why Spain repeatedly ranks in the world's top destinations in terms of arrivals and receipts (Cabrini, 2003).

Turisme de Barcelona, the city's DMO, is a member-based organisation. Therefore its approach to tourism marketing is to support its members, mainly tourist operators and event organisers, by developing promotional techniques and tools, such as brochures, websites and advertising. This has been successful to date, as all industry stakeholders have leveraged off the profile and branding of the city of Barcelona to promote their own products, be it an event, attraction or tourism activity (Barcelona Turisme, 2006, 2007).

Tourism marketing campaigns that promote the characteristics of a destination, such as showcasing its creative industries, can engender curiosity, interest and loyalty, which result in longer-term relationships between the consumer and the destination (Holt, 2004). Developing a connection between tourists and a particular destination can achieve increased visitation, return visits, word-of-mouth recommendations, and inspiration as a future holiday destination (Nanda *et al.*, 2006). However, establishing this emotional relationship is not easily achieved through the short-term marketing activities so often produced by the tourism industry, such as promotional brochures, product launches and television advertisements (Kavaratzis, 2005).

Marketing academics and practitioners emphasise the importance of targeting audiences through the use of creativity, especially 'stories' (Kavaratzis & Ashworth, 2005), and many have embraced this concept to develop and position a brand (Roberts, 2004). Brand stories and stories told through marketing activities, such as advertising, events and social networking tools, are particularly effective in reaching and engaging youth consumers aged between 17 and 25 (Dane & Yoon, 2009). Similarly, even younger consumers, aged 8–14 (those considered in this chapter), are engaged by marketing that tells a story (Belch *et al.*, 2012; Gregory Thomas, 2007). However, regulations and social concerns in marketing to this younger cohort (Quester *et al.*, 2011) can lead to industries disregarding them as potential consumers.

Creative tourism marketing is relevant for a young, aware audience for several reasons:

- the buying power of young people;
- the growing influence that young people have on deciding where families holiday;
- the continual need for DMOs to market their destination so as to increase visitation;
- the need to support sustainable tourism so that cultural attractions can remain for future generations;
- the wishes of young students to learn about history and culture in an experiential and more creative way.

It is therefore appropriate to consider a marketing strategy that can support all of these elements. One approach is to consider ways to advance creative tourism marketing specifically to those aged between 8 and 14 years (the tweens), as it has been demonstrated that young people are engaged through creativity and experience and, as identified, they are a target audience who cannot be ignored, if only because how they see and experience their holidays will affect their future destination selection.

## Conclusion: Empowering the Young Consumer, the Current Tourist and the Future Tourist

This chapter has discussed how young people are current and future consumer markets (Sutherland & Thompson, 2001). It has highlighted that young people do have the ability to coerce and influence adults' current spending, including where their family will holiday. What influences their young imaginations, especially through creativity and experiences on their holidays, can determine what they will explore as the future, adult tourists. It is worth considering 'that culture is not only at the root of tourism … but also a key source of motivation in becoming a tourist' (Boniface, 1999: 288). Therefore, it is timely for destinations to develop strategic marketing plans specifically aimed at young tourists, in an effort to support long-term tourism. This can and should be achieved by combining a range of marketing approaches that incorporate creative tourism and cultural education. Destinations such as Barcelona have a distinctive culture especially when displayed through entertaining activities produced from the creative industries that can engage a young audience. As a reminder from the perspective of Cullingford (1995) and Sutherland and Thompson (2001), young tourists have the power to influence now and into the future.

## References

Barcelona Turisme (2006) *Estadístiques de Turisme a Barcelona*. Barcelona: Ajuntament de Barcelona and Cambra de Comerç de Barcelona.

Barcelona Turisme (2007) *Memòria 2007 – Turisme de Barcelona*. Barcelona: Ajuntament de Barcelona and Cambra de Comerç de Barcelona.

Beder, S. (1998) Marketing to children. In *Proceedings from Caring for Children in the Media Age National Conference* (pp. 101–111). Sydney: New College Institute for Values Research.

Belch, G.E., Belch, M.A., Kerr, G. and Powell, I. (2012) *Advertising: An Integrated Marketing Communication Perspective* (2nd edition). Sydney: McGraw-Hill Australia.

Bilbao Metropoli-30 (1997) *Memoria Informe de Progreso*. Bilbao: Asociación para la Revitalización del Bilbao Metropolitano.

Blichfeldt, B.S., Pedersen, B.M., Johansen, A. and Hansen, L. (2011) Tweens on holidays. In-situ decision-making from children's perspective. *Scandinavian Journal of Hospitality and Tourism*, 11(2), 135–149.

Boniface, B. and Cooper, C. (2001) *Worldwide Destinations: The Geography of Travel and Tourism*. Oxford: Butterworth-Heinemann.

Boniface, P. (1995) *Managing Quality Cultural Tourism*. London: Routledge.

Boniface, P. (1999) Tourism and cultures: consensus in the making? In M. Robinson and P. Boniface (eds), *Tourism and Cultural Conflicts* (pp. 287–306). London: CABI.

Bronner, F. and de Hoog, R. (2008) Agreement and disagreement in family vacation decision-making. *Tourism Management*, 29(5), 967–979.

Brooks, K. (2008) *Consuming Innocence: Popular Culture and Our Children*. Queensland: University of Queensland Press.

Cabrini, L. (2003) *Cultural Tourism: Opportunities and Challenges*. Madrid: UN World Tourism Organization.

Clark, A. (2008) *History's Children: History Wars in the Classroom*. Sydney: University of New South Wales Press.

Cullingford, C. (1995) Children's attitudes to holidays overseas. *Tourism Management*, 16(2), 121–127.

Dane, J. and Yoon, H. (2009) Lynx: the challenges of lad culture. In H. Powell, J. Hardy, S. Hawkin and I. Macrury (eds), *The Advertising Handbook* (pp. 91–98). London: Routledge.

Demetriou, D. (2004) Optimistic, responsible and political: the face of today's teens. *Independent*, 31 March.

Ekstrom, K., Tansuhaj, P. and Foxman, E. (1986) Children's influence in family decisions and consumer socialization: a reciprocal view. In M. Wallendorf and P. Anderson (eds), *Advances in Consumer Research* (vol. 14, pp. 283–288). Provo, UT: Association for Consumer Research.

Future Laboratory (2004) Sunshine teens. In *Viewpoint #14*. London: Future Laboratory.

Gmelch, S.B. (2004) *Tourists and Tourism*. Long Grove, IL: Waveland Press.

Gregory Thomas, S. (2007) *Buy, Buy Baby: How Big Business Captures the Ultimate Consumer – Your Baby or Toddler*. London: Harper Collins.

Guilliatt, R. (2008) Why kids hate Australian history article. *Weekend Australian Magazine*, 23 February.

Holt, D.B. (2004) *How Brands Become Icons: The Principles of Cultural Branding*. Boston, MA: Harvard Business School Press.

Kavaratzis, M. (2005) Place branding: a review of trends and conceptual models. *Marketing Review*, 5(4), 329–342.

Kavaratzis, M. and Ashworth, G.J. (2005) City branding: an effective assertion of identity or a transitory marketing trick? *Royal Dutch Geographical Society KNAG*, 96(5), 506–514.

Lindstrom, M. (2004) *Brand Child* (2nd edition). London: Kogan Page.

Mayo, E. and Nairn, A. (2009) *Consumer Kids: How Big Business Is Grooming Our Children For Profit*. London: Constable.

Nanda, D., Hu, C. and Bai, B. (2006) Exploring family roles in purchasing decisions during vacation planning: review and discussion for future research. *Journal of Travel and Tourism Marketing*, 20(3–4), 107–125.

National Trust (2010) *2009/10 Annual Report*. Retrieved 14 July 2011 from http://www.nationaltrust.org.uk/main/w-trust/w-thecharity/w-annualreport2010.htm.

Neal, C., Quester, P. and Hawkins, D. (2000) *Consumer Behaviour: Implications for Marketing Strategy*. Sydney: Irwin/McGraw-Hill.

Pike, S. (2005) Tourism destination branding complexity. *Journal of Product and Brand Management*, 14(4), 258–259.

Quester, P., Pettigrew, S. and Hawkins, D. (2011) *Consumer Behaviour: Implications for Marketing Strategy* (6th edition). Sydney: Irwin/McGraw-Hill.

Ritchie, B. and Uzabeaga, S. (2005) *Discover What It Means To Be Australian in Your National Capital: Size and Effect of School Excursions to the National Capital*. Canberra: Centre for Tourism, University of Canberra, National Capital Educational Tourism Project.

Roberts, K. (2004) *Lovemarks: The Future Beyond Brands*. New York: PowerHouse Books.

Schor, J.B. (2005) *Born to Buy*. New York: Scribner.

Seaton, A.V. and Bennett, M.M. (1996) *Marketing Tourism Products*. London: Thomson Business Press.

Smith, A. (2007) Monumentality in 'capital' cities and its implications for tourism marketing: the case of Barcelona. *Journal of Travel and Tourism Marketing*, 22(3–4), 79–93.

Su, C., Fern, E.F. and Ye, K. (2003) A temporal dynamic model of spousal family purchase-decision behavior. *Journal of Marketing Research*, 40(3), 268–281.

Sutherland, A. and Thompson, B. (2001) *Kidfluence: The Marketers Guide to Understanding and Reaching Generation Y – Kids, Tweens and Teens*. Toronto: McGraw-Hill Ryerson.

Thornton, P.R., Shaw, G. and Williams, A.M. (1997) Tourist group holiday decision-making and behaviour: the influence of children. *Tourism Management*, 18(5), 287–297.

UNESCO Creative Cities Network (1 November 2006) *Towards Sustainable Strategies for Creative Tourism. Discussion Report of the Planning Meeting for 2008 International Conference on Creative Tourism, Santa Fe, New Mexico, USA, October 25–27 2006* (CLT/CEI/CID/2008/RP/66). Paris: UNESCO. Retrieved 19 March 2012 from http://unesdoc.unesco.org/images/0015/001598/159811E.pdf.

UNWTO (2011) Tourism highlights. Retrieved 5 July 2011 from http://www.unwto.org/facts/menu.html.

VisitBritain (2006) *Families Research*. London: VisitBritain. Retrieved 5 July 2011 from http://www.visitengland.org/Images/Family%20holidays%202006_tcm30-19731.pdf .

Weaver, D. and Lawton, L. (2006) *Tourism Management*. Milton: Wiley.

# 11  Investigating the 'Family Life Cycle' Model in Tourism

## Elisa Backer

## Introduction

The 'family life cycle' (FLC) model is considered to be a set of stages that most people go through during their adulthood. It is frequently used for explaining consumer behaviour and market segments and is used for understanding travel patterns. However, the traditional FLC model is becoming increasingly outdated. The natural progression from singles, to couples, to having children, retiring and being a solitary survivor is a depiction of life in the 1950s. However, an increasing proportion of people exist outside this model. Some people remain single with no children (called SINKs – Single Income No Kids), while others elect not to have (or leave it too late to have) children (DINKs – Double Income No Kids). Even couples with children do not necessarily holiday together. There are also other people who sit outside of the FLC model – gay and lesbian couples, and people whose spouse dies at an early age. The issue of evaluating the FLC is not new, and the model itself has been redefined numerous times by various researchers since it was first used in 1903. However, despite attempts to redefine the FLC model to consider those groups left out, the traditional FLC model from 1966 continues to dominate in tourism. While its limitations have been discussed for 80 years, few studies have considered what proportion of travellers fall outside of the traditional FLC model. The aim of the research reported in this chapter was to consider what proportion of travellers in four regions of Australia's state of Victoria – Ballarat, Bendigo, Geelong Otway and Yarra Valley – were not captured by the traditional FLC model.

## Literature Review

The FLC is essentially a set of stages that most people are expected to go through during their adult life. A history of the development of the FLC

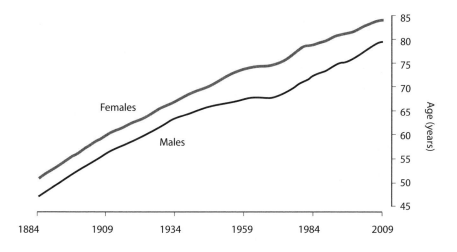

**Figure 11.1** Life expectancy at birth in Australia. *Source*: Australian Bureau of Statistics (2011a: 1)

highlights that the model has been presented in a large number of variations. The area of study can be traced back to 1903, when Rowntree (1903) used the structure of FLC to examine poverty patterns in England (Murphy & Staples, 1979). Since it originated, various researchers have altered it, expanded it and changed it. More recent contributions in the field have reflected societal trends (e.g. expanding the model to include single parents). However, some of the earlier FLC model expansions partly reflected the extended life expectancy, which created time for more stages to develop. Extended life expectancy has allowed a shift in the median age for women entering the FLC. This has been responsible for 'the continuing postponement of marriage' (Glick, 1977: 5).

Life expectancy has increased more than 30 years over the past 130 years in Australia (see Figure 11.1). At the time the FLC was created, in 1903, the average life expectancy in Australia was around 55 for males. By the mid-1930s this had risen to around 65, and to around 67 in the 1960s. Thus, an extended life allowed for more stages in life.

The influence of extended life span can be seen through the development of the FLC model from the 1930s to the 1960s. The 1930s is the period in which a number of researchers started to actually evaluate the FLC, resulting in some amendments to it. In that decade, three different versions of the FLC model evolved. The first of the three 1930s papers published described the four stages as being: married couples; couples with at least one child; couples with at least one adult child; couples growing old (Sorokin *et al.*, 1931). A similar model was presented by Kirkpatrick *et al.* (1934) but it described the four stages as: a family with children at pre-school, grade school, then high school; then all adults. Two years later, a modification was made by Loomis (1936) that specified children's age ranges, with stages being: childless couple, eldest child under 14; eldest children between 14 and 36; old families.

In the 1940s, further analysis of the FLC model was undertaken and more stages were introduced, so that the four stages became seven stages in three key works (Bigelow, 1942; Duvall & Hill, 1948; Glick, 1947). A pre-family stage of establishment was added by Bigelow (1942), who also included a recovery and a retirement stage after the various children's stages. Glick (1947) made a stark change to the FLC by stating that the first stage was a first marriage. The focus on single marriage was maintained by Duvall and Hill (1948), who considered that stage 1 of the FLC was childless. After the progression of children, stage 6 was recognised as 'ageing companions' – with the assumption was the marriage was still intact. This was followed by a final stage where one partner was remaining after the other had died.

In the 1960s and early 1970s stages were interrogated further, with specifics of children's ages added, resulting in some complicated and highly detailed modifications to the FLC. During that phase, the terms 'full nest', 'empty nest' and 'solitary survivor' were introduced (Wells & Gubar, 1966). While the FLC model had by that time been used for decades in sociology, Wells and Gubar's (1966) study represented a major contribution in the marketing arena. Despite contributions to the area of FLC during the 1980s and 1990s (e.g. Cosenza & Davis, 1981; Derrick & Lehfeld, 1980; Glick, 1989; Lawson, 1991; Murphy & Staples, 1979; Schnittger & Bird, 1990), the Wells and Gubar (1966) study has remained popular and is the basis for what is currently presented in several major tourism textbooks.

The most popular tourism textbook in Australia, that by Weaver and Lawton (2010), presents an adaptation of the Wells and Gubar (1966) model (Figure 11.2). The FLC model describes very simply how many people will typically go through eight stages during their life and uses those terms coined by Wells and Gubar (1966) such as full nest, empty nest and solitary survivor. The Wells and Gubar (1966) model is used in Richardson and Fluker's (2008) tourism textbook. An adaptation of the Wells and Gubar (1966) was used by Lumsdon (1977) and a similar version is used in the tourism textbook by Page and Connell (2009). A number of other tourism textbooks (e.g. those by Cooper *et al.*, 2008; and Hall, 2007) have created new versions of the traditional FLC model. However, the inclusion of the FLC in the foundations of tourism teaching is evident, and 'the concept has been enormously influential in consideration of tourism motivations and stages of travel' (Hall, 2007: 109).

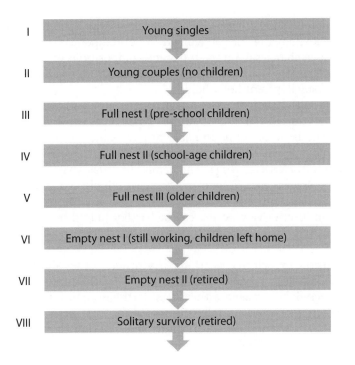

**Figure 11.2** The Weaver and Lawton adaptation of the family life cycle model.
*Source*: Weaver and Lawton (2010: 164)

While the importance of recognising and understanding the FLC model is emphasised in tourism, its limitations must also be appreciated. The model does leave out some groups of people. Not everyone gets married; not every marriage lasts forever; some people choose not to have (or cannot have) children; sometimes partners die at an early age. It also assumes people remain in a good state of health. For instance, women who have family histories of breast or ovarian cancer, and therefore have a higher risk of developing these diseases, often feel 'a great sense of urgency' (Werner-Lin, 2008: 428) to enter the FLC stages. Despite attempts to recreate the FLC model over the past few decades to include some of these groups (e.g. Gilly & Enis, 1982; Murphy & Staples, 1979), these 'modernised' FLC models have failed to make a significant impression.

Murphy and Staples discussed childless families and also the growing rates of divorce and remarriage, stating the 'necessity' to recognise divorce in the FLC (Murphy & Staples, 1979: 15). Gilly and Enis highlighted the shortcomings of the earlier FLC models, explaining that they failed 'to recognise the changing role of women in contemporary society and the impact of such changes upon the types and compositions of families' (Gilly & Enis, 1982: 271). Their redefined FLC model took into account childless couples and single-parent households.

More recently, the choice of some couples not to have children has received attention in the FLC literature. While an abundance of literature surrounds the issue of couples unable to have children due to infertility, couples who are child-free by choice had hitherto received very little focus (Pelton & Hertlein, 2011). The 'family life cycle may not adequately describe the stages' that voluntarily childless couples go through during their relationship (Pelton & Hertlein, 2011: 39). These couples can often be treated in an insensitive way and can be harshly judged by society (Pelton & Hertlein, 2011):

> We think they're selfish ... we think they're rigid ... they are self-absorbed, hypochondriacal, competitive, anxious.... My child-free chums name their dogs Baby', celebrate their cats' birthdays and bury them all in pet cemeteries.... Are mortally obsessed with cysts, moles, sunburn, and cellulite.... Some of them are on antidepressants (my diagnosis is Empty Futuritis). (Stern, 1994: 62; cited in Pelton & Hertlein, 2011: 43)

Indeed, the replacement of children through pet ownership is not new. Some commercial accommodation providers allow pets to stay in order to cater for this growing market segment (Weaver & Lawton, 2010). Such providers have developed niche strategies aimed at those in society who want to holiday but who do not want to separate from their pets (who, for some, are like their children). In fact, the role of pets throughout the FLC has also been considered in the literature (e.g. Turner, 2005).

The applications of the FLC model are broad. It has been studied in terms of its implications in medicine, sociology, marketing, economics and tourism. The FLC has been found to be more correlated with the purchase of leisure activities (including tourism) than social class or age (Hisrich & Cheng, 1974). Some further research investigating the relationship between the FLC and travel behaviour followed Hisrich and Cheng's (1974) study (e.g. Hong et al., 2005; Lawson, 1991; Lin & Lehto, 2006; Zimmerman, 1982).

Zimmerman analysed travel frequency along the stages of five different household types, or models. A 12-stage 'typical family life cycle' (Zimmerman, 1982: 57) was developed along with a separate six-stage single-parent cycle. A seven-stage model was set up to accommodate married couples without children. The other two models were for a single-person household and a household with individuals not related to each other. Life cycle stages could be seen to influence travel behaviour. However, the complexity of the research, by accommodating the range of household types in modern society,

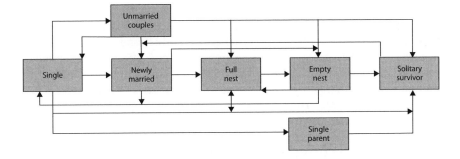

**Figure 11.3** Bojanic's modernised FLC model. *Source*: Bojanic (2011: 408)

was a deficiency. Zimmerman (1982) acknowledged this, stating that as 'the life cycle ... is more complex than is usually assumed, one may wonder why it should be used at all in travel research'. A condensed yet modernised FLC model was put forward by Bojanic (2011), which also highlighted an important point, that people can reach the end of the FLC and go back to earlier FLC stages (Figure 11.3).

The deficiencies of the traditional FCL model in tourism were highlighted through Lawson's (1991) seminal paper. Using the Wells and Gubar (1966) model as his framework, Lawson examined the linkage between the FLC and tourist behaviour. Based on examining tourist behaviour in New Zealand, he was able to assign the number of observed cases of tourists across each of the FLC stages. Of greatest significance, 1359 individuals in his sample (40%) did not fit into any of the FLC stages. This work was seen as important in tourism because it highlighted not only the proportion of cases not reflected in the traditional FLC model, but also which FLC stages accounted for the most cases, and in which stage people spent the most money on their vacation.

Using a slightly altered version of the traditional FLC to include single parents, Hong *et al.* (2005) observed similar findings to Lawson (1991). They found that couples who were married without children and 'empty nest' couples travelled more often than people at all other FLC stages. Those groups who travelled less often were found to be single parents and solitary survivors (Hong *et al.*, 2005). However, while these FLC groups were found to be observed less often, they can often be missed in some travel collection. For example, single travellers have been found to be significantly more likely to visiting friends and relatives (VFR) than other travellers, and as such may not be reflected in some data-sets that focus on commercial accommodation (Backer, 2011).

The findings in the FLC literature that has considered the relationship with travel frequency are not unexpected. Studies have observed low-travel frequency in 'full nest' FLC stages, particularly full nest I (see Figure 11.2). Such findings seem axiomatic. Parents with pre-school children are unlikely to want to travel far, or often, with very young children, who are likely to require frequent naps, high chairs, nappies, cots, booster seats, and other facilities that are bulky to transport.

However, of greatest significance from the tourism-related FLC studies is Lawson's (1991) finding that 40% of travellers did not fit into any FLC stage. Lawson's study was undertaken in New Zealand, and as such may not reflect broader behaviours. It was also undertaken over two decades ago and as such it is reasonable to expect that an even higher proportion of travellers do not fit into the traditional FLC model now. The study reported here aimed to consider the specific area of what proportion of travellers in four regions within Australia's state of Victoria fitted into the traditional FLC model. The Wells and Gubar (1966) model was used as the conceptual framework, following the model used by Lawson (1991), which is also found in current popular tourism textbooks, as detailed above.

## Method

In order to ascertain what proportion of travellers were not reflected in the traditional FLC model, four regions in Victoria were selected. The four regions were Ballarat, Geelong, Bendigo and Yarra Valley. These regions are identified on the map of Victoria (Figure 11.4).

The four regions in which surveying for this research occurred are each no more than two hours from Victoria's capital city, Melbourne. Geelong is the largest of the four regions, with a population of 216,330 (City of Greater Geelong, 2011). Geelong is about 70 kilometres south-west of Melbourne's central business district (CBD). Ballarat has a population of around 96,000 (Australian Bureau of Statistics, 2011b) and is around 110 kilometres from Melbourne's CBD. Bendigo is furthest from Melbourne, at around 150 kilometres. Its population is slightly more than 100,000 (Australian Bureau of Statistics, 2010). Yalla Valley is a large and diverse shire, with a population of around 147,000 (Yarra Ranges Council, 2011). However, the township and surrounding area in which the regional visitor information centre (VIC) has a population of only around 3,400 (Yarra Ranges Council, 2011). Yarra Valley is about 70 kilometres from the CBD of Melbourne.

These four regions all have destination marketing organisations (DMOs) that operate VICs. Permission from the organisations was obtained to conduct a short paper-based survey for this research in their information centres. Surveying took place for the four months from the beginning of March through to the end of June 2011. Tourists to the four regions who

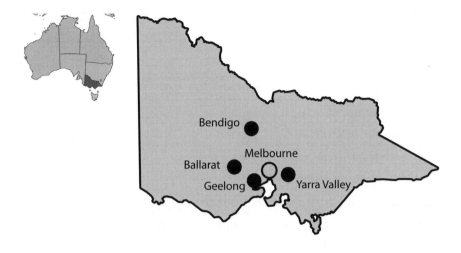

**Figure 11.4** Map of Victoria identifying the four regions for the study of travellers within Australia's state of Victoria and the traditional family life cycle model. *Source*: Adapted from Total Travel (2011)

came into the VIC were invited to participate in the survey. Data were entered into SPSS v.19.

## Results

In total, 174 responses to the survey were collected from the four regions: 43 from Ballarat, 64 from Bendigo, 38 from Geelong and 27 from Yarra Valley. An expanded FLC model had been used for the survey instrument. The traditional FLC model (Wells & Gubar, 1966) was used as the framework, and additional FLC stages were added to reflect a more modern lifestyle. The results for the expanded FLC can be seen in Table 11.1.

Despite best attempts to capture people through an expanded FLC model, 9.2% felt that no group represented their FLC position. Some examples included widowers who were still working, people aged over 35 who were separated and had no children, 'retired' and 'pensioner'. Some people are on pensions from a young age – such as disability pensions – and some of those in the survey did not feel that any of the options captured their situation. Similarly, an individual who has retired and married but does not have children was not represented adequately in the options. As

**Table 11.1** Tourist categorisations in an expanded family life cycle (FLC) model

| FLC stage | Responses |
|---|---|
| Young singles (less than 35 years old) | 27 (15.5%) |
| Young couples (no children) (female less than 35 years old) | 21 (12.1%) |
| Gay couple (no children) | 4 (2.3%) |
| Gay couple (with children) | 2 (1.1%) |
| Older couple (no children) (female 35+ years of age) | 7 (4.0%) |
| Single parent (children still at home) | 6 (3.4%) |
| Older single (never been married, no children) (35+ years old) | 0 |
| Couple with pre-school children (youngest child not at school) | 14 (8.0%) |
| Couple with school-aged children (youngest child at school) | 22 (12.6%) |
| Couple with older children (all children finished school) | 15 (8.6%) |
| Empty nest I (still working, children left home) | 18 (10.3%) |
| Empty nest II (retired, children left home) | 21 (12.1%) |
| Widower (widower who is not working and partner is deceased) | 1 (0.6%) |
| Other | 16 (9.2%) |

such, some of these 'other' types were captured in the 'other' category. Of the total number of responses, 138 (80.2%) fitted into a traditional FLC stage, but the remaining 34 responses (19.8%) did not fit into any stage of the traditional FLC model.

These data were then disaggregated according to each region from which the tourist had visited, to examine whether there was any difference in the FLC versus non-FLC ratio based on regions (Table 11.2).

Based on disaggregation by region, Bendigo had the highest proportion of respondents, at 28.1%, who did not fit into the traditional FLC. The second highest proportion of non-FLC respondents in the Yarra Valley, with 18.5%, followed by Geelong (15.8%) and then Ballarat (11.6%). A chi-square test revealed no overall difference at the 95% confidence level, and $z$-tests at the 95% confidence level revealed no significant difference between the regions.

Respondents were asked whether they were staying with friends and relatives, staying in commercial accommodation, or were day trippers. The purpose of this question was to ascertain whether the ratio of FLC versus non-FLC respondents was different based on these accommodation types

**Table 11.2** FLC versus non-FLC by region

|  | Ballarat | Bendigo | Geelong | Yarra Valley |
|---|---|---|---|---|
| FLC | 88.4% (*n*=38) | 71.9% (*n*=46) | 84.2% (*n*=32) | 81.5% (*n*=22) |
| Non-FLC | 11.6% (*n*=5) | 28.1% (*n*=8) | 15.8% (*n*=6) | 18.5% (*n*=5) |
| Total | 43 | 64 | 38 | 27 |

$\chi^2$=5.021, d.f.=3, $p$>0.05

**Table 11.3** FLC versus non-FLC by accommodation type

|  | VFR | Commercial | Day tripper | Total |
|---|---|---|---|---|
| FLC | 22% (*n*=30) | 51.5% (*n*=70) | 26.5% (*n*=36) | 136 |
| Non-FLC | 31.4% (*n*=11) | 62.9% (*n*=22) | 5.7% (*n*=2) | 35 |
| Total | 41 | 92 | 38 | 171 |

**Table 11.4** Number of nights staying in destination and FLC versus non-FLC, by region

|  | Ballarat* | Bendigo | Geelong | Yarra Valley |
|---|---|---|---|---|
| FLC | 4.52 | 3.35 | 3.83 | 1.77 |
| Non-FLC | 5.40 | 2.00 | 4.00 | 2.25 |

*Significant at the 95% confidence level

(Table 11.3). The majority of FLC respondents were staying in commercial accommodation (51.5%) followed by day-trippers (26.5%) and then VFRs. The majority of non-FLC respondents were also staying in commercial accommodation (62.9%) followed by VFRs (31.4%). Few non-FLC respondents were day-trippers (5.7%).

Respondents were also asked how long they were staying in the region. The means across each region were considered and examined based on being FLC or non-FLC. The results are presented in Table 11.4.

In order to test for statistical significance, *t*-tests were performed at the 95% confidence level. These tests revealed no significant different between FLC and non-FLC stages for Bendigo, Geelong or Yarra Valley. However, non-FLCs were found to stay significantly longer than traditional FLCs in Ballarat (5.40 compared with 4.52).

## Discussion

Since the FLC was first used as the basis for research in 1903, it has undergone many changes and has been used across numerous research areas. As life expectancy has increased, living longer has provided more stages for people to explore. People have increasingly had more time to explore single life before getting married. This has allowed for the option to delay starting a family to work longer, save more money and travel first. A longer life expectancy has also allowed people more time after their children have left home. An increased life expectancy linked with changes in social views has necessarily influenced the nature of the FLC model. People could marry more than once. Just as people approaching the empty nest I stage they may remarry and find themselves back in full nest I stage.

Not everyone has children; some do not want to, and some are not able to. Not every family has two parents – single parents are now common. And there are also parents who are same-sex couples. Today, there are so many different types of parents and families that the traditional FLC model becomes increasingly limited. In fact, it is not uncommon for there to be vast age differences within couples. The assumption of the traditional FLC model is that couples are around the same age and go through the stages together. Significant age gaps are, though, seen in society – made famous by various celebrity couples such as Catherine Zeta-Jones and Michael Douglas, with a 25-year age gap. Rod Stewart and Penny Lancaster have a 26-year age difference. Woody Allen and Soon-Yi Previn are 35 years apart in age, while Billy Joel and Katie Lee have a 32-year age gap. Peter Stringfellow and Bella Wright are 43 years apart in age. These are examples of people who are not following the traditional FLC model. The vastly younger partner could be left as a solitary survivor at an early age, leaving them plenty of time to revisit an earlier stage of the FLC by finding a new partner.

While the deficiencies in the traditional FLC model are axiomatic, the traditional FLC model is still widely used in tourism and other circles. However, its limitations in tourism are clearly highlighted in market segmentation discussions. An interesting issue surrounding the traditional FLC model is that, despite its limitations, it has not been replaced by a modernised model. Various versions have been developed through the decades, but they have not yet managed to overtake the traditional models. One explanation for this could be the complexity of the modernised FLC models, when graphically depicted. The simplified modern FLC model (Bojanic, 2011) may have added appeal for future applications. It contains only seven stages while still allowing single parents and unmarried couples to be represented. It condenses all children's ages in a simplified stage of 'full nest' to reduce

**Table 11.5**  An extended range of FLC stages

| FLC stage |
| --- |
| Young singles (less than 35 years old |
| Young couples (no children) (female less than 35 years old) |
| Gay couple (no children) |
| Gay couple (with children) |
| Older couple (no children) (female 35+ years of age) |
| Older retired couple (no children from current marriage) |
| Age-gap couple (children from current relationship, with or without children from previous relationship) |
| Age-gap couple (no children from current relationship, with or without children from previous relationship) |
| Older divorced single (no children) |
| Single parent (children still at home) |
| Older single (never been married, no children) (35+ years old) |
| Couple with pre-school children (youngest child not at school) |
| Couple with school-aged children (youngest child at school) |
| Couple with older children (all children finished school) |
| Empty nest I (still working, children left home) |
| Empty nest II (retired, children left home) |
| Widower (widower who is not working and partner is deceased) |
| Widower (still working) |

the number of full-nest stages. Whether the simplification is considered problematic for marketers is yet to be examined.

In the present research, despite expanding the traditional FLC to incorporate more stages – 13 stages – 9.2% of respondents still ended up in an 'other' category, which opened up several additional further stages. Thus, it can be said that the 13 stages used as a framework for this research was insufficient. A possible range of stages that can be considered more inclusive is set out in Table 11.5.

Historically, more accurate (and complicated) depictions of the range of stages today's individual may go through have not been popular. More complicated diverse 'modern' FLC models are more inclusive but even so are still not perfect representations of the diverse modern society. The traditional FLC model is still popular in tourism despite its limitations, perhaps because it is simple and represents a useful model for explaining a process.

## Conclusion

The results of this research have shown that the traditional FLC model leaves out a significant proportion of travellers. Across the four regions in which this study was conducted, almost 20% of respondents did not fall into any recognised category in the traditional FLC model. An expanded FLC framework revealed gay couples either with or without children, older couples without children, single parents, widowers who were still working, and pensioners (who may be on pensions from a very early age – for example disability pensions).

In 1991, Lawson found that 40% of travellers in New Zealand did not fit into the traditional FLC model. The results from this research, conducted two decades later, are surprisingly low by comparison.

The four destinations have high proportions of travellers in the VFR market. As such, it is possible that the proportion of people not fitting into the FLC would be even higher in other destinations with smaller VFR markets. That is, destinations such as capital cities may attract a broader and more diverse mixture of tourists. Thus, the proportion of respondents who did not fit the traditional FLC model in the present study may be lower than what could be found in other regions. In addition, this research was conducted by surveying tourists in a VIC. The people who visit VICs may be more likely to fit into the traditional FLC model and so, again, the study may not have accurately captured the proportion of FLC tourists.

Certainly, further research along the lines of that conducted in this study and by Lawson (1991) would be valuable in creating a better understanding of what proportion of tourists are not captured by the traditional FLC model. As that model continues to be taught in tourism, it is important to understand its limitations in terms of the implications in tourism. Operators with 'family' prices are typically talking to the traditional family of two adults and two children, but today's family can also be a gay couple with children or a single parent with four children. By teaching the traditional FLC model uncritically, it is possible that the future tourism marketers and managers will not accurately capture the market correctly, through a lack of understanding of the number of people left out.

This research highlights the importance of understanding the complexities of today's and tomorrow's 'family' and has theoretical and practical implications. People do not necessarily follow the FLC stages, or may revisit some of the stages several times during their lives. It is important to understand these points, or increasingly tourism operators may not be sending the right message to their markets. If in four conservative regional communities 20% of the tourists are essentially 'forgotten', this has considerable implications both for regions with broader markets and for the future. Further research examining this issue in more detail would add greatly to the limited literature in this field as well as offering practical benefits to tourism operators globally.

## References

Australian Bureau of Statistics (2010) *National Regional Profile: Greater Bendigo*. Canberra: ABS.

Australian Bureau of Statistics (2011a) *Australian Social Trends March 2011: Life Expectancy Trends — Australia. Statistics.* Canberra: ABS.

Australian Bureau of Statistics (2011b) *Regional Population Growth, Australia.* Canberra: ABS.

Backer, E. (2011) VFR travellers of the future. In I. Yeoman, C. Hsu, K. Smith and S. Watson (eds), *Tourism and Demography* (pp. 74–84). Oxford: Goodfellow.

Bigelow, H. (1942) Money and marriage. In G. Becker and R. Hill (eds), *Marriage and the Family* (pp. 382–386). Boston, MA: Health and Company.

Bojanic, D.C. (2011) The impact of age and family life experiences on Mexican visitor shopping expenditures. *Tourism Management*, 32(2), 406–414.

City of Greater Geelong (2011) City statistics. Retrieved 30 September 2011 from http://www.geelongaustralia.com.au/business/statistics.

Cooper, C., Fletcher, J., Fyall, A., Gilbert, D. and Wanhill, S. (2008) *Tourism: Principles and Practice* (4th edition). Harlow: Prentice-Hall.

Cosenza, R.M. and Davis, D.L. (1981) Family vacation decision making over the family life cycle: a decision and influence structure analysis. *Journal of Travel Research*, 20(2), 17–23.

Derrick, F.W. and Lehfeld, A.K. (1980) The family life cycle: an alternative approach. *Journal of Consumer Research*, 7(2), 214–217.

Duvall, E. and Hill, R. (1948) *Report on the Committee on the Dynamics of Family Interaction.* Washington, DC: National Conference on Family Life.

Gilly, M.C. and Enis, B.M. (1982) Recycling the family life cycle: a proposal for redefinition. *Advances in Consumer Research*, 9(1), 271–277.

Glick, P.C. (1947) The family cycle. *American Sociological Review*, 12(2), 164–174.

Glick, P.C. (1977) Updating the life cycle of the family. *Family Relations*, 39(1), 5–13.

Glick, P.C. (1989) The family life cycle and social change. *Family Relations*, 38(2), 123–129.

Hall, C.M. (2007) *Introduction to Tourism in Australia* (5th edition). Frenchs Forest: Pearson Education.

Hisrich, R. and Cheng, E. (1974) Selecting the superior segmentation correlate. *Journal of Marketing*, 38(3), 60–63.

Hong, G.-S., Fan, J.X. and Palmer, L. (2005) Leisure travel expenditure patterns by family life cycle stages. *Journal of Travel and Tourism Marketing*, 18(2), 15–30.

Kirkpatrick, E., Cowles, M. and Tough, R. (1934) *The Life Cycle of the Farm Family in Relation to Its Standard of Living.* Research Bulletin 121. Madison, WI: University of Wisconsin Agricultural Experiment Station.

Lawson, R. (1991) Patterns of tourist expenditure and types of vacation across the family life cycle. *Journal of Travel Research*, 29(4), 12–18.

Lin, Y.-C. and Lehto, X. Y. (2006) A study of female travelers' needs trajectory and family life cycle. *Journal of Hospitality and Leisure Marketing*, 15(1), 65–88.

Loomis, C. (1936) The study of the life cycle of families. *Rural Sociology*, 1(2), 180–199.

Lumsdon, L. (1977) *Tourism Marketing*. London: Thomas International Business Press.

Murphy, P.E. and Staples, W.A. (1979) A modernized family life cycle. *Journal of Consumer Research*, 6(1), 12–22.

Page, S. and Connell, J. (2009) *Tourism: A Modern Synthesis*. China: South-Western Cengage Learning.

Pelton, S.L. and Hertlein, K.M. (2011) A proposed life cycle for voluntary childfree couples. *Journal of Feminist Family Therapy*, 23(1), 39–53.

Richardson, J. and Fluker, M. (2008) *Understanding and Managing Tourism* (2nd edition). Frenchs Forest: Pearson Education.

Rowntree, B. (1903) *Poverty: A Study of Town Life*. London: Macmillan.

Schnittger, M.H. and Bird, G.W. (1990) Coping among dual-career men and women across the family life cycle. *Family Relations*, 39(2), 199–205.

Sorokin, P., Zimmerman, A., Carle, C. and Galpin, C. (1931) *A systematic Sourcebook in Rural Sociology* (2nd edition). Minneapolis, MN: University of Minnesota Press.

Total Travel (2011) Map of Victoria. Retrieved 30 September 2011 from http://au.totaltravel.yahoo.com/destinations/maps/australia/vic.

Turner, W.G. (2005) The role of companion animals throughout the family life cycle. *Family Life*, 9(4), 11–22.

Weaver, D. and Lawton, L. (2010) *Tourism Management* (4th edition). Milton: Wiley.

Wells, W.D. and Gubar, G. (1966) Life cycle concept in marketing research. *Journal of Marketing Research*, 3(4), 355–363.

Werner-Lin, A. (2008) Beating the biological clock: the compressed family life cycle of young women with BRCA gene alterations. *Social Work in Health Care*, 47(4), 416–437.

Yarra Ranges Council (2011) Population forecasts. Retrieved 3 October 2011 from http://forecast2.id.com.au/Default.aspx?id=125&pg=5180.

Zimmerman, C. (1982) The life cycle concept as a tool for travel research. *Transportation*, 11(1), 51–69.

# 12 The Future of Family Tourism: A Cognitive Mapping Approach

## Ian Yeoman and Heike Schänzel

## Introduction

Families travelling with children represent one of the largest and most constant markets for the tourism industry and yet tourism research has rarely taken notice of children's and families' holiday experiences (Carr, 2011; Obrador, 2012). For example, family holidays in Britain generate over a third of receipts within the wider travel industry (Mintel, 2004) and these are predicted to grow, albeit in different forms (Yeoman, 2008). Predictions for the future of families highlight: increasing longevity, leading to stronger multigenerational ties; trends to smaller family units, which may strengthen family networks and social cohesion outside the immediate family; and increasing blurring between various forms of partnerships (Organisation for Economic Co-operation and Development, 2008). Studies should seek to show what is likely to continue or to change and what is novel, by providing a systematic and pattern-based understanding of past and present. This chapter suggests some likely future trends with regards to tourism and families.

There is scant tourism literature on the future of families, although work on demography and family structures (Glover & Prideaux, 2011; Yeoman, 2008) has predicted an increased emphasis on fewer children and more multigenerational travel. Instead, most future studies in tourism are concerned with destination management (Butler, 2009; Dwyer et al., 2009) rather than specific markets. This chapter looks at the drivers that represent family tourism, which are slow-moving social trends, including changes in direction. To date, quantitative research has predominated in tourism, resulting in mainly individual interpretations of group behaviour unsuitable to account for the thick sociality present in the collective experience of family groups (Obrador, 2012; Schänzel, 2010). Additionally, most family tourism research is market- and consumer-driven (Lehto et al., 2009), with few studies including children (Blichfeldt *et al.*, 2011). Specialised studies on social tourism are coming out of Europe (McCabe *et al.*, 2011; Minnaert *et al.*, 2009) and families form part of travel undertaken to visit friends and relatives (VFR) (Backer, 2012). However, there is a lack of research into broader experiential dimensions and ideologies. The meaning of holidays for children is under-researched (Carr, 2011; Hilbrecht *et al.*, 2008; Small, 2008) and research on fatherhood in tourism is only just emerging (Schänzel & Smith, 2011), despite traditions of research with children and fathers in other disciplinary areas (Daly, 1996; Galinsky, 1999; Jeanes, 2010; Kay, 2009). Family structures and societal values have changed substantially in recent decades (Carr, 2011), which could have strong influences on family tourism behaviour. However, family tourism research has not kept up with the changes in family forms and a reconceptualisation of families that takes account of diversity and difference (Shaw, 2010; Yeoman, 2008) is yet to emerge. There is increasing research on everyday family leisure life and ideological influences (Daly, 2004; Shaw, 2010), yet this has not been extended to an away-from-home dimension. These omissions are a reminder not only that tourism research is lagging behind other social research but also that the literature on family tourism is fragmented, incomplete and individualised.

This chapter identifies the contributions from Chapters 2–12, as well as the key themes that emerge from the text. A cognitive mapping approach has been used, as previously applied in tourism (Yeoman *et al.*, 2006; Yeoman & Watson, 2011). Each chapter theme has been interpreted through a cognitive map and then a final conceptual or merged map has been produced that represents the contribution made to the subject domain of family tourism. The principal purpose of this chapter is to identify the changes and trends that are occurring in family tourism, based upon current research, to demonstrate the connections between concepts and to provide a more holistic interpretation of family holidays for the future, using a cognitive mapping approach.

# Research Method: Explaining Cognitive Mapping

## The bricolage

When subjective research is done, with the researcher acting as a filter or interpretation device, it is important to understand the context of the researcher and the phenomena being researched. Where the researcher is faced with a range of viewpoints about family tourism, a useful approach is to view the researcher as a bricoleur. A bricoleur is a:

> Jack of all trades or a professional 'do it yourself' person. (Levi-Strauss, 1966: 17)

It is the researcher as the bricoleur who pieces together the research as a set of cognitive patterns which represents a map of the future (here, of family tourism). Such a pattern is called a bricolage (Levi-Strauss, 1966), which represents a series of findings that 'make sense' to the researcher (Weick, 1979). Guba's (1990) assumption that all research is interpretative places the bricoleur at the centre of the research. This paradigm of constructivist interpretation (Schwandt, 1994) is based upon ontology, where the reality of knowledge is predominantly specific and local. It is a form of knowledge that is expertise and grounded in practice. This epistemology views knowledge in a subjective and transactional manner as merely suggesting directions along which to look, rather than providing descriptions of what to see (Blumer, 1954). This methodological stance is founded upon subjectivity and interpretation, in which the bricoleur explores the mind of the researchers in order to construct a cognitive map of the future.

Fundamentally, the constructivist interpretative paradigm believes that the world of events and meaning must be interpreted (Schwandt, 1994). This process of construction is about clarifying, through reflection and debate, the language of those researched. The process is about 'questioning' and 'searching' for a construction, where the bricoleur has a 'knowing' and 'being', rather than being concerned with methods (Wolcott, 1988, 1992). These constructions, according to Guba and Lincoln (1989), are about 'making sense' of the research, where making sense is a process of debate between the researchers, to the point at which the researchers feel comfortable with the construction of the cognitive map, often described as a 'eureka' moment.

## The cognitive map

Cognitive maps (also known as mental maps, mind maps, cognitive models, or mental models) are a type of mental processing composed of a series of psychological transformations by which an individual can acquire, code, store, recall and decode information about the relative locations and attributes of phenomena in their everyday or metaphorical spatial environment (Eden & Ackermann, 1998). Applied as a research methodology they are used to represent a cognition of researched thoughts through a series of links as a map or picture.

Jones (1993: 11) states that a cognitive map:

Is a collection of ideas (concepts) and relationships in the form of a map. Ideas are expressed by short phrases which encapsulate a single notion and, where appropriate, its opposite. The relationships between ideas are described by linking them together in either a causal or connotative manner.

The method used by the authors is drawn from Eden and Ackermann's (1998) use of cognitive mapping in strategic management and management science, which used personal construct theory (Kelly, 1955). The personal construct theory of personality was developed by the psychologist George Kelly in the 1950s to help patients to uncover their own 'constructs' with minimal intervention or interpretation by the therapist. The repertory grid was later adapted for various uses within organisations, including decision-making and interpretation of other people's world views. Eden and Ackermann's approach to cognitive mapping involves the idea of concepts. These are short phrases or words which represent a verb in which ideas are linked as cause/effect, means/end or how/why, meaning a cognitive map is a representation of a particular person's perceptions about a situation in terms of bipolar constructs, where the terms are seen as a contrast with each other. For example, 'family holidays in the sun' may lead to 'increased family tensions … increased family happiness'. The result is not unlike an influence diagram or causal loop diagram, although it is explicitly subjective and uses constructs rather than variables (Mingers, 2011). Eden and Ackermann (1998) suggest that cognitive mapping can be used as a mind map in problem solving. It may also be used to record transcripts of interviews or other documentary evidence in a way that promotes analysis, questioning and understanding. However, the literature on the application of cognitive mapping (Yeoman, 2004) is bastardised as researchers adapt the theory based upon their own skills and research philosophies.

## Decision Explorer (DE)

A computer-assisted qualitative data analysis (CAQDAS) approach, according to Barry (1998), aids in the automation of processing data and the capturing of concepts. A CAQDAS approach helps the bricoleur view relationships of phenomena and data through the ability to trace and track data, hence supporting the principle of the bricoleur as a constructivist interpreter. A CAQDAS approach provides a formal structure for notes and memos to develop an analysis platform which is consistent with triangulation and grounded theory (Strauss & Corbin, 1994). Decision Explorer (DE) is an interactive tool for assisting and clarifying problems (Jenkins, 1998), using the principles of cognitive mapping (Eden & Ackermann, 1998) within the realm of CAQDAS. DE allows a visual display and analysis of cognitive maps in such a manner that it permits 'multiple viewpoints', 'holding of concepts', 'tracing of concepts' and 'causal relationship management'.

Decision Explorer is a rich interactive tool that allows for the movement of concepts and connections in order that the bricoleur can be in the centre of the meaning of the research area (here, family tourism), in order to draw conclusions and construct a meaningful view of the future. DE helps the bricoleur produce the bricolage. This is where the bricoleur pieces together the research to produce a close set of practices and interpretations that present a series of findings and that 'make sense' (Levi-Strauss, 1966; Weick, 1979). The most important feature of DE (Eden & Ackermann, 1998) is the ability to categorise concepts, values and emergent themes. DE allows the bricoleur to elicit data and code concepts, for example using 'set management' commands.

# Observations from Family Tourism

Each chapter has been interpreted through a conceptual mapping approach, resulting in 10 main themes, highlighting and visualising the current knowledge and key trends with regard to tourism and families. The first three chapters or themes provide a context to family tourism (Chapters 2–4), while the next five chapters or themes explore the experiences of family holidaying (Chapters 5–9) and the last two chapters/themes (Chapters 10 and 11) focus more specifically on the future of family tourism. These chapter themes then result in a final conceptual or merged map, representing the contribution made to the subject domain of the future of family tourism.

## Chapter 2 – Society and Ideology

Chapter 2 highlighted the influence that society and the dominant ideology of parenting exerts on family holiday experiences. The cognitive map (Figure 12.1) reveals that higher valuation of family time and togetherness has led to a new orthodoxy about leisure and tourism. This is founded on the urban myth of the decline of the family when in fact most studies of time use suggest that families are spending more time together than previous generations, adding to their perceived busy-ness. The changing roles of parents are exemplified through intensive mothering and generative fathering, giving rise to more goal-directed childhoods. This entails an increased emphasis placed by parents on structured time with their children, to provide them with a world of activities and experiences. Holidays are part of this purposive aspect of family leisure time which disguises individual needs for personal leisure and own time. The key contribution of this theme is that a departure from idealistic notions of family holidays is required, with a reorientation towards more realistic understandings of individual needs, based on gender and generational differences.

## Chapter 3 – Demography and Societal Changes

This chapter addressed slow-moving social structural and demographic changes and drew out four prominent trends that are significant for the future (Figure 12.2). Longevity and smaller core size have led to families becoming more vertical in form rather than horizontal. Fewer children in

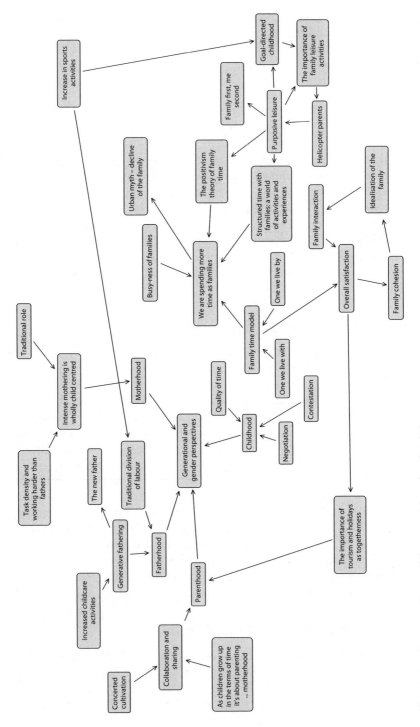

**Figure 12.1** Conceptual map of demographic and societal changes

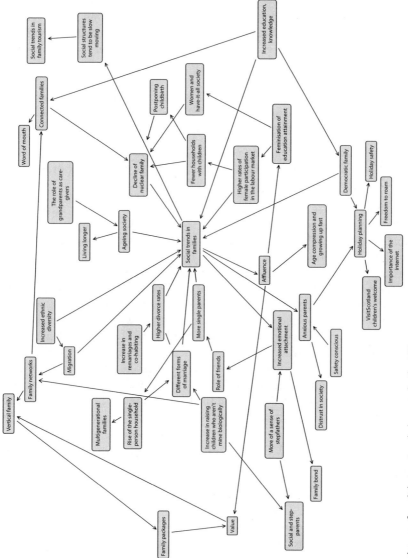

**Figure 12.2** Conceptual map of social structural changes in the UK

society and increased emotional attachment to them mean children will become a luxury themselves as they become scarcer and more important. As society ages and families are more mobile, the elderly population has an important care-giving role in looking after their grandchildren and providing a safe environment. Families have less time to relax and play together with higher rates of female participation in the labour market; therefore time together becomes the new luxury and tourism is the facilitator of family bonds through increased quality time. The key contribution of this theme is identifying family tourism as 'social glue', by increasing the opportunity for family interaction and also through multigenerational holidays, 'grandtravel', extended family travel and VFR travel.

## Chapter 4 – UK Family Tourism: Past, Present and Future Challenges

This chapter traced the historical development of family tourism in the UK through to the future (Figure 12.3). It highlighted the growing importance of the family tourism market in the UK despite the prevailing economic climate, by tracing historical shifts in working-class culture, the influence of children on tourism demand and the changing make-up of families. Not only are families considered the fundamental social group in society but also the presence of children has a major influence on tourism participation and patterns. The significance of the holiday was explored in the context of disadvantaged families and social tourism. It was noted that family relationships are improved by increased quality family time and enhanced engagement with learning occurs as a result of family holidays providing a key argument for the 'term-time holiday'. The key contribution of this theme is the bringing together of different influences, historical, social and financial, that currently shape the family tourism market in the UK and into the future.

## Chapter 5 – Inclusion of Fathers, Children and the Whole Family Group

This chapter theme adds the role of the father, the emphasis placed by the children on what they want from a holiday and the internal group dynamics to the understanding of family holiday experiences. From the conceptual map (Figure 12.4), it is argued that the inherent sociality present in family groups requires more holistic and critical methodological approaches to tourism research. A whole-family methodology was used to highlight the role of fathers as the main entertainer of the children, the importance placed by children on the social aspect of fun and the group dynamics of compromise, cooperation and conflict on holiday. The key contribution of the chapter is the provision of more inclusive familial perspectives that explore gender, generational and group dynamic dimensions in tourism. From this

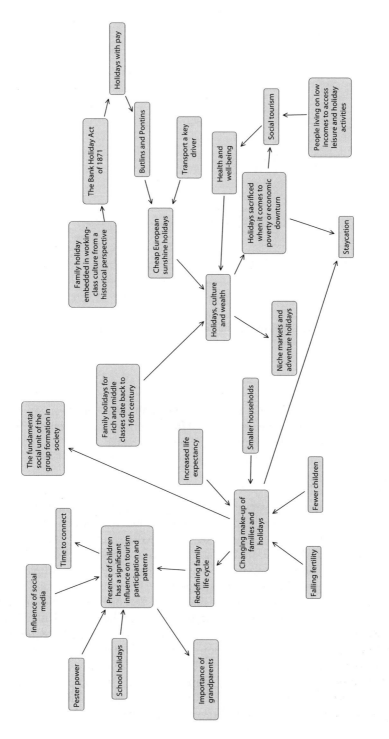

**Figure 12.3** Conceptual map of UK family tourism: Past, present and future challenges

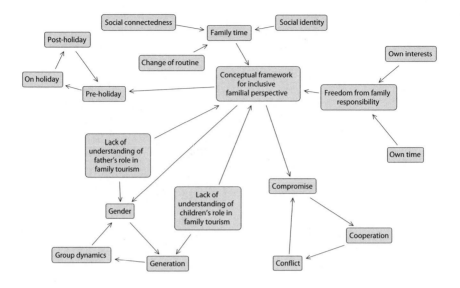

**Figure 12.4** Conceptual map of inclusion of fathers, children and the whole family group

it emerged that a balance is needed between an overt emphasis on family time based on social connectedness and freedom from family responsibilities based on pursuing all family members' own interests.

## Chapter 6 – VFR Travel

Despite the decade-long trend in declining domestic holidays in Australia, this chapter argued that the proportion of people undertaking VFR travel has increased in the majority of destinations in Victoria. This supports the notion that the VFR market may be an appropriate choice to assist in 'buffering' against economic downturns, especially when coupled with natural disasters and a strong exchange rate. The conceptual map (Figure 12.5) highlights that destinations may need to consider developing VFR strategies such as marketing to 'Aunt Betty' or local hosts, particularly with recessionary conditions, increased social media exposure and greater availability of international travel options. The key contribution was outlining the long-term robustness of the VFR market, as not only is reconnecting with family and friends socially important but also people will always travel to reconnect. In addition, VFR will have a growing role in terms of migration and possibly inbound international travel to Australia. Further

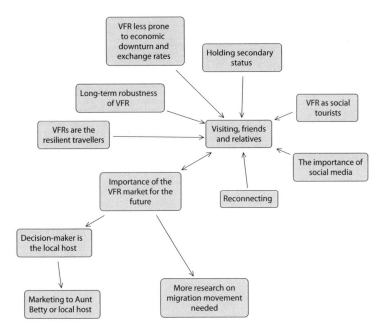

**Figure 12.5** Conceptual map of VFR travel

research on migration movements would add to the limited literature that has touched on these issues.

## Chapter 7 – Value of Social Tourism

This chapter theme is illustrated in several countries in Europe that facilitate access to tourism for disadvantaged families through social policy. From the conceptual map (Figure 12.6) social tourism emerges as tourism with added moral value for families who are physically or financially deprived and as a means to counteract social disintegration. It stresses the increasing diversification of family forms, such as single-sex parents and 'blended' families. Social tourism is shown to have a range of benefits for participating families, exemplified by the development of social and family capital, mainly in the form of closer bonds and relationship-building and by providing new learning opportunities. The key contribution of this chapter is highlighting how family tourism, instead of a frivolous activity, can be seen as a central building block for strong families – a function that is of particular importance to disadvantaged families.

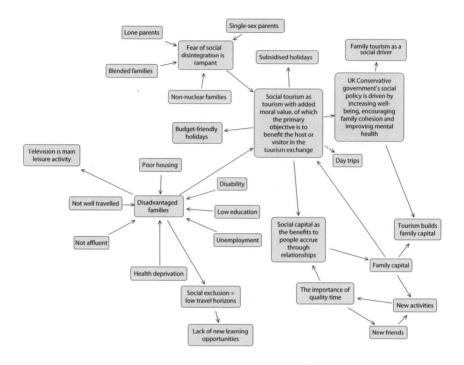

**Figure 12.6** Conceptual map of value of social tourism

## Chapter 8 – Stress of the Family Holiday

While the tourism industry focuses on the family market, this chapter showed that the expectations of parents are not always met by operators (Figure 12.7). Stress levels can be high for parents in everyday life, particularly for those with larger families and younger children. Societal pressure is often placed on families to have holidays but holidays can give rise to financial hardship. The greater expense for families and their possible reliance on single incomes require more effort in planning and saving up, which can result in substantial disappointments if the holiday is not relaxing. This is accompanied by moral issues of good parenting in putting children first and feelings of guilt when conflicts arise on holiday, especially for mothers. The study found that stress levels were often raised during and after the family holiday, and were often exaggerated by minor inconveniences from tourism providers. The key contribution of this chapter is highlighting

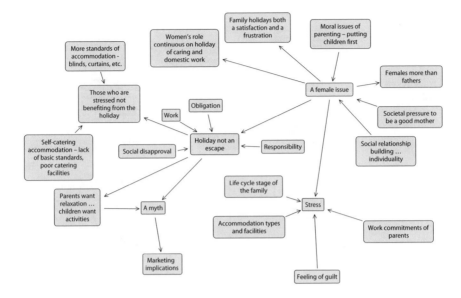

**Figure 12.7** Conceptual map of stress of the family holiday

the need for better linking between what families need and what tourism operators provide, in order to reduce stress for families (their main purpose of holidaying).

## Chapter 9 – Gay and Lesbian Family Travel

This chapter considered the potential for gay and lesbian family tourism in respect to market size, disposable income and particular requirements (Figure 12.8). It emphasised the contested nature of gay and lesbian marriage, which can lead to added stress and lack of acknowledgement from tourism providers. 'The gay and lesbian family holiday' has particularly significant potential for strengthening and consolidating sexual identities and family relationships but its market size is difficult to identify, due to a lack of empirical data. Gay and lesbian families may avoid commercial providers in order to obtain privacy and avoid tension but may not desire a separate product either. The key contribution of this chapter is highlighting the challenges of the tourism industry to overcome the fears and concerns of gay and lesbian families and tap into the needs of this growing market.

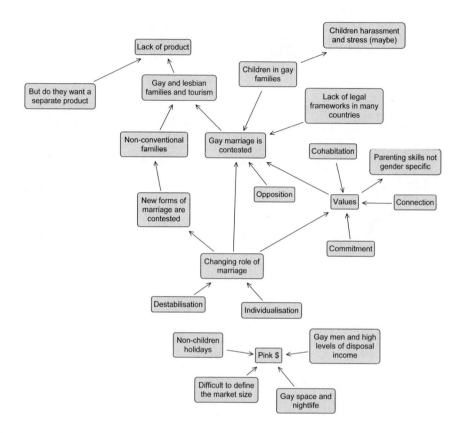

**Figure 12.8** Conceptual map of gay and lesbian family travel

## Chapter 10 – Consumer Kids and Tourists

This chapter discussed the importance of marketing to young tourists, who are often missed by destination marketing organisations (DMOs) (Figure 12.9). DMOs need to address this by developing strategic marketing campaigns for this persuasive target group. The concept of creative tourism marketing was suggested as a means to connect with young consumers, who can be more cynical about mainstream advertising and are prone to switch off when unengaged. Consumer kids desire information about destinations, especially as they are the current tourists and strong influencers on family travel decisions. Half of holiday choices can be influenced by children through what is often referred to as pester power. The key contribution of

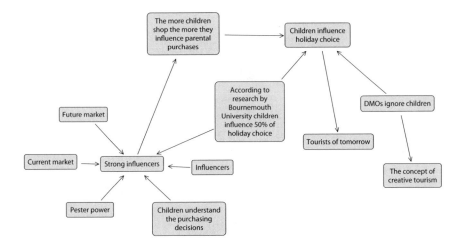

**Figure 12.9** Conceptual map of consumer kids and tourists

this chapter lies in highlighting the importance of targeting young tourists and how this can be achieved by appealing and engaging; this is essential, as their experiences will affect future family holiday patterns as they are the next generation of travellers.

## Chapter 11 – Future Family Life Cycle

This chapter explored the traditional family life cycle (FLC) model, suggested that it is becoming increasingly outdated and questioned its continued usefulness (Figure 12.10). The FLC was based mainly on US family structures and perceives consumers as having differentiated patterns based on the successive stages in the model. While the natural progression from singles, to couples, to having children, retiring and being a solitary survivor is a depiction of life in the past, an increasing proportion of people exist outside this model, making it potentially obsolete. Increasingly, people remain single with no children (SINKs) or couples elect not to have children (DINKs), and there are also families with different sexual orientations who do not fit the model. This chapter is based on an Australian survey study conducted in 2011 which found that 19.8% of respondents did not fit the FLC. The key contribution of this chapter is highlighting the need for new life cycle models to be developed to reflect societal changes.

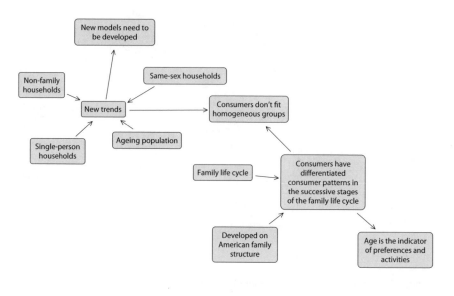

**Figure 12.10** Conceptual map of future family life cycle

# Emerging Futures – The Development of a Cognitive Map of Families and Tourism

From the analysis of the preceding chapters, the authors have developed a merged cognitive map of families and tourism, which displays the key themes that emerged (Figure 12.11). As a consequence of the cognitive mapping analysis, the contribution of this chapter to the literature of family tourism lies in nine clusters, discussed under separate headings below.

## New family structures as a consequence of demography

Family holidays are no longer exclusively about nuclear families but reflect changes in family structures and societal values. There is increasing diversity of family forms in tourism: single-parent families, gay and lesbian families, blended families and extended families, among other forms. The increasing life span of people coupled with fewer children in society leads to families being more vertical, meaning that in the future there will be more multi-generational travel and 'grandtravel'. It also needs acknowledgement that through immigration families are increasingly from diverse ethnic backgrounds. Tourism in the future needs to be reconceptualised as reflecting that diversity in families.

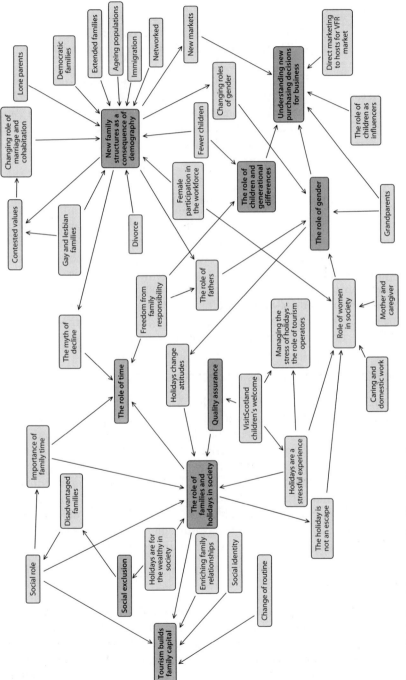

**Figure 12.11** Cognitive map of families and tourism

## The role of children and generational differences

Increasing emphasis is placed on fewer children born than in previous generations, which leads to more democratic decision-making in families. The role that children play as influencers of tourism purchasing decisions is increasingly recognised. There are also growing demands for understanding that the needs of children differ from those of their parents or even grandparents and that these generational differences need to be addressed by tourism operators. Children cannot be considered as a homogeneous group and age is a big differentiator. Catering to the nuances of the young family tourist as the next generation of travellers is vital in ensuring the sustainability of tourism businesses.

## The role of gender and parenting behaviour

The change in gender roles and parenting behaviour can have significant influences on family holiday experiences. Societal changes have led to intensive mothering and involved fathering, implying a more concerted effort in raising fewer children than previous generations. This implies that the traditional roles of parents are extended to encompass a wider variety of parental behaviour towards children on holiday. Recognition is needed of the complex gender relations in tourism and how gender imperatives for both fathers and mothers are affecting holiday needs and outcomes.

## Understanding new purchasing decisions for business

Tourism businesses require better understandings of the complex purchasing decisions involved, especially in relation to the changing family market. There are new forms of families and they are from diverse cultural backgrounds; these need to be considered along with changes in gender and parenting roles, children's greater influence and family travel increasingly involving the extended family and VFR. This should lead to more creative and innovative marketing campaigns that engage the young tourist, appeal to gay and lesbian families or relate directly to the local VFR hosts. To capture future travel purchasing behaviour will require account to be taken of the rising diversity, multivocality and fluidity of families.

## The role of time

Increasing societal importance is placed on family time, especially by the middle classes. Holidays can take on a purposive nature by facilitating family togetherness. This is contrasted with the myth of decline, when, in fact, families today spend more leisure time together than previous generations. On holiday, family members also seek freedom from family responsibilities: mothers from domestic work, fathers from entertainment imperatives and children from parental restrictions. The role of time in the future involves acknowledging that a balance is needed between family time and family members pursuing their own interests on holiday, which requires more realistic understandings of individual needs, away from ideological orthodoxy.

## Social exclusion

Holidays are generally perceived as being for the wealthy and healthy in society, which can come at the exclusion of disadvantaged families. Family holidays can facilitate the expansion of social connection or social capital, provide new learning opportunities and change behaviours for the better. Families who are unable to take holidays are thus excluded from such potential benefits. Social tourism initiatives in the future will be able to broaden the travel horizons of a wider diversity of families. But more importantly, those families can accrue benefits through relationship building and social integration if family tourism is established as an essential element of contemporary society.

## The role of families and holidays in society

Families have an important role to play in society despite the demise of traditional family models. There is a myth of decline of the family when in fact families today are just differently connected than previously. Holidays can serve an important social role in enriching family relationships within the immediate and extended family by overcoming increasing mobility issues. Family travel and VFR travel make up a substantial market size and are more resilient than other forms of tourism, as people will always travel to reconnect. Having extended family on holiday also aids in making the experience less stressful for parents and providing more of an escape.

## Tourism builds family capital

Family tourism is widely accepted as aiding in the strengthening of family relationships. The term 'family capital' is used to reflect the bonding between parents and children and the social identification that is facilitated on holiday. Holidays provide a change of routine when families can engage in different activities from those of everyday life. This can aid in the building of family capital, and holidays can take an important social role here. With the increase in extended family travel, grandtravel and VFR travel, more opportunities are provided for family capital formation, which goes beyond parent–child relationships.

## Quality assurance

Holidays are considered as offering a break from everyday life. Family holidays, however, can prove to be more stressful than staying at home, especially with regard to domestic considerations. Parents and children have unique requirements on holiday that are unlike those arising in other markets, due to family group dynamics. Family travel holidays are not only becoming more diverse but also contain constantly changing gender and generational expectations. The role of the tourism operators in the future is to provide more family-friendly quality assurance that reflects the changing needs of modern family structures and behaviours.

# Concluding for the Future

The merged cognitive map (Figure 12.11) shows the slow-moving changes that are occurring within family tourism, whether it is the role of time or purchasing behaviour. These observations are of interest to a number of parties. For researchers, a reconceptualisation of tourism is required that takes account of increasing diversity and difference in family forms (Shaw, 2010; Yeoman, 2008). Although the family market makes up a substantial and robust market size, especially when VFR travel is included (Backer, 2012), this is not reflected in tourism research (Carr, 2011; Obrador, 2012). In the future, tourism research needs to reflect more the complex realities of individual needs present in a social group than the highly idealised focus on quality family time (Schänzel, 2010). In particular, the changing role of the father on holiday needs acknowledgement (Schänzel & Smith, 2011). The benefits of family capital formation through travel need greater recognition, especially in light of substantial VFR travel (Backer, 2012) and increasing forms of extended family travel. This expands to social tourism needing wider acceptance as a form of social inclusion and a means of extending the benefits of family tourism beyond the realms of the middle classes (Minnaert et al., 2009). For business, an emphasis on marketing and product development is necessary in relation to the needs and decision-making power of children (Blichfeldt et al., 2011; Carr, 2011) by giving a voice to a heterogeneous group of young tourists as the next generation of travellers. This means that marketing campaigns and products in the future need to be more creative and innovative to capture the increasing diversity, multi-vocality and fluidity of families who travel. If business can get it right and minimise inconveniences for families, success will follow as currently many tourism operators misunderstand the stresses and dynamics involved when families travel.

   This chapter has shown the connections between a wide variety of concepts and has thereby presented a more holistic interpretation of the future of family tourism than has been previously attempted. Significant gaps in current knowledge have been recognised, alongside emerging trends. Suggestions for future research have been made. Nine main themes have been identified that provide steerage for the future major tourism market that families will represent. From these contributions it is evident that understanding of families is vital for future industry developments. However, the authors are aware that we have managed to cover only some of the current research developments in this book and would suggest the following areas for further research:

- the Asian family market as a representation of the rising middle classes in Asia;
- a detailed examination of the single-parent family market;
- the travel behaviours of families from ethnic or indigenous backgrounds;
- differentiation in the understanding of children on holiday as represented by age and gender;
- a detailed examination of multigenerational differences and needs in family travel;
- further analysis of the supply side of family tourism, with tourism operator perspectives on catering for the family market;
- the economic impact on tourism of changes to family structures and forms.

In addition, it is recognised that each one of the clusters in the cognitive map require further study. We hope that you have enjoyed reading the various chapters in this book, which demonstrate the application of the study of families to tourism.

## References

Backer, E. (2012) VFR travel: it is underestimated. *Tourism Management*, 33(1), 74–79.

Barry, C.A. (1998) Choosing qualitative data analysis software: Atlas/ti and Nudist compared. *Sociological Research Online*, 3(3). Retrieved from http://socresonline.org.uk/3/3/4.html.

Blichfeldt, B.S., Pedersen, B.M., Johansen, A. and Hansen, L. (2011) Tweens on holidays. In-situ decision-making from children's perspective. *Scandinavian Journal of Hospitality and Tourism*, 11(2), 135–149.

Blumer, H. (1954) What is wrong with social theory? *American Sociological Review*, 19(1), 3–27.

Butler, R. (2009) Tourism in the future: cycles, waves or wheels? *Futures*, 41(6), 346–352.

Carr, N. (2011) *Children's and Families' Holiday Experiences*. London: Routledge.

Daly, K. (1996) Spending time with the kids: meanings of family time for fathers. *Family Relations*, 45(4), 466–476.

Daly, K. (2004) *The Changing Culture of Parenting*. Ottawa: Vanier Institute of the Family.

Dwyer, L., Edwards, D., Mistilis, N., Roman, C. and Scott, N. (2009) Destination and enterprise management for a tourism future. *Tourism Management*, 30(1), 63–74.

Eden, C. and Ackermann, F. (1998) *Making Strategy: The Journey of Strategic Management*. London: Sage.

Galinsky, E. (1999) *Ask the Children*. New York: Harper Collins.

Glover, P. and Prideaux, B. (2011) An ageing population and changing family structures. In I. Yeoman, C. Hsu, K. Smith and S. Watson (eds), *Tourism and Demography* (pp. 41–54). Oxford: Goodfellow.

Guba, E.G. (1990) The alternative paradigm dialog. In E.G. Guba (ed.), *The Paradigm Dialog* (pp. 17–30). London: Sage.

Guba, E.G. and Lincoln, Y.S. (1989) *Fourth Generation Evaluation*. London: Sage.

Hilbrecht, M., Shaw, S.M., Delamere, F.M. and Havitz, M.E. (2008) Experiences, perspectives, and meanings of family vacations for children. *Leisure/Loisir*, 32(2), 541–571.

Jeanes, R. (2010) Seen but not heard? Examining children's voices in leisure and family research. *Leisure/Loisir*, 34(3), 243–259 (doi:10.1080/14927713.2010.520490).

Jenkins, M. (1998) The theory and practice of comparing causal maps. In C. Eden and J.C. Spencer (eds), *Managerial and Organizational Cognition* (pp. 231–250). London: Sage.

Jones, M. (1993) *Decision Explorer: Reference Manual Version 3.1*. Glasgow: Banxia Software Limited.

Kay, T. (ed.) (2009) *Fathering Through Sport and Leisure*. London: Routledge.

Kelly, G.A. (1955) *The Psychology of Personal Constructs*. New York: Routledge.

Lehto, X.Y., Choi, S., Lin, Y.-C. and MacDermid, S.M. (2009) Vacation and family functioning. *Annals of Tourism Research*, 36(3), 459–479.

Levi-Strauss, C. (1966) *The Savage Mind*. Chicago, IL: University of Chicago Press.

McCabe, S., Minnaert, L. and Diekmann, A. (eds) (2011) *Social Tourism in Europe*. Bristol: Channel View.

Mingers, J. (2011) Soft OR comes of age – but not everywhere! *Omega*, 39(6), 729–741.

Minnaert, L., Maitland, R. and Miller, G. (2009) Tourism and social policy: the value of social tourism. *Annals of Tourism Research*, 36(2), 316–334.

Mintel (2004) *Family Holidays, Leisure Intelligence, June*. London: Mintel International Group.

Obrador, P. (2012) The place of the family in tourism research: domesticity and thick sociality by the pool. *Annals of Tourism Research*, 39(1), 401–420.

Organisation for Economic Co-operation and Development (2008) *The Future of the Family to 2030 – A Scoping Report*. Paris: OECD International Futures Programme.

Schänzel, H.A. (2010) Whole-family research: towards a methodology in tourism for encompassing generation, gender, and group dynamic perspectives. *Tourism Analysis*, 15(5), 555–569.

Schänzel, H.A. and Smith, K.A. (2011) The absence of fatherhood: achieving true gender scholarship in family tourism research. *Annals of Leisure Research*, 14(2–3), 129–140.

Schwandt, T.A. (1994) Constructivist, interpretivist approaches to human inquiry. In N.K. Denzin and Y.S. Lincoln (eds), *Handbook of Qualitative Research* (1st edition) (pp. 118–137). Thousand Oaks, CA: Sage.

Shaw, S.M. (2010) Diversity and ideology: changes in Canadian family life and implications for leisure. *World Leisure Journal*, 52(1), 4–13.

Small, J. (2008) The absence of childhood in tourism studies. *Annals of Tourism Research*, 35(3), 772–789.

Strauss, A. and Corbin, J. (ed.) (1994) Grounded methodology: an overview. In N. Denzin and Y. Lincoln (eds) *Handbook of Qualitative Research* (pp. 262–272). Sage: London.

Weick, K.E. (1979) *The Social Psychology of Organizing*. New York: Random House.

Wolcott, H.F. (1988) Ethnographic research in education. In R.M. Jaeger (ed.), *Complementary Methods for Research in Education* (pp. 187–249). Washington, DC: American Educational Research Association.

Wolcott, H.F. (1992) Postering in qualitative inquiry. In M.D. Lecompte, W.L. Milroy and J. Preissle (eds), *The Handbook of Qualitative Research in Education* (pp. 3–52). New York: Academic Press.

Yeoman, I. (2004) *The Development of a Conceptual Map of Soft Operations Research*. Unpublished doctoral dissertation, Napier University, Edinburgh.

Yeoman, I. (2008) *Tomorrow's Tourist: Scenarios and Trends*. Oxford: Elsevier.

Yeoman, I., Munro, C. and McMahon-Beattie, U. (2006) Tomorrow's: world, consumer and tourist. *Journal of Vacation Marketing*, 12(2), 174–190.

Yeoman, I. and Watson, S. (2011) Cognitive maps of tourism and demography: contributions, themes and further research. In I. Yeoman, C.H.C. Hsu, K.A. Smith and S. Watson (eds), *Tourism and Demography* (pp. 209–236). Oxford: Goodfellow.

# Index